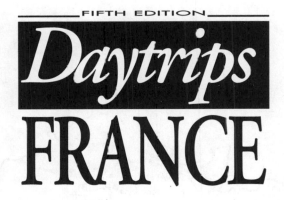

FIFTH EDITION

Daytrips
FRANCE

Amiens

Deauville
Honfleur
Bayeux
Caen
Rouen
Giverny
Senlis
Chantilly
Reims
Versailles
PARIS
Chartres
Provins
Fontainebleau
Moret
Auxerre
Angers
Blois
Amboise
Tours
Bourges
Dijon
Beaune
Lyon
Var
Vence
St. Paul
Èze
Menton
Villefranche
Monaco
Nîmes
Avignon
Grasse
NICE
Arles
Aix
Antibes
Cagnes
Cannes
MARSEILLE
St. Tropez

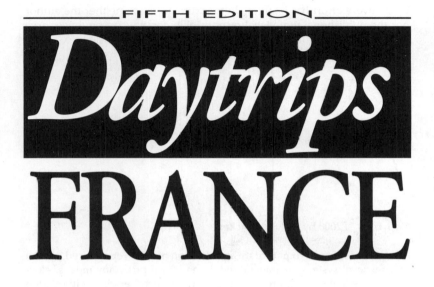

FIFTH EDITION

Daytrips
FRANCE

48 *one day adventures*
by rail, bus or car
includes Paris walking tours

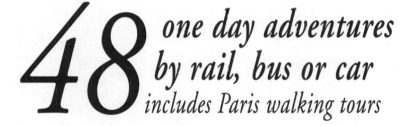

EARL STEINBICKER

HASTINGS HOUSE
Book Publishers
Norwalk, Connecticut

ISBN: 0-8038-2006-2
Cover design and book layout by Mark Salore.
Printed in the United States of America.
10 9 8 7 6 5 4 3 2

Comments? Ideas?

We'd love to hear from you. Ideas from our readers have resulted in many improvements in the past, and will continue to do so. And, if your suggestions are used, we'll gladly send you a complimentary copy of any book in the series. Please send your thoughts to Hastings House, Book Publishers, 9 Mott St., Norwalk CT 06850, or fax us at (203) 838-4084, or e-mail to info@upub.com.

Contents

Introduction

Visitors to France can choose from an enormous range of experiences. There are magnificent cities and medieval towns to explore, splendid châteaux and quaint fishing villages to visit, history to be relived and wines to be tasted. Few nations can match its scope of art, architecture, cuisine, or natural splendor. What's more, the overwhelming majority of France's most exciting attractions can easily be enjoyed on a daytrip basis with absolutely no need for frequent hotel changes. This book takes a careful look at 48 of the most intriguing destinations and tells you, in step-by-step detail, exactly how to go about probing them on your own.

Daytrips in France is not intended to be a comprehensive guide to the entire nation. It focuses, instead, on four broad areas of maximum tourist interest—walking tours of Paris, daytrips from Paris, daytrips in Provence, and daytrips along the Riviera. The most logical bases for these one-day adventures are Paris, Marseille, and Nice; although other towns could be substituted as suggested in the text.

Daytrips have many advantages over the usual point-to-point touring, especially for short-term visitors. You can sample a far greater range in the same time by seeing only those places that really interest you instead of "doing" the regions town by town. This can lead to a more varied diet of sights, such as spending one day on a Normandy beach, the next back in Paris, and the third in medieval Beaune. They are also ideal for business travelers with a few free days interspersed between meetings.

There is no need to pre-plan every moment of your vacation since with daytrips you are always free to venture wherever you please. Feel like seeing Antibes today? Ah, but this is Tuesday, when its sights are closed, so maybe it would be better to head for Monaco instead, or take a glorious rail excursion through the Var Valley. Is rain predicted for the entire day? You certainly don't want to be in Deauville in a shower, so why not try the wonderful museums in Dijon? The operative word here is flexibility; the freedom of not being tied to a schedule or route.

All of the daytrips in this book may be taken by public transportation, and all but those within the base cities themselves by private car. Full information for doing this is given in the "Getting There" section of each trip. A suggested do-it-yourself tour is outlined in both the text and on the local map provided. Time and weather considerations are included, along with price-keyed restaurant recommendations, background data, and sources of additional information.

The trips have been arranged in a geographic sequence following convenient transportation routes. In several cases it is possible to combine two trips in the same day. These opportunities are noted whenever they are practical.

Destinations were chosen to appeal to a wide variety of interests, and include some new discoveries along with the proven favorites. In addition to the usual cathedrals, castles, and museums there are wine centers, boat cruises, Roman ruins, elegant resorts and major cities, great seaports and quaint fishing villages, preserved medieval towns, caves, exquisite gardens, splendid châteaux, places where history was made, homes of famous artists, natural beauty spots and even an exciting railfan excursion.

Many of the attractions have a nominal entrance fee—those that are free will come as a pleasant surprise. Cathedrals and churches will appreciate a small donation in the collection box to help pay their maintenance costs.

Finally, a gentle disclaimer. Places have a way of changing without warning, and errors do creep into print. If your heart is absolutely set on a particular sight, you should check first to make sure that it isn't closed for renovations, or that the opening times are still valid. Phone numbers for the local tourist information offices are included for this purpose.

One last thought—it isn't really necessary to see everything at any given destination. Be selective. Your one-day adventures in France should be fun, not an endurance test. If it starts becoming that, just stroll over to the nearest sidewalk café, sit down, and enjoy yourself. There will always be another day.

Happy Daytripping!

Section I

DAYTRIP
STRATEGIES

The word "Daytrip" may not have made it into dictionaries yet, but for experienced independent travelers it represents the easiest, most natural, and often the least expensive approach to exploring a European country. This strategy, in which you base yourself in a central city and probe the surrounding country on a series of one-day excursions, is especially effective throughout most of France.

ADVANTAGES:
   While not the answer to every travel situation, daytrips offer significant advantages over point-to-point touring following a set plan. Here are a dozen good reasons for considering the daytrip approach:
1. Freedom from the constraints of a fixed itinerary. You can go wherever you feel like going whenever the mood strikes you.
2. Freedom from the burden of luggage. Your bags remain in your hotel while you run around with only a guidebook and camera.
3. Freedom from the anxiety of reservation foul-ups. You don't have to worry each day about whether that night's lodging will actually materialize.
4. The flexibility of making last-minutes changes to allow for unexpected weather, serendipitous discoveries, changing interests, new-found passions, and so on.
5. The flexibility to take breaks from sightseeing whenever you feel tired or bored, without upsetting a planned itinerary. Why not sleep late in your base city for a change?
6. The opportunity to sample different travel experiences without committing more than a day to them.
7. The opportunity to become a "temporary resident" of your base city. By staying there for a week or so you can get to know it in depth, becoming familiar with the local restaurants, shops, theaters, night life, and other attractions—enjoying them as a native would.

8. The convenience of not having to hunt for a hotel each day, along with the security of knowing that a familiar room is waiting back in your base city.
9. The convenience of not having to pack and unpack your bags each day. Your clothes can hang in a closet where they belong, or even be sent out for cleaning.
10. The convenience (and security!) of having a fixed address in your base city, where friends, relatives, and business associates can reach you in an emergency. It is often difficult to contact anyone who changes hotels daily.
11. The economy of staying at one hotel on a discounted longer-term basis, especially with airline package plans. You can make reservations for your base city without sacrificing any flexibility at all.
12. The economy of getting the most value out of a railpass. Daytripping is ideally suited to rail travel since the best train service operates out of base-city hubs. This is especially true in the cases of Paris, Marseille, and Nice.

Above all, daytrips ease the transition from tourist to accomplished traveler. Even if this is your first trip abroad, you can probably handle an uncomplicated one-day excursion such as the one to Versailles on your own. The confidence gained will help immensely when you tackle more complex destinations, freeing you from the limitations of guided tours and putting you in complete control of your own trip.

DISADVANTAGES:
For all of its attractions, the daytrip concept does have certain restrictions. There are always a few areas where geography and the available transportation have conspired to make one-day excursions impractical, or at least awkward. In France, these include Alsace, Lorraine, Brittany, Languedoc-Roussillon, and the Alps.

Another disadvantage is that you will have to forego the pleasures of staying at remote country inns. Should this deter you from making daytrips, you can still get the most from this guidebook by traveling directly between destinations without using bases. All of the walking tours and other information are still valid. You might also consider using daytrips part of the time and touring the rest.

CHOOSING A BASE CITY

Most of France's best attractions can be experienced on one-day excursions from either **Paris**, **Marseille**, or **Nice**—or from towns close to them. All three of these bases are natural transportation hubs, with a dense network of rail lines and highways radiating out from them. They are also convenient gateway cities for air travelers coming from overseas or other points in Europe. Paris is in itself one of the world's greatest destinations, while both Marseille and Nice offer a good range of worthwhile sights.

Paris is the natural base for daytrips to most of **central France**, which is covered in sections II to VI of this book. Section VII deals with **Provence**, for which Marseille, Arles, or Avignon make the best bases. The **Riviera**, or Côte d' Azur, described in Section VIII, is most conveniently explored by basing yourself in or around Nice.

ACCOMMODATIONS:

All three base cities tend to be tight on desirable hotel space at certain times, especially in summer. For this reason it is always best to make advance reservations for at least the first few days of your stay. Doing this in connection with an airline package plan can also save you money.

France offers the widest possible choice of accommodations, ranging from some of the most luxurious hotels in the world to some more practical choices, such as The Grand Hotel du Danemark near Gare de L'Est in Paris, ☎ 01-4607-2020. There's also a large selection of youth hostels. Another possibility, if you're staying in a base city for a week or more, is to rent a furnished apartment—a move that both cuts cost and allows you to feel more like a native. Arrangements for this should be made well in advance and secured with a deposit. For current information, check with an overseas branch of the French Government Tourist Office (see page 24), or with the classified ads in such publications as *International Travel News*. There are several Internet sites on this subject that can be accessed via links from the main tourist site, www.francetourism.com.

It is not necessary to stay in the base city itself; you may prefer the suburbs, which are usually well-served by commuter rail lines, and which are especially attractive if you're driving instead of traveling by rail. This option is often less expensive and may actually be more enjoyable.

Should you arrive in a city without reservations, head directly to the nearest local tourist information office, which probably has a branch at the airport or in or near a major train station. Their locations and phone numbers are given in the "Practicalities" section of each trip. Most of these offices can, for a small fee, find you a place to stay even at the last moment. They may even be able to get you bargain rates if the hotels happen to have a surplus of empty rooms at that time.

GETTING AROUND

BY RAIL:

The French love to travel by rail, which comes as no surprise as they are blessed with the fastest and some of the most modern trains in the world. Rail is almost invariably the quickest way to cover the medium distances outlined in the following chapters. The **French National Railroads**

(Société Nationale des Chemins de Fer Français, or **SNCF**) operates an average of 1,500 passenger trains a day over a dense network of more than 20,000 miles of track, serving some 4,000 stations. Many of its lines radiate in all directions from Paris, making daytrips from the capital exceptionally fast and easy. In an energy-conscious age it has been the policy of the French government to encourage rail travel by constantly improving the service with expanded schedules and state-of-the-art technology; and by making it readily affordable for both citizens and visitors.

A new era of rail transportation dawned in 1981 when the first **TGV** trains began service between Paris and Lyon. Presently operating at speeds of 186 mph on their own dedicated lines, one of these speed demons has actually been clocked during trials at a phenomenal 317 mph, a new world record! The expanded TGV fleet now serves many other destinations as well, sometimes running partly on regular tracks at reduced speed. The TGV *Atlantique*, operating from Montparnasse Station in Paris, runs to Angers and Nantes, as well as Rennes, Brest, Bordeaux, Toulouse, and Spain. TGV service from Nord Station in Paris goes to Lille and Calais; and as the **EuroStar** to London in three hours flat, non-stop via the Channel Tunnel. Recent expansions include **Thalys** service to Brussels, Amsterdam, Cologne, and Düsseldorf. Meanwhile, the running times of other express trains have been improved, with some routinely cruising at 125 mph.

Seasoned travelers often consider riding trains to be one of the best ways of meeting the local people and making new friends. It is not unusual to strike up an engaging conversation that makes your trip all the more memorable. You also get a marvelous view of the passing countryside from the large windows, and have time to catch up on your reading. Then too, you are spared the worries of driving, especially after having a few glasses of wine with your meals.

All trains belong to one of the following categories, as indicated on schedules and departure platforms:

TGV—*Train à Grande Vitesse.* The world's fastest trains offer a smooth, quiet air-conditioned ride between Paris (Lyon, Montparnasse and Nord stations) and many destinations throughout France, as well as to neighboring countries. Both first- and second-class accommodations are available. Reservations are an absolute requirement, and these may be made for a fee up until five minutes before departure, either at the reservation window or from special machines in the stations. There is a surcharge during peak travel times, which is waived for railpass users. Meal service at your seat is available for first-class passengers, but must be arranged for when you reserve your seat. A bar car for both classes provides light meals, sandwiches, snacks, and beverages.

EuroStar—Operated by a consortium of the French, British, and Belgian railways, these TGV-type trains offer extremely high-speed service via the Channel Tunnel from Paris (Nord Station) to London (Waterloo Station). Downtown to downtown, it's faster than flying. Reservations are required.

Thalys—Another consortium using TGV-type trains, provides extremely fast service from Paris to Brussels, Amsterdam, Cologne, and Düsseldorf. Reservations are required.

EC—*EuroCity.* High-speed international expresses with modern comforts. Both first- and second-class seating is offered, and there's a supplementary fare that's covered by the various Eurailpasses and by the France Railpass within France only. Those EC trains going to Geneva, Lausanne, or Bern are often of the TGV type, above, which require reservations. Reservations may be made for other EC trains if desired.

IC—*Intercité.* Fast international trains serving many towns in France with modern equipment. Both first- and second-class seating is available. A supplemental fare is charged, but not to users of railpasses. Reservations can be made if desired.

Express—These trains make more stops and frequently use modern equipment. The category also includes a number of foreign trains that may or may not measure up to French standards of comfort. Both classes of seating are available.

Omnibus—Often not given any particular designation, these locals make many stops and can take you to smaller, off-beat destinations. Much of the equipment is old and sometimes rather quaint, although there are modern omnibus trains. First class is not always offered.

In addition, you may want to use these services:

RER—Commuter trains operating on a very frequent schedule in and around Paris, which connect with the Métro subway system. They are operated by RATP, the Paris transit system, and in general do not accept railpasses. The equipment is modern and consists of both first- and second-class cars.

Buses—*Autocars,* operated by or for the French National Railroads and marked "SNCF," connect certain rural areas with train stations in larger towns; and fill in for some rail services during off-peak hours. Railpasses are valid on these—but not other—buses.

SCHEDULES for all SNCF services are available at the stations. Generally, the easiest way is to ask at the train information window, usually marked *Renseignements.* The personnel there may not always speak English, but you will have no trouble if you write out the name of your destination and the time you would like to leave, using the 24-hour clock. Doing this avoids the confusion caused by towns with similar-sounding names, such as Cannes, Cagnes, or Caen. It also prevents misunderstandings of day-to-day variations when, for example, a particular train only runs on Saturdays in summer. At the same time, always check the return schedule so you won't wind up stranded.

All schedules are stated in terms of the 24-hour clock, thus a departure at 3:32 p.m. would be shown as 15.32. Free printed pocket schedules *(Fiches-Horaires)* are available for popular destinations, and schedules are also posted throughout the stations. Be careful of any footnotes on these, as they often refer to variations. The **glossary** on page 291 will be helpful in making translations, as will a pocket French-English dictionary. The regional schedule books *(Indicateur Officiel),* available at station news-stands, are complete but very bulky to use. The smaller **Thomas Cook European Timetable,** sold in some travel book stores in America, by mail from the Forsyth Travel Library (P.O. Box 280800, Kansas City, MO 64148-0800, (1-800-FORSYTH, Internet: www.forsyth.com), or at Thomas Cook offices in Britain, is very useful although it does not list every local service. Information directly from the railroad is available on the **Internet** at www.sncf.fr.

   RESERVATIONS are required for all TGV trains and can be made up to two months in advance of, and up to five minutes before, departure time if seats are still available. There is a charge for this. Travelers who can read simple French may prefer the handy coin-operated TGV reservation machines, which are valid only for departures within the next hour. You may want to make reservations for other rail trips, particularly on the often-crowded trains to the Normandy coast in high season. One advantage to reservations is that you can specify a smoking or non-smoking section, and a window or aisle seat. Otherwise, reservations are not really necessary for the daytrips in this book other than those by TGV. Passengers traveling without them should be careful not to sit in someone else's reserved seat, which is marked by a card at the compartment entrance or above the seat.

   PARIS has many train stations, a legacy from the days before nationalization when just about every route was operated by a different company. The map on page 15 shows the general location of those that are of interest to tourists. All of them are connected by the Métro subway system and can be easily reached. Be sure you know which station you're leaving from before starting out on the day's adventures.

   It is always best to arrive at the station *(Gare)* a little early in order to acquaint yourself with its layout. On the departure platform *(Quai)* you will usually find a sign marked *Composition des Trains* that shows the make-up of each express leaving from that platform, including the location of each car. This serves two purposes. First, you won't have to make a last-minute dash when you discover that the first-class cars stop at the opposite end of a long platform. Secondly, and more important, it shows which—if any—cars are dropped off en route to your destination.

   The routing and final destination of each car is usually shown just outside its door as well as in its vestibule. First-class cars are marked with the numeral "1" near the door, and usually with a yellow stripe above the windows.

   Most express trains offer a **food and beverage service** of some sort, as indicated on the schedules. Riding in a regular dining car, bar car, or *Gril-Express* car can be a delightful experience, but beware the pushcarts in other cars that sell well-shaken cans of warm beer. You are much better off stocking up on snacks and refreshments at the station and bringing them

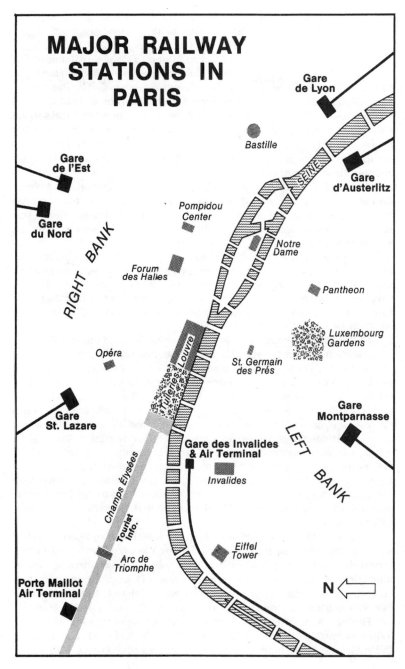

MAJOR RAILWAY STATIONS IN PARIS

along with you, as most Europeans do. Establishments offering take-out food and drinks are usually marked with the word *Emporter*.

RAILPASSES can be a bargain if you intend to do any real amount of train travel. Ask your travel agent about them before going to France, as they are difficult if not impossible to purchase once there. The French National Railroads (**SNCF**) accepts the following passes:

EURAILPASS—The best-known pass, allows unlimited first-class travel throughout 17 European countries, excluding Great Britain. It is available for periods of 15 or 21 consecutive days, or 1,2, or 3 months. The Eurailpass includes a wide variety of fringe benefits, and a discount on EuroStar Channel Tunnel service.

EURAIL FLEXIPASS—Allows unlimited first-class travel on any 10 or 15 days within a 2-month period. It is valid in the same 17 countries and has the same benefits as the regular Eurailpass. This is an attractive deal if you intend to spend time exploring the base cities as well as making daytrips from them.

EURAIL SAVERPASS—An economical version of the Eurailpass offering the same first-class benefits for groups of two to five people traveling together. This pass is available for periods of 15 or 21 consecutive days, or one, two, or three consecutive months, and the travel must *always* be done as a group. There is also a Flexi version valid for any 10 or 15 days in two months.

EURAIL YOUTHPASS—This low-cost version of the Eurailpass is available to anyone under the age of 26 and allows unlimited *second-class* travel in the same 17 countries for periods of 15 days, or one, two, or three months. There is also a **Eurail Youth Flexipass** valid for any 10 or 15 days within a two-month period.

EURAIL DRIVE PASS—A complex program that combines rail travel with car rentals at an attractive price, tailored to meet your specific needs.

EUROPASS—This mini-Eurailpass allows unlimited rail travel in France, Germany, Switzerland, Italy, and Spain. Adults travel in first class; the youth rate (under 26) is for second class. For an extra price, the following countries may be added: Austria/Hungary, Benelux, Greece, and Portugal. Durations of any 5 to 15 days within a 2-month period may be selected. There is also a **Europass Drive** arrangement combining rail travel with car rentals.

FRANCE RAILPASS—Valid for unlimited travel in France only (and to Monaco), this flexible pass is available for any 3 to 6 days within a 1-month period. It is offered in both first- and second-class versions, for either adults or for children between the ages of 4 and 11. Depending on the version purchased, it can represent a significant saving over the similar Eurail Flexipass and should be considered if your travels are limited to France.

FRANCE RAIL 'n DRIVE—A flexible arrangement that combines the France Railpass with a rental car at attractive rates. There is also a **France Rail 'n Fly** pass combining rail travel with flights within France, and for the ultimate in versatility, the **France Fly, Rail 'n Drive Pass.**

All railpasses must be **validated** at the information window of a train station on the first day of actual use. The first and last days of validity will be entered on the pass at that time. Be certain that you agree with the dates *before* allowing the agent to write them in.

If you intend to take several of the daytrips in this book, and especially if at least one of them is to a distant location such as Lyon, Dijon, or Angers, a railpass will probably wind up saving you a considerable amount of money. Even if the savings are less than that, a pass should still be considered for the convenience it offers in not having to line up for tickets, and for the freedom of just hopping aboard most trains at whim. Possession of a railpass will also encourage you to become more adventurous, to seek out distant and offbeat destinations. And, should you ever manage to get on the wrong train by mistake, your only cost will be your time.

The various Eurailpasses, Europasses, and France Railpasses are sold by most travel agents in North America, who also have current information and prices. Alternatively, you could contact the North American agent for the French Railroads, **Rail Europe**, at 226 Westchester Ave., White Plains, NY 10604, ☎ toll-free 1-800-438-7245, Internet: www.raileurope.com. They will happily supply you with a booklet of current French and European fares, useful in determining whether to buy a railpass, and a catalog of custom travel programs. The French National Railroads also has offices in London and throughout Europe.

Those who have decided against a railpass can purchase tickets *(billets)* at ticket windows *(guichets)* in the stations, or from automatic vending machines. There is usually no saving to be had by buying a round-trip ticket. Be sure to **validate** your ticket—*compostez votre billet*—before use by inserting it into one of the orange ticket-stamping machines *(composteur)* located near the platforms. Round-trip *(aller et retour)* tickets must also be stamped on the return journey. Failure to validate could result in a fine, since the SNCF operates on an honor system with only a few spot checks made, and unvalidated tickets could be used over and over again or even redeemed for cash.

If you meet the age requirements and are staying in France long enough, you might want to invest in a discount card. Typically, these are valid for one year but will pay for themselves long before that. They offer a 50% reduction on point-to-point tickets during non-rush "blue" periods, and 20% off during busier "white" periods. There is no discount during the rare ultra-peak "red" periods. Youths between 12 and 25 can get the **Carte 12-25** card, valid for both themselves and up to three companions of the same age range. Seniors over 60 qualify for the **Carte Senior**, valid for the named traveler only. Both are sold in major train stations in France.

BY BUS:

A few of the daytrips in this book are to destinations not served by the railroad. To reach them by public transportation, you should first take a train to the nearest town on a rail line and then continue on by connecting bus. Instructions for doing this are given in each case. Railpasses are valid on buses operated by or for the SNCF; others require payment of a fare. Buses, often called *Autobus* or *Autocar,* usually depart from a bus station *(gare routière),* most often located next to or near the train station.

BY CAR:

Many tourists prefer to explore France by car, which may be more economical when several people are traveling together. Although slower, cars offer a complete freedom from schedules. All of the daytrips in this book (except those within Paris) can be made this way, with distances and road directions provided for each. In addition to a car you will need a valid driver's license and, to play it safe, an International Driving Permit. The latter is issued in America by the AAA, in Canada by the CAA, and by other automobile clubs. While not strictly required, this multi-language translation of your license can smooth things over in a sticky situation. You'll also need a good regional road map. Those published by Michelin are excellent and highly detailed.

Driving in France is essentially the same as in the U.S.A. or Canada, but attention should be paid to a few points. Seat belts are compulsory at all times for both the driver and front-seat passenger, with children under 12 confined to the rear seat. Failure to heed this rule could result in a fine. Similarly, the penalties for driving while intoxicated can be quite severe. Be particularly wary of the notorious *priorité à droite* rule, in which vehicles coming from the right have the right-of-way. While there are many exceptions to this, you should always be careful and never try to bluff a French driver—they know their rights and take them very seriously.

Roads in France are excellent and well marked. *Autoroutes,* designated by the letter "A" preceding their number, are usually limited-access toll *(péage)* roads with a 130-kph (80 mph) speed limit. This may be lower in some areas, or in bad weather. Other main roads, known as *Routes Nationales* or "N" roads, are free and most often have a 90-kph limit (60-kph in built-up areas). To get the real flavor of the country, however, you should at least occasionally drive on the *Routes Départementales* (letter "D"), local roads that meander from village to village. If you have the time, you might find it more enjoyable to use minor roads instead, following a good local road map. An **Internet** site to check for route planning is: www.iti.fr.

A brief **glossary** for drivers is provided on page 292. For more comprehensive automotive terms, you may want to use a pocket-size phrase book, such as *French for Travellers* by Berlitz.

CAR RENTALS *(Location de Voitures)* should be arranged in advance through your travel agent or one of the major chains such as Hertz, Avis, National, or Budget. There are also many local firms that might charge less, but which may impose severe restrictions on drop-off possibilities and other conveniences. Among the best deals available are the fly/drive plans offered by various airlines in conjunction with their transatlantic flights. Check with your travel agent about this as arrangements must be made in advance. If you intend to rent a car for over 17 days it will pay to consider **leasing**—an arrangement that is exempt from the stiff tax on rentals and which saves money on insurance. Finally, in estimating your expenses, remember that gasoline (essence) costs several times as much in France as in America. Before returning a rental car, be sure to fill up the tank to avoid a high refilling charge.

BY AIR:

You may prefer air travel for the long haul between major base cities in France, particularly from Paris to Nice. There are frequent flights on this route, as well as an extensive network of domestic services between all major cities in France, with competition from several regional carriers.

Paris has two major airports, **Charles de Gaulle** *(also called Roissy)*, north of the city; and **Orly**, to the south. Most transatlantic flights land at Charles de Gaulle. Air France operates buses from each, which can be used by passengers on other airlines as well. These connect CDG airport with Gare Montparnasse, the Arc de Triomphe, and Porte Maillot in Paris; and Orly with Gare Montparnasse and Invalides, also in Paris. Taxis are a more convenient way of getting into town and have the advantage of taking you directly to your destination. There are also combination bus/train services called "Roissy Rail" and "Orly Rail," which are convenient if you don't have too much luggage. They go to/from Nord and Austerlitz stations respectively.

On the Riviera, the Nice-Côte d'-Azur Airport is so close to downtown Nice that taxis are practical for all but the slimmest budgets. There is also a local bus service.

FOOD AND DRINK

Several choice restaurants are listed for each destination in this book. Most of these are long-time favorites of experienced travelers and serve French cuisine. Their approximate price range, based on the least expensive complete meal offered, is indicated as follows:

$	—	Inexpensive, but may have fancier dishes available.
$$	—	Reasonable. These establishments may also feature daily specials.
$$$	—	Luxurious and expensive.
$$$+	—	Very expensive.
X:	—	Days or periods closed.

Those who take their dining very seriously should consult an up-to-date restaurant and hotel guide such as the classic red-covered *Michelin France*, issued annually in March.

It is always wise to check the prices posted outside the restaurant before entering. Remember that in France the word **"menu"** refers to a fixed-price *(prix-fixe)* set meal, consisting of several courses, often with a range of choices for each, and possibly including a drink *(boisson comprise)*. Ordering from the *menu* is almost invariably the most economical way to dine. Most restaurants offer several *menus* in which complexity increases with price. The cheapest of these is often called the *menu touristique* and the most expensive the *menu gastronomique* or the *menu dégustation*, which is a sampling of small portions of the chef's best dishes. **A la carte**, on the other hand, means that each item is individually priced, affording a greater choice but usually costing quite a bit more. These items are listed on the *carte*.

The word **entrée** does not have the same meaning as in North America; rather it designates a course served between the appetizer *(hors d'oeuvre)* and the main course. **Meats** in France are not cooked as thoroughly as most Americans are accustomed to. If you want a steak well done *(bien cuit)*, be sure to tell the waiter. **Coffee** is *never* consumed during a meal and its cost is not included in the *prix-fixe*. Wait until after the dessert, then enjoy a small cup of *café express*, a black brew as delicious as it is strong. **Water** may be drunk during the meal, with or without wine. You can order a mineral water *(eau minérale)*, either sparkling *(gazeuse)* or still *(non-gazeuse)* for a small cost; or just plain tap water *(eau fraîche, une carafe d'eau)*, which is free. A **salad**—frequently just lettuce with a dressing—is generally served after the main course, unless it is an appetizer such as *crudités*. A selection of cheeses *(plateau de fromage)* is almost always offered just before the dessert or as the dessert.

Menus and ***cartes*** are usually written in French only. While the waiter can often be of help, it is much better if you understand the names of various dishes. The simplified **Menu Translator** beginning on page 286 and the **Glossary of Dining Terms** on page 290 cover the most basic names and terms, while the more adventurous may want to use a pocket-sized translator book such as the *Marling Menu Master for France*, which will help you to try unfamiliar dishes without anxiety.

Tips are often included in the price of the meal *(service compris, s.c., or prix net)*. If not *(service non compris, or s.n.c.)*, an amount—usually 15%—will be added to the bill *(L'addition)*. The policy of the restaurant is noted on the menu or carte, although sometimes cryptically. Asking about this is perfectly proper and will offend no one. Leaving a small additional tip is an accepted way of saying "thank you" for good service.

One of the secrets to keeping your restaurant bills within reason is to order the **house wine** *(vin de maison)* rather than the more expensive choices. In any good restaurant the chef is proud of his cooking and selects the house wine as a complement to it, so you really can't go wrong.

These wines, often served in an open pitcher *(carafe* or *pichet),* half-bottle *(demi-bouteille)* or whole bottle *(bouteille)* are usually available in red *(rouge),* white *(blanc),* or rosé.

Unless you are familiar with French vintages, it is best to consult the waiter before choosing a more complex wine. He has the experience to suggest the right wine for the meal you ordered. Nearly every corner of France has its own type of wine, and most of these go very well with the local cuisine. French **beers** can be quite good, especially those from Alsace. Beers imported from nearby Germany, Belgium, and Holland are also very popular.

Those in a hurry to get on with their sightseeing will find that there are many low-cost alternatives to restaurant dining. These range from the traditional *pique-nique* lunch made from ingredients purchased at nearby markets to having a *croque-monsieur* or other sandwich at a café; or whatever catches your eye in a self-service cafeteria, or even a French hamburger and *crudités* at one of those ubiquitous fast-food outlets.

If you are not completely famished but would still like a traditional French meal, why not stop in at a *crêperie?* The specialties there include *galettes* (pancakes stuffed with meat, cheese, vegetables, or fish), dessert *crêpes* and hard cider. These places are often quite atmospheric and very inexpensive. Pizzerias are also extremely popular with the French.

PRACTICALITIES

PACKAGE PLANS:

The cost of your trip to France can be cut substantially by selecting one of the many attractive package plans that combine transatlantic airfares with local hotel accommodations and/or car rentals. Since the details of these programs, as well as the airfares, change frequently you should consult with a reliable travel agent well ahead of time, or check them out on such Internet sites as: www.Travelocity.com.

HOLIDAYS:

Legal holidays *(Fêtes Légales)* in France are:

January 1	July 14 (Bastille Day)
Easter Monday	August 15 (Assumption Day)
May 1 (Labor Day)	November 1 (All Saints' Day)
May 8 (V-E Day)	November 11 (Armistice Day)
Ascension Day	Christmas
(40 days after Easter)	
Whit Monday (Second Monday	
after Ascension)	

In addition, the Principality of Monaco celebrates:

January 27 (Feast of St.- Dévote)	November 19 (National Day)

Trains operate on holiday schedules on these days, and some attractions may be closed. Banks close at noon on the day preceding a holiday. When any of these falls on a Sunday, the following Monday is taken as a holiday.

MONEY MATTERS:

Traveler's Checks are the safest way to protect your money while abroad. They often, however, entail service charges both when you buy them and again when you convert them into *Francs* (or *Euros* after 2002) in France. Avoid dealing with storefront money changers that thrive wherever tourists gather. Regular commercial banks are your best bet for changing money, whether cash or traveler's checks. Changing relatively large sums at one time will take some of the sting out of service charges.

Automated Teller Machines (ATMs) *(guichets automatiques)* offer the best exchange rates to be found anywhere, and allow you to take money directly out of your home bank account as you need it. They are usually open 24 hours a day, are conveniently located all over France, and yield cash in Francs (Euros after 2002). Check with your issuing bank before leaving home to make sure that your PIN code will work in France.

Credit cards are widely accepted at the more expensive establishments throughout France, but less often by budget hotels and restaurants. They may also be used to yield cash advances from ATM machines *(guichets automatiques)*, provided you have a compatible PIN code. The most commonly accepted cards are Visa *(Carte Bleue)* and MasterCard *(EuroCard)*, with American Express a distant third.

TELEPHONES:

To phone ahead from anywhere in France, you must dial the complete 10-digit number. All numbers in Paris begin with 01, all numbers outside of Paris begin with 02 to 04. Calling ahead is useful if the whole reason for your daytrip hinges on seeing a particular sight that might possibly be closed, or perhaps to check the weather.

A few pay phones in France still use coins—just load up the slot with small denominations and any that are not used will be returned. The newer type of pilfer-proof pay phones accept no coins but are operated by inserting a "Télécarte" card, available in various denominations at any post office or from most "Tabac" shops, many cafés, newsstands, and so on. The cost of each call is electronically subtracted from the value of the card as it is used.

SUGGESTED TOURS

The do-it-yourself walking tours in this book are relatively short and easy to follow. Walking is almost always the best way to explore the old towns of France, and certainly the healthiest, although you may want to use local transportation for the occasional steep hill or long stretch. Details about this are mentioned whenever they might apply. On the assumption that most readers will be arriving by public transportation, the tours always begin at the local train station, bus or Métro stop. Those going by car can make a simple adjustment. Suggested routes are shown by heavy broken lines on the maps, while the circled numbers refer to major attractions or points of reference along the way, with corresponding numbers in the text.

Trying to see everything in any given town could easily become an exhausting marathon. You will certainly enjoy yourself more by being selective and passing by anything that doesn't catch your fancy in favor of a friendly sidewalk café. God will forgive you if you don't visit *every* church.

Practical information, such as the opening times of various attractions, is as accurate as was possible at the time of writing. Everything is, of course, subject to change. You should always check with the local tourist office if seeing a particular sight is crucially important to you.

As a way of estimating the time any segment of the walking tour will take, you can look at the scale on the map and figure that the average person covers about 100 yards in one minute. The maps, by the way, were drawn to best fit the page size. North does not necessarily point to the top, but is always indicated by an arrow.

*OUTSTANDING ATTRACTIONS:

An * asterisk before any attractions, be it an entire daytrip or just one exhibit in a museum, denotes a special treat that in the author's opinion should not be missed.

TOURIST INFORMATION

Virtually every French town of any tourist interest has its own information office, usually called a *Syndicat d'Initiative* or *Office de Tourisme,* which can help you with specific questions, furnish maps and brochures, or book local accommodations. They almost invariably have at least one person on staff who speaks English. Sometimes these offices are closed on Sundays, holidays, or over the noon meal period.

The location of the offices is shown on the town maps in this book by the word "info.," or the symbol **i** and repeated along with the phone number under the "Practicalities" section for each trip. Wherever relevant, the **Internet** address is also given. Some of these World Wide Web sites are good, while others are just too commercial, but at least they will give you some free information in advance of your trip, or on the road if you're toting a computer. New sites are constantly being added, so if one is not listed just enter the town's name followed by .fr, perhaps throwing in the word tourism, visit, or the like. Most offer English text by clicking on an image of a British or American flag. You can also use a search engine such as AltaVista or Yahoo.

ADVANCE PLANNING INFORMATION:

The **French Government Tourist Office** *(Maison de la France)* has branches throughout the world that will gladly help you in planning your trip. In North America these are located at:

444 Madison Ave., **New York** NY 10022
676 North Michigan Ave., **Chicago**, IL 60611
9454 Wilshire Blvd., **Beverly Hills**, CA 90212
1981 Ave. McGill College, Suite 490, **Montreal**, P.Q. H3A 2W9, Canada

☎ for **information requests** (410) 286-8310, or use the **Internet:** www.france tourism.com

In **England,** they are at 178 Piccadilly, London W1V OAL, ☎ (0171) 6399-3500.

Section II

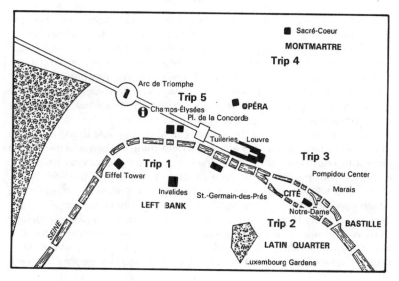

- Sacré-Coeur
  MONTMARTRE
  Trip 4

Arc de Triomphe
Trip 5
Champs-Élysées ● OPÉRA
Pl. de la Concorde
Tuileries Louvre
Trip 3
Trip 1 Pompidou Center
Eiffel Tower Marais
Invalides CITÉ
LEFT BANK St.-Germain-des-Prés
Notre-Dame
Trip 2 BASTILLE
LATIN QUARTER
SEINE
Luxembourg Gardens

DAYTRIPS WITHIN PARIS

Paris is quite simply the most beautiful city on Earth, and exploring it in depth could easily become a lifelong passion. Like most visitors, you probably don't have that much time available, but still want to see some of its best and most famous sights within a period of a few days. The five walking tours in this section are efficiently organized to provide a good overall impression of the city at a fairly leisurely pace by connecting the major attractions with routes that lead along some of the most interesting streets. Each tour is intended to last the better part of one day, depending on the amount of time you spend at stops along the way, having lunch, and just sitting at outdoor cafés or in parks. There is no need to rush—the actual walking time should never be much more than one hour.

Each tour begins where the previous one left off, which is always at a Métro (subway) station. Truly ambitious walkers could continue on and do part or all of the next tour. After completing the five routes you will have seen most of the main sights of Paris, but only begun to nibble at the visual feast it offers. To experience the best of what remains you should refer to the "Additional Attractions" chapter beginning on page 70.

GETTING AROUND PARIS

The **Métro** (subway) is by far the fastest, easiest, and cheapest way of getting around Paris. For convenience, all of the walking tours described in the next five chapters begin and end at a Métro station. Wherever you are in Paris, you're never more than a few minutes from one of the 360 stations spread along 120 miles of tracks. The trains run frequently between about 5:30 a.m. and 12:30 the following morning. They are cleaner than you might expect in a large city, and plagued with very little actual crime other than occasional pickpockets. Hang onto your wallet.

Despite its complexity, the Métro is amazingly simple to use once you master a few basic rules. First, you must determine the name of the station closest to your destination, then trace a route on the subway map to it. Continue your tracing in the same direction to the end of the line *(ligne)*, where you will see the name of its last station. This is the *direction* in which you should travel. The *lignes* also have numbers, but these are seldom referred to. It may be necessary to make a change *(correspondence)* of trains en route, in which case you should note the *direction* of the first line, the name of the station at which the change is made, and the *direction* of the second line. In a very few cases a second change may be needed.

All Métro stations have system-wide maps on their walls. In addition, major stations have electric maps where you press a button for your final destination and the best route automatically lights up. Some stations have computer terminals that give you a printout of the quickest route to your destination. A pocket-size map *(Plan de Métro)* of the system is available free at major stations.

Fares are the same regardless of the distance traveled, with a few exceptions for stations well out of town. You can save quite a bit of money by purchasing a pack of ten tickets, called a *carnet*. It is also possible to buy a **Formule 1** card valid for one day of unlimited travel on the Métro, RER, city buses, and suburban SNCF trains; or a **Paris Visite** card valid for 2, 3 or 5 consecutive days. Both cards are offered in a range of zones, the most expensive also covering the airports. They are sold at major Métro stations and at the main Paris tourist office.

The magnetically-encoded tickets operate electric turnstiles and are then returned to you. Be sure to retain them until the end of the trip as occasional spot checks are made. Once in the station, follow the *direction* signs to the proper platform. Change of trains are made by following the orange *correspondence* signs, while the blue *sortie* signs lead to the exits.

The **RER** is a commuter rail service that runs as an express subway within Paris and continues on the surface to outlying towns such as Versailles, St.-Germain-en-Laye, both airports, and even Disneyland Paris. Métro tickets may be used for second-class travel within the city limits of Paris, but otherwise a special ticket to your particular destination is needed, or you can use the Formule 1 or Paris Visite card assuming that they cover the appropriate zones. All RER trains carry both first- and second-class cars. Most of its stations within Paris connect directly to the Métro.

Buses are a slow but picturesque way to get around Paris. They are operated by the same RATP authority and use regular Métro tickets—one for short distances and 2, 3, or 4 for longer ones. If you're not sure about this, just ask the driver. Tickets must be punched in the canceling machine near the entrance. Do not punch the ticket that comes with the Formule 1 or Paris Visite card as this invalidates it. Be sure to keep your ticket as you may have to show it to an inspector. A system map *(Plan d'Autobus)* is available free at major Métro station information booths, and a route diagram posted at each bus stop. In general, city buses operate between about 6:30 a.m. and 8:30 p.m., while some run later and a few continue all night long.

Taxis are a reasonable way of getting around Paris, especially if two or three people are traveling together. They usually do not cruise looking for passengers, but can be found parked at taxi ranks marked *Tête de Station* or *Arrêt Taxis.* Be aware that there are day (7 a.m. to 7 p.m.) and night fares plus additional charges for stopping at train stations or airports, and for excess luggage. For your own safety use metered cabs only. A tip of 15% is expected.

By car, in a word—don't. Driving (and parking!) in Paris is at best an experience to avoid.

PRACTICALITIES

WHEN TO GO:

Any time is a good time to visit Paris, but the city is probably at its best in late spring and early fall. Many Parisians take their lengthy vacations in July and August, leaving the streets to the tourists. Quite a few of the attractions are closed on Tuesdays, and others on Mondays. These are noted in the "Practicalities" section for each walking tour.

FOOD AND DRINK:

A selection of good restaurants and cafés in different price categories has been included for each of the five Paris walking tours. All of these are on or near the suggested route. For a more comprehensive list covering more of Paris you should refer to one of the many published dining guides to the city.

MONEY SAVER:

An attractions pass called the **Carte Musées et Monuments** is available at major museums, monuments, Métro stations, and the main Paris tourist office. It allows unlimited visits with free admission to some 65 museums and monuments in and around Paris, including the Louvre, the Musée d'Orsay, Versailles, and many others. One great advantage to this pass, besides saving money, is that you avoid having to stand in lines for admission. The pass is available for periods of one, three, or five consecutive days.

TOURIST INFORMATION:

The main Paris tourist office is located at 127 Avenue des Champs-Élysées, ☎ 01-4952-5354, Internet: www.paris.org. There are also branches at the Nord and Lyon train stations, and at the Eiffel Tower in season. Most of these offices can make last-minute hotel reservations for you, as well provide information.

*The Left Bank

Nothing is more symbolic of Paris than the Eiffel Tower, so it seems appropriate to begin your walks with the classic view of it, perhaps ascending to the top for a sweeping panoramic survey of the city. The suggested tour described in this chapter continues on through the most interesting neighborhoods *(quartiers)* of the Left Bank *(Rive Gauche)* but stops short of the Latin Quarter, which is covered in the next chapter. Along the way you will be able to visit some of the greatest sights in Paris, including the Invalides, the Rodin and Orsay museums, the picturesque quays along the Seine, and the colorful St.-Germain-des-Prés district. The walk ends in a delightful area that is especially rich in outdoor cafés, where you can relax in the traditional Parisian fashion.

GETTING THERE:

The quickest way to get to the starting point of this walk from most parts of Paris is to take the **Métro** to Trocadéro. You can also reach it via **bus** routes 22, 30, 32, or 63. Buses 72 and 82 stop at the foot of the bridge opposite the Eiffel Tower. By **taxi**, ask the driver for Place du Trocadéro.

PRACTICALITIES:

This walking tour can be taken on any day, but note that the Orsay and Rodin museums are closed on Mondays, and the Delacroix Museum on Tuesdays.

FOOD AND DRINK:

There is no shortage of restaurants and cafés along or near the suggested route, while you find a particularly good selection around Place St.-Germain-des-Prés. Some outstanding choices in all price categories are:

Allard (41 Rue St.-André-des-Arts, 3 blocks west of Place St. Michel) A longtime favorite of Parisians, ☎ 01-4326-4823 for reservations. X: Sun., Aug. $$$

Brasserie Lipp (151 Blvd. St.-Germain, a block west of the Church of St.-Germain-des-Prés) A famous old café with an intellectual clientele. Alsatian specialties. ☎ 01-4548-5391. $$$

Vagenende (142 Blvd. St.-Germain, 2 blocks east of the Church of St.-Germain-des-Prés) Serving traditional cuisine in a Belle Époque setting since 1898. ☎ 01-4326-6818. $$

Le Procope (13 Rue de L'Ancienne-Comédie, 5 blocks east of the Church of St.-Germain-des-Prés) A café since 1686, now a restaurant. Voltaire dined here, as did Benjamin Franklin. ☎ 01- 4046-7900. $$

Thoumieux (79 Rue St.-Dominique, 3 blocks northwest of the Invalides) Fine traditional cuisine in a turn-of-the-century atmosphere. ☎ 01-4705-4975. $ and $$

Aux Charpentiers (10 Rue Mabillon, 2 blocks south of the Church of St.-Germain-des-Prés) This is what Left Bank bistros were like decades ago. ☎ 01-4326-3005. X: Sun. $ and $$

Restaurant des Beaux-Arts (11 Rue Bonaparte, by the Beaux-Arts school) Good food and very crowded. A great value. ☎ 01-4326-9264. $

Petit Saint-Benoît (4 Rue Saint-Benoît, 2 blocks northwest of the Church of St.-Germain-des-Prés) A simple neighborhood bistro with low prices. ☎ 01-4260-2792. $

SUGGESTED TOUR:

Numbers in parentheses correspond to numbers on the map.

Begin your walking tour at the Trocadéro Métro Station (1). Next to this stands the massive Palais de Chaillot, a Neo-Classical structure left over from the Paris Exposition of 1937. Built in two symmetrically-curved wings, it now houses a theater and four museums that you might want to visit on another day. These are the Naval Museum *(Musée de la Marine)*, the Museum of Mankind *(Musée de l'Homme)*, the Museum of French Monuments, and the Museum of the Cinema.

Step out onto its central terrace for the most spectacular view of the Eiffel Tower possible, then continue straight ahead, going down steps past the gardens and fountains. The Pont d'Iéna, built by Napoleon in 1814 to commemorate a victory over the Prussians, spans the Seine and leads to the Left Bank. Rising dramatically in front of you is the:

*EIFFEL TOWER *(Tour Eiffel)* (2), ☎ 01-4411-2323, Internet: www.eiffel-tower.com. *Open daily 9:30 a.m. (9 in spring and summer) to 11 p.m. (midnight from early July–early Sept.). Lift tickets to first level 21FF, second level 43FF, third level 60FF; children 4–12 are almost half-price. Use the west and north pillars. If you prefer to walk up the stairs (south pillar) to the first and second levels, the cost is 15FF.*

It may be hard to imagine Paris without its beloved symbol, but at first many leading Parisians didn't think so. In fact, there was a strong movement to have it torn down, and the tower was saved only after the French Army discovered its strategic use as a radio antenna, a function it still serves. When it was built for the World's Fair of 1889 it was, at 1,051 feet, the tallest structure on Earth, and it retained that record for decades. The tower is named after its designer, Gustave Eiffel, a structural engineer who also built the inner framework of the Statue of Liberty in New York.

You can ascend the tower for a birds-eye *view of Paris and the surrounding countryside, but expect long lines for the elevator during the tourist season. Actually, the view is better around sunset when the lights of Paris come on, so you might want to return here later in the day.

From the base of the tower a large open park called the **Champ-de-Mars**, originally a military parade ground, spreads southeast to the imposing **École Militaire**. Built in the 18th century, this famous military academy had among its graduates a young artillery lieutenant named Napoleon Bonaparte, who it predicted would "go far under favorable circumstances."

Napoleon, of course, did go far, but today he rests just around the corner at **Les Invalides** (3). Built by Louis XIV in the late 17th century as a retirement home for wounded war veterans, this monumental complex now houses several attractions. Along its southern end stands the **Church of the Dome**, an outstanding structure in the French Classical style designed by the most important architect of the time, Jules Hardouin-Mansart. Inside, in an open circular crypt, is a red porphyry sarcophagus containing the mortal remains of Napoleon. The great emperor is still deeply revered by the French people. Other notable soldiers buried here include Vauban and Marshal Foch.

The same complex includes the **Museum of the Army**, one of the greatest military museums on Earth. Part of it is on the east side of the inner courtyard and is devoted to the history of the French Army, while the section on the west side has a fine collection of medieval armor, weapons, and intriguing exhibits dealing with the two world wars of this century. Connecting with it is the **Museum of Relief Maps**, which features superb scale models of French strongholds from 1668 to 1870. ☎ *01-4442-3767, Internet: www.invalides.org. Open daily 10–4:45, closing at 5:45 from April–Sept. Adults 38FF, seniors, students, children 28FF.*

Continue on through the complex and follow the map to one of the most enchanting sights in Paris, the ***Rodin Museum** (4). Housed in a small 18th-century mansion called the Hôtel Biron and surrounded by delightful private gardens, the museum is devoted to the works of the renowned sculptor Auguste Rodin, who worked here from 1908 until his death in 1917. Even if you don't care for museums, you'll probably love this place. The house contains his own works, personal collection, and furnishings; while scattered around the gardens are such masterpieces as *The Thinker, Balzac*, the *Burghers of Calais*, and the fabulous *Gates of Hell*. Their strength and vitality is astonishing, especially in so marvelous a setting. ☎ *01-4705-0134. Open Tues.–Sun., 9:30–4:45, remaining open until 5:45 from April–Sept. Adults 28FF, seniors and youths 18–25 18FF, under 18 free. Reduced admission on Sun. Garden alone 5FF. Gift shop. Café.*

The route now leads through the elegant **Faubourg-Saint-Germain**, a district of gracious mansions presently occupied by government ministries and foreign embassies. Next to the river is the **Palais Bourbon**, an 18th-century palace built by a daughter of Louis XIV and later embellished

Paris
The Left Bank

M = Métro Station

1,000 Yards

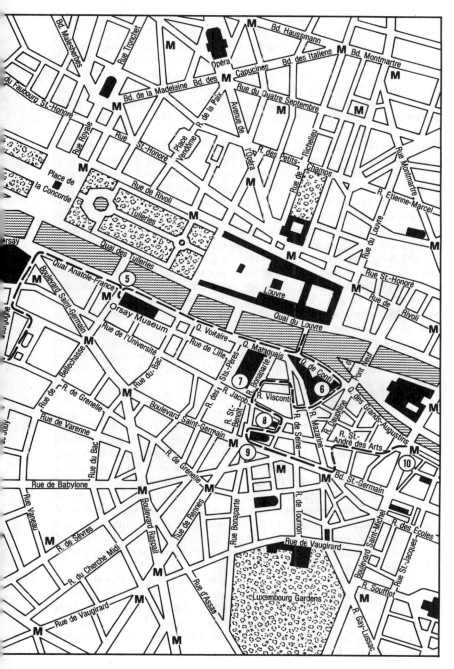

by Napoleon. Since 1827 it has housed the National Assembly, the lower house of the French Parliament.

A right turn on the Quai Anatole-France takes you along the Seine to the **Gare d'Orsay**, a former railroad station built around 1900. Alas, its platforms proved to be too short for express trains and after 1939 it fell into virtual disuse. There were plans to demolish the noble structure, but reason prevailed and after a variety of more-or-less artistic uses, it was converted into a museum in 1986. No visitor to Paris should miss the fabulous:

*MUSÉE d'ORSAY (5), ☎ 01-4049-4814, recording 01-4549-1111, Internet: www.musee-orsay.fr. *Open Tues.–Sun., 10 (9 on Sun. and in summer) to 6, closing at 9:45 on Thurs. Adults 40FF, seniors and youths 18–25 30FF, under 18 free. Tickets valid for re-entry all day. Separate admission for special exhibitions. Guided tours in English, 11 a.m. Tues.–Sat., 40FF. Audio guides 30FF. English guidebook 95FF. Restaurant. Gift shop.*

Despite a storm of controversy raised by critics, this is certainly one of the most popular attractions in town. Covering the entire scope of art from 1848 to 1914, it bridges the immense gap between the Classical collections of the Louvre and the modern works in the Pompidou Center. Many of its Impressionist paintings are from the old Jeu de Paume Museum, but there is a great deal more than this. In addition to painting and sculpture, you will find sections on the decorative arts, photography, cinema, architecture, and town planning. Everything is linked chronologically with counterpart movements in literature, music, sociology, politics, and economics. A visit here takes several hours, so you may prefer to return when you can devote the amount of time that it deserves. Expect crowds during the tourist season.

Continue along the quai, which becomes even more colorful as you approach the ***Pont des Arts**, a charming iron footbridge across the Seine that was opened in 1803. Just beyond it is the **Institut de France**, home of the venerable Académie Française, a prestigious body charged with protecting the purity of the French language. This is surely a hopeless task in the land of le week-end and le hamburger. Four other learned societies also meet beneath its majestic dome. Adjacent to it is the former Royal Mint, the **Hôtel des Monnaies** (6). This now houses the small **Museum of Coins and Medals**, covering the entire scope of French minting from ancient to modern times. ☎ *01-4046-5535. Open Tues.–Fri., 11–5:30 and weekends noon–5:30. Adults 20FF, seniors and students 15FF, under 16 free. Free for all on Sun.*

From here the route gets a bit tricky, so you will have to follow the map carefully. It leads through some very old and colorful streets to the **School of Fine Arts** (*École des Beaux-Arts*) (7), founded in the early 19th century on the site of a former monastery. Although not generally open to the public, there are occasional exhibitions of works by the students that you might be able to see.

Turn left on Rue Bonaparte and left again on Rue Jacob, continuing on to the tiny **Place de Fürstemberg**. This is easily among the most charming and romantic small squares in Paris, with an atmosphere right out of the 17th century. On its west side is the house where the artist Eugène Delacroix lived and worked until his death in 1863. It has been preserved as he left it, and is now the **Delacroix Museum** (8). Don't miss seeing this remarkable little gem. ☎ *01-4441-8650. Open Wed.–Mon., 9:30–5:30. Adults 22FF (15FF on Sun.), seniors, students, children 15FF.*

A right turn into the quiet Rue de l'Abbaye brings you to **Place St.-Germain-des-Prés**, one of the main centers of activity on the Left Bank. This is a great place to sit down at an outdoor café and just watch the world go by, perhaps at the famous **Deux Magots** or the **Flore**. Facing the square is the 11th-century **Church of St.-Germain-des-Prés** (9), whose origins go back to the 6th century and which ranks as the oldest church in Paris. Originally this was part of an enormous Benedictine abbey whose 42,000 acres of land were surrounded by a defensive moat and extended all the way to the Seine. During the French Revolution the abbey was broken up and much of its church was vandalized. An unsatisfactory restoration in the 19th century didn't help matters, but the interior is still worth visiting for its interesting mixture of Romanesque, Gothic, and later styles.

Continue down the lively Boulevard St.-Germain. Many of the narrow streets leading off this thoroughfare in either direction are worth exploring if you have the time. When you get to the Odéon Métro stop, turn left into the well-hidden **Cour du Commerce St.-André**, a tiny alleyway lined with old shops. There is so much to see around here by just poking into the little passageways and following your instincts. When you tire of this, turn down the delightful Rue St.-André-des-Arts to its eastern end, where some nice outdoor cafés provide the perfect spot to relax at the end of this walk. From here it is only a few steps to the **St.-Michel Métro Station** (10), where you can get a subway or RER train back to your hotel. If you happen to be still bursting with energy, you might want to begin the next walk, described in the following chapter.

Trip 2
Paris

*The Latin Quarter and the Cité

This walking tour takes you through the very oldest sections of Paris. The Latin Quarter, first settled by the Romans around the time of Christ, is on the Left Bank while the still more ancient Île de la Cité, an island in the Seine, has been inhabited for well over 2,000 years. Although many changes have occurred during their long histories, the neighborhoods covered in this walk are still charged with a romantic atmosphere that is quite different from that of the rest of Paris. This is mostly due to the presence of the Sorbonne and other colleges, whose students bring a youthful vitality to a venerable district.

Some of the highlights passed along the suggested walking route include the Cluny Museum, the Luxembourg Gardens, the Panthéon, the Conciergerie, the Sainte-Chapelle, Notre-Dame Cathedral, and the Île St.-Louis. Seeing all of them could take the better part of a day, but by skipping by a few you might be able to continue on and do part of the next tour, or at least have more time for relaxing at an outdoor café or in one of the gardens.

GETTING THERE:

The start of this walking tour may be easily reached by taking the **Métro** to Saint-Michel. It is also served by **bus** routes 21, 27, 38, 85, and 96. By **taxi**, ask the driver for Place St.-Michel.

PRACTICALITIES:

This walk can be made on any day in good weather, although you should note that the Cluny Museum is closed on Tuesdays, and the Sainte-Chapelle on some holidays.

FOOD AND DRINK:

There is a wide choice of restaurants and cafés along the entire walking route, including:

IN THE LATIN QUARTER:

Au Pactole (44 Blvd. St.-Germain, on the Left Bank, 3 blocks south of Notre-Dame) Known for its inventive cuisine. ☎ 01-4633-3131. X: Sat.

lunch, Sun. $$$

La Rôtisserie du Beaujolais (19 Quai de la Tournelle, across from Ile St.-Louis) Under the same management as its esteemed neighbor, the Tour d'Argent. ☎ 01-4354-1747. X: Mon. $$ and $$$

Polidor (41 Rue Monsieur-le-Prince, a block east of the Odéon Theater) Very famous for its old-fashioned cooking and Left Bank atmosphere. ☎ 01-4326-9534. $$

Chez Toutoune (5 Rue de Pontoise, on the Left Bank, 3 blocks southeast of Notre-Dame) Specializes in Provençal cuisine. ☎ 01- 4326-5681. X: Mon. lunch. $$

Atelier Maître-Albert (1 Rue Maître-Albert, 4 blocks east of St.-Julien-le-Pauvre Church) Great value, homey atmosphere. ☎ 01-4633-1378. X: Sun., Mon. lunch, holidays $$

Chez Maître-Paul (12 Rue Monsieur-le-Prince, 2 blocks northeast of the Odéon Theater) Hearty provincial fare with a modern touch. ☎ 01-4354-7459. X: Sun., Mon. lunch, July-Aug. $$

Jardin des Pâtes (4 Rue Lacépède, south of the Arènes de Lutéce) Organic healthy foods, mostly pasta and vegetarian dishes. ☎ 01-4331-5071. X: Mon. $

Lina's (27 Rue. St.-Sulpice, just east of the Church of St.-Sulpice) A chain restaurant noted for its great sandwiches, soups, and the like. ☎ 01-4329-1414. $

AROUND THE CITÉ:

Paul (15 Place Dauphine, near Square du Vert-Galant) An old-fashioned bistro on the Ile de la Cité. ☎ 01-4354-2148 for reservations. X: Mon., Aug. $$

Le Trumilou (84 Quai de l'Hôtel-de-Ville, on the Right Bank, 4 blocks northeast of Notre-Dame) An unpretentious bistro with huge servings of home cooking. ☎ 01-4277-6398. X: Mon. $

Brasserie de l'Île Saint-Louis (55 Quai de Bourbon, next to Pont St.-Louis) This typical Alsatian brasserie offers superb *choucroute garnie* along with a view. ☎ 01-4354-0259. X: Wed., Thurs. lunch, Aug. $

For a special treat, don't miss the **Berthillon** ice cream shop at 31 Rue St.-Louis-en-l'Île on the Île St.-Louis.

SUGGESTED TOUR:

Numbers in parentheses correspond to numbers on the map.

This walking tour begins where the previous one left off, at **Place St.-Michel** (1). Carved out of a medieval warren of tiny alleyways in the 19th century, the large and highly animated square is embellished with a huge fountain at its southern end. From here, the Boulevard St.-Michel, popularly known as the *Boul' Mich*, leads into the heart of the Latin Quarter. That term derives from the language spoken by early scholars, not from the fact that this was once the Roman town of *Lutetia*.

Very little remains of the Roman era, but some sections of its 2nd-century baths can be seen within the **National Museum of the Middle Ages**

(Musée National du Moyen Âge or *Thermes de Cluny) (2),* which incorporates parts of the ancient ruins. Actually, bits of this are visible from the street, but a visit to the museum is highly worthwhile for its stunning collection of medieval art and treasures. The present structure was built in the 15th century as a town mansion for the abbots of Cluny, who frequently traveled to Paris. Today it is regarded as one of the finest examples of late medieval domestic architecture in France. Parts of the museum spill over into the adjacent **Roman Baths** *(Thermes),* some of which is still in good condition. Among the many treasures on display is a remarkable series of 15th-century ***tapestries** called the *Lady and the Unicorn,* thought to symbolize the five senses and the mastery of them. Also not to be missed is the **Chapel** with its superb Gothic decorations. Enter through a small courtyard on the side street. ☎ *01-5373-7800. Open Wed.–Mon. 9:15–5:45. Adults 30FF, seniors and youths 18–25 20FF. Reduced admission on Sun.*

Now cross Boulevard St.-Michel and stroll down Rue Racine to the **National Theater of the Odéon** (3), built in 1782 as a suitable home for the French Comedians. After the Revolution this theatrical group moved to the Right Bank and the present theater, rebuilt after a fire in 1807, was used for drama—a role it continues today.

Continue on, following the map, to the **Church of St.-Sulpice** (4). Begun in 1646 on the site of earlier churches, it acquired its present monumental façade in 1766. The church is famous for its organ concerts, and its interior has some noted murals by Delacroix in the first chapel on the right. A metal strip embedded in the floor of the transept runs due north and south, marking the equinoxes and solstices as the sun strikes different points. The Lady Chapel has an excellent statue of the *Virgin and Child* by Jean-Baptiste Pigalle, and there are two rather enormous holy-water stoups from Venice.

Exit into the attractive Place St.-Sulpice and follow around to the **Luxembourg Gardens** (5), an utterly delightful park where children sail toy boats on the pond and watch puppet shows in a little theater near the southwest corner. All over the park are scattered countless statues of prominent French men and women, while the **Medici Fountain** near the northeast corner attracts lovers and strollers alike. The **Luxembourg Palace** at the north end was built in the early 17th century for Marie de Medici, widow of Henri IV. She disliked living in the Louvre and had this grandiose mansion designed in the style of the Pitti Palace in Florence to remind her of home. Used as a prison during the Revolution, it is now the seat of the Senate, the upper house of the French parliament.

Leave the park and follow Rue Soufflot to the **Panthéon** (6), where many of France's heroes are entombed. Begun as a church by Louis XV in fulfillment of a vow, the monumental structure alternated back and forth between religious and secular uses, but in 1885 it was permanently taken over by the State as a final resting place for the remains of Victor Hugo. Other notables interred in its crypt include Emile Zola, Voltaire, and

Rousseau. You can visit them on a guided tour and also examine the marvelous 19th-century frescoes depicting mythical scenes from the early history of Paris; these on the main floor. Be warned in advance, however, that all-in-all, it's a pretty gloomy experience. ☎ *01-4354-3451. Open daily except major holidays, 10–6. Adults 35FF, youths 12–25 23FF, under 12 free.* Just north of it is the **Sorbonne**, one of the oldest and most famous universities in Europe.

Continue on past the fascinating **Church of St.-Étienne-du-Mont** (7), a 16th-century structure in a wild variety of styles whose interior is enlivened with a strange rood screen, the only one left in Paris; and with some exquisite stained-glass windows in the apse. A right turn on Rue Descartes leads to **Place de la Contrescarpe** (8). This pleasantly seedy little square was famous in the Middle Ages for its rowdy character, and still preserves the somewhat rustic ambiance of the old Latin Quarter in years gone by. The Rue Mouffetard, leading south from it, is a lively place noted for its eclectic selection of good cheap restaurants.

From here you might want to make a short side trip to one of Paris' lesser-known sights, the **Arènes de Lutèce** (9). Located in a tranquil public park, this partially-restored Gallo-Roman amphitheater probably dates from about AD 200 and once provided some 15,000 spectators with typical Roman entertainments. It was destroyed by the Barbarians around 280 and lay buried until being rediscovered in 1869 during construction of the adjacent Rue Monge. Now used mostly by local residents for quiet games of *boules*, it makes a lovely resting place away from the hubbub of the city.

The route now leads downhill towards the Seine, passing through the attractive Place Maubert before continuing down the narrow Rue de Bièvre to the river. Stroll partly across the bridge for the classic rear view of Notre-Dame Cathedral, then follow the map to the **Church of St.-Julien-le-Pauvre** (10). The aura of medieval Paris hangs heavy in this utterly delightful neighborhood, and the simple church seems transplanted from a distant time and place. The present structure dates from the 12th century although there were previous churches on the site as far back as the 6th century. Since 1889 it has belonged to the Melchite (Greek Catholic) faith. Step inside for a look at the unusual choir screen with its icons, and the beautifully carved pillar capitals. The garden next to the church, Square René Viviani, offers a remarkable view of Notre-Dame.

In just a few steps you will come to another great medieval church, that of **St.-Séverin** (11). Built in the 13th century and later enlarged, it has an unusual interior layout featuring a double ambulatory filled with a veritable thicket of elegant columns. The stained-glass windows, some from the 15th century, are particularly fine and make a wonderful setting for the musical concerts that are frequently given here.

Return to nearby **Place St.-Michel** (1), the starting point of this walk, where you might want to take a break at one of the many attractive outdoor cafés. Now cross the bridge over the Seine to the **Île de la Cité**, an island where Paris began in the 3rd century BC as a settlement of the

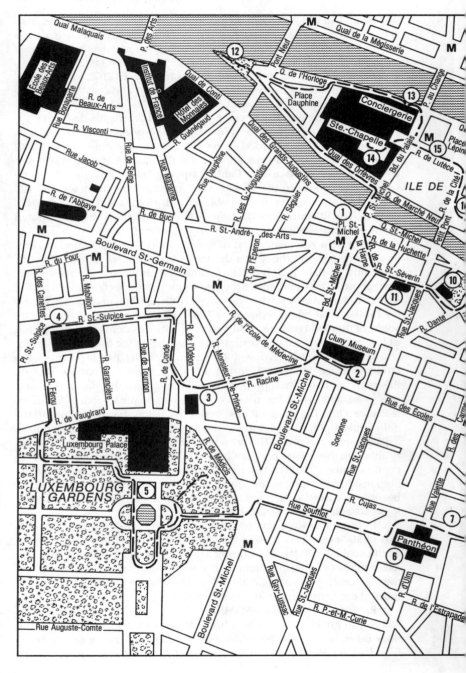

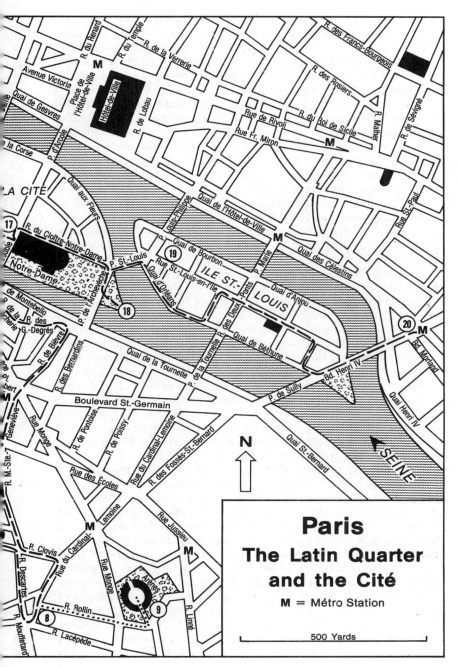

Paris

The Latin Quarter
and the Cité

M = Métro Station

500 Yards

Parisii tribe—a defensive place well protected against marauding tribes. During the Middle Ages it was a densely packed warren of little alleyways holding a population of some 25,000 along with the Royal Palace and the Cathedral of Notre-Dame. A massive rebuilding program in the late 19th century has left it what it is today; primarily the home of several govern- ment agencies spread between broad streets and open squares.

Turn left along the Quai des Orfèvres to the **Pont Neuf** which, despite its name (meaning "new"), is the oldest existing bridge in Paris. Completely spanning both arms of the Seine, it was opened in 1607 and appears today much as it did then. Although the colorful vendors, enter- tainers, and pickpockets who once lined its sidewalks are gone, it is still one of the most interesting and possibly the most beautiful of the 33 bridges that span the Seine within Paris.

A flight of steps behind the equestrian statue of Henri IV descends to the delightful **Square du Vert-Galant** (12), a green spit of land jutting out into the river. Named in honor of France's most beloved king, Henri IV, it is among the nicest places in Paris for relaxing and taking in the riverside view. Don't miss this special treat.

Return to the bridge level and amble into Place Dauphine, which still retains a touch of its quiet 17th-century charm. Continue around on the Quai de l'Horloge to the dreaded **Conciergerie** (13), where thousands of unlucky souls spent their last hours before going to the guillotine during the Revolution. Dating in part from the early 14th century and originally a section of the former royal palace, it is now incorporated into the massive Palais de Justice (Law Courts) complex. You can visit the impressive Salle des Gens d'Armes, the dungeons, the cell of Queen Marie Antoinette (who lost her head on October 16, 1793), and the Girondin's Chapel—now a small museum displaying a rather unsharp guillotine blade and similar Revolutionary memorabilia. What's best about this chilling place is that you can emerge from it a free person. ☎ *01-5373-7850. Open daily 10–5, remaining open until 6:30 from April–Sept. Adults 35FF, youths 12–25 23FF. Combination ticket with Sainte Chapelle (below), 50FF.*

Turn right on Boulevard du Palais and right again into the courtyard of the **Palais du Justice**. This labyrinth of buildings evolved from the former medieval royal palace and still includes quite a few parts of it. While it is perfectly possible to visit the courts on weekdays from 1:30 to 4 p.m. and perhaps sit in on a public trial, the main attraction of the complex is the ***Sainte-Chapelle** (14), reached through a passageway to the left. Built in the mid-13th century by the Crusader King Louis IX (popularly known as St. Louis), this exquisite church is one of the most sparkling gems of Paris and should not be missed. Its Lower Chapel, used by commoners, is impres- sive enough, but the nobility's Upper Chapel is the supreme embodiment of what Gothic was all about. It was here that the supposed Crown of Thorns and relics of the True Cross, purchased by St. Louis from the rulers of the East, were kept in a setting that seems to consist solely of gorgeous stained glass, glowing like the inside of a fine jewel. The precious relics are now in Notre-Dame Cathedral as the brilliantly restored Sainte-Chapelle is seldom used for religious ceremonies. ☎ *01-5373-7851. Open daily 10–5 (6:30 from April–Sept.). Adults 35FF, youths 12–25 23FF. Combination ticket with Conciergerie, above, 50FF.*

Little of the island's former charm seems to have escaped the urban renewal schemes of the last century, but one spot that is still a joy for the eye is **Place Louis Lépine** (15), where the picturesque **Flower Market** *(marché aux fleurs)* is held daily all year round, except that on Sundays the posies are replaced with a chirping bird market *(marché aux oiseaux).*

Stroll over to the nearby **Place du Parvis** (16), a large open area in front of Notre-Dame Cathedral. Until the mid-19th century this neighborhood was crowded with small buildings and narrow lanes, leaving only a tiny square in front of the cathedral—an entirely different view than the one you have today. Much of ancient and medieval Paris still lies buried beneath this, and was rediscovered during construction of an underground parking garage. Since 1980 the subterranean ruins have been open to the public as the **Crypte Archéologique**, entered from the west end of the square. You can walk among the Gallo-Roman remains, ancient ramparts, and cellars from the Middle Ages, all dramatically lit and explained in English. This superb and imaginative trip into the forgotten past can be made on any day except major holidays. A bronze plaque on the square above it marks the *"kilomètre zéro,"* the point from which all distances in France are measured. ☎ *01-4329-8351. Open daily 10–5, remaining open until 6 from April–Sept. Adults 35FF, youths 12–25 23FF, under 12 free. Combination ticket with Notre Dame's North Tower (below) 40FF.*

Rising in front of you stands the magnificent:

*NOTRE-DAME CATHEDRAL (17), ☎ 01-4234-5610. *Open daily 8–6:45 (7:45 on weekends). Free. Treasury open Mon.–Sat. 9:30–6:30, adults 15FF, students 10FF. Tower open daily 10–6 (10–5 from Oct.–March), adults 35FF, youths 12–25 23FF, under 12 free, combination ticket with Crypte Archéologique, above, 40FF. Guided tours in English of the cathedral at noon on Wed. and Thurs., 2:30 Sat., 2:30 daily in Aug., free.*

Man has worshiped on the site of Notre-Dame Cathedral since pagan times, with Celtic gods followed by Roman deities, then by a succession of Christian churches. The present Gothic structure was begun in 1163 and not really completed until the mid-14th century. It is the most important church in France, long used as the setting for many of the major ceremonies that have punctuated the nation's history. Tourists flock here by the thousands, but their presence does not seriously detract from the splendor of the building or its setting.

Notre-Dame was not always held in such high regard. During the Renaissance the Gothic style had fallen out of favor and disastrous alterations were made to "improve" the cathedral. With the Revolution of the late 18th century it was thoroughly ransacked and turned first into a "Temple of Reason," with a resident goddess, and then allowed to decay.

When Napoleon crowned himself emperor here in 1804 the walls had to be covered with tapestries to disguise their dilapidated condition. Ironically, Notre-Dame's salvation came principally from the writings of a professed atheist, the author Victor Hugo, whose novel *The Hunchback of Notre Dame* focused public attention on the glory that was fast falling into ruin. Feeling compelled to act, the government in 1841 entrusted a complete restoration to the noted architect Viollet-le-Duc, who spent the next 23 years directing a splendid rehabilitation. He has often been criticized for going too far, but the cathedral today looks very much as it did in medieval drawings.

Notre-Dame's front *façade is a triumph of the early Gothic style, despite the two somewhat squat towers. It must be remembered that the cathedral was intended to be seen from the small square then in front of it, not from the vast open area of today—which gives a very different perspective. A better view will be had from the rear or from across the Seine, where the majestic **flying buttresses**—those slender supports that transfer weight away from the walls, thus allowing greater window space—add so much to the cathedral's beauty.

Three elegant doorways grace the front façade. From left to right, these are known as the portals of the Virgin, of the Last Judgement, and of St. Anne. They are elaborately decorated with appropriate carvings, which were once painted in brilliant colors against a gilt background. Some of these are modern replacements as many of the originals were mutilated during the Revolution. Above them is the **Kings' Gallery**, a row of 28 statues of the kings of Judea, destroyed in 1793 when a mob mistook them for the hated kings of France. They were reconstructed later in the 19th century. The **Rose Window**, over 30 feet in diameter, is centered between this and the **Great Gallery**, richly festooned with fantastic gargoyles of various demons.

The interior of Notre-Dame is enormous, easily accommodating a crowd of 9,000, and served as the prototype for all of the major Gothic cathedrals. Most of the stained-glass windows are modern replacements, executed according to medieval techniques, although there is original 13th-century glass in the rose window of the north transept, said to be a gift from St. Louis. To the right of the center of the transept, just before the chancel, is a marvelous 14th-century statue of the *Virgin and Child*, which fortunately was in another church when the revolutionary mobs attacked. More violence occurred on August 26, 1944 during the Liberation *Te Deum* service, when the Germans opened fire on a congregation that included General De Gaulle, who refused to duck and remained unhurt.

A doorway along the south ambulatory leads to the **Treasury**, whose precious objects—including what is believed to be a fragment of the True Cross—are on display.

You may want to round out your visit to Notre-Dame by climbing the **Towers** for a close look at the gargoyles and for a splendid low-level view of medieval Paris. Ascents—on foot—begin from the outside of the north tower and continue across the open west gallery.

If Notre-Dame has whetted your appetite for French Gothic cathe-drals, there are several others that can be seen on the daytrips described in other sections of this book. Those generally regarded as being the most beautiful in the country are at Chartres, Amiens, Reims, and Bourges.

Walk around to Square Jean XXIII, a lovely garden with an unsur-passed view of the east end of Notre-Dame. Just behind this, at the tip of the island, steps lead down to the touching **Deportation Memorial** (18), an underground crypt built in remembrance of the 200,000 French victims of Nazi concentration camps.

You have now seen all of the major sights along this walking tour. By continuing on to the Métro station at Sully-Morland, however, you will discover one of the most delightful areas in Paris, the Île St.-Louis (19). Happily, there are several attractive outdoor cafés and restaurants there, along with the best ice cream shop in France (Berthillon, at 31 Rue St.-Louis-en-l'Île).

Trailing right behind the Île de la Cité, the Île St.-Louis has a com-pletely different atmosphere. Created in the mid-17th century by joining together two smaller islands, it has always been a residential area where many of France's leading citizens such as Voltaire, Jean-Jacques Rousseau, Baudelaire, Cézanne and, more recently, Georges Pompidou, lived in quiet understated elegance. A number of foreigners, especially writers, continue to call it home.

Cross over to the island via the Pont St.-Louis, a pedestrian span that has recently been reconstructed, and follow the lovely Quai d'Orléans along the river's edge. There are no particular sights to see, but the route on the map takes you through some of the most interesting streets. When you reach the park at its eastern end, turn left onto the Pont de Sully and cross it to the **Sully-Morland Métro Station** (20). This is the end of this walk-ing tour and the beginning of the next—which you will probably want to save for another day.

*From the Bastille to the Opéra

You'll find an exceptionally broad range of fascinating sights along the route of this walking tour, which covers the oldest and most historically interesting *quartiers* of the Right Bank *(Rive Droite)*. Beginning near the site of the Bastille, it meanders through the marvelously picturesque Marais district, then follows colorful old streets to the stunningly modern Pompidou Center and the up-to-the minute Forum des Halles. It then continues on past the Louvre, the Palais Royal, the delightful Tuileries Gardens, the fashionable streets around Place Vendôme, and ends up at the Opéra, in the center of a smart shopping area.

Along the way you will have to chance to see some of the most exciting museums in Paris, most of which are located in historic buildings. Which of these you actually stop at will depend on your particular interests and the amount of time available, although you should really save the Louvre for later as even a cursory visit there requires the better part of a day.

GETTING THERE:

Those continuing on from the previous walking tour will begin at the Sully-Morland Métro Station, from which a short stroll up the Boulevard Henri IV leads to the real start of this route, Place de la Bastille. If you're coming from another part of town, just take the **Métro** directly to Bastille. This is also served by **bus** routes 20, 29, 65, 69, 76, 86, 87, and 91. By **taxi**, ask the driver for Place de la Bastille.

PRACTICALITIES:

This walk can be enjoyed on any fine day, but note that the Victor Hugo and Carnavalet museums are closed on Mondays and some holidays, while the Picasso Museum, Pompidou Center, the Louvre, and some of the smaller museums are closed on Tuesdays and a few holidays.

FOOD AND DRINK:

You will pass a very broad selection of restaurants and cafés along

nearly all of this walking route, including:
IN THE MARAIS:
L'Ambroisie (9 Place des Vosges) Superb dining in quiet elegance, one of the best restaurants in France. Reservations needed, ☎ 01-4378-5145. X: Sun., Mon., Aug. $$$+

Bofinger (5 Rue de la Bastille, a blocks west of Place de la Bastille) A beautiful turn-of-the-century brasserie with Alsatian specialties. ☎ 01-4272-8782. $$

Robert et Louise (66 Rue Vieille du Temple, just east of the National Archives) An unpretentious classic bistro with consistently good food. ☎ 01-4278-5589. X: Sun. $$

Jo Goldenberg (7 Rue des Rosiers, 3 blocks southeast of the Carnavalet Museum) A favorite place for Jewish deli food since 1920. ☎ 01-4887-2016. $$

FROM POMPIDOU CENTER TO FORUM DES HALLES:
Ambassade d'Auvergne (22 Rue du Grenier St.-Lazare, 2 blocks north of Pompidou Center) Hearty dishes from the Auvergne in rustic surroundings. ☎ 01-4272-3122 for reservations. X: Sun., July-Aug. $$$

Au Pied de Cochon (6 Rue Coquillière, just west of St.-Eustache Church) A landmark restaurant from the glory days of Les Halles. ☎ 01-4013-7700. $$

Le Grizzli (7 Rue St.-Martin, near Pompidou Center) This 1902 bistro has plenty of atmosphere, as well as good food. ☎ 01-4887-7756. X: Sun. $$

FROM THE LOUVRE TO THE OPÉRA:
Le Grand Café (4 Blvd. des Capucines, a block southeast of the Opéra) Classic French cuisine in a grand old brasserie of the Belle Époque. ☎ 01-4312-1900. $$$

Palais Royal (110 Galerie de Valois, in the Palais Royal garden) Delightful contemporary dining, indoors or on the garden terrace. ☎ 01-4020-0027. X: Sat. lunch, Sun. $$ and $$$

Chez Georges (1 Rue du Mail, 3 blocks northeast of the Palais Royal) A traditional bistro with real French cooking. ☎ 01-4260-0711. X: Sun., Aug. $$

Le Soufflé (36 Rue du Mont-Thabor, 2 blocks south of Place Vendôme) Featuring a wide variety of soufflés. ☎ 01-4260-2719. X: Sun. $$

Hippopotamus Opéra (7 Blvd. des Capucines, near the Opéra) A favorite place for grilled meats at modest prices, part of a chain. ☎ 01-4742-7570. $

Those in a hurry to get on with the walk may want to refuel at one of the many familiar fast-food outlets around Pompidou Center and Forum des Halles.

SUGGESTED TOUR:

Numbers in parentheses correspond to numbers on the map.

If you are continuing on from the previous tour you should take a short walk up Boulevard Henri IV to the start of this walk, **Place de la**

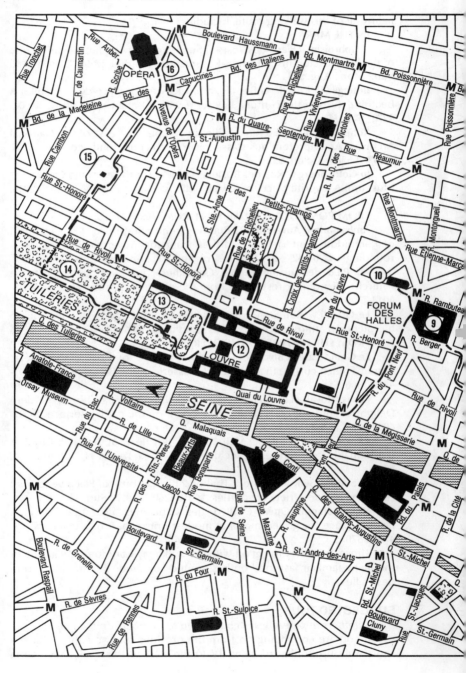

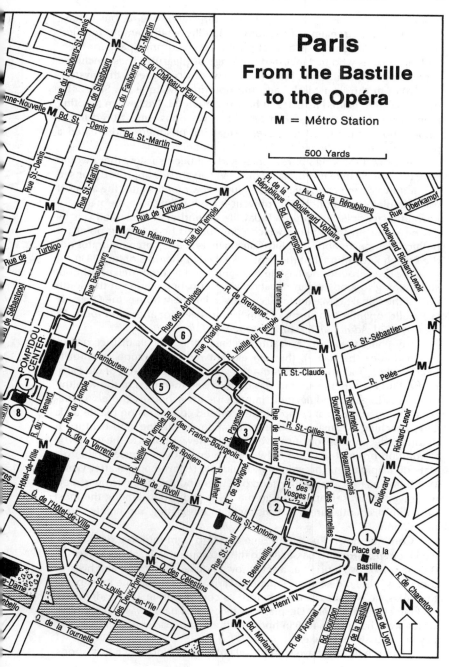

Paris
From the Bastille
to the Opéra

M = Métro Station

500 Yards

Bastille (1). Otherwise, you can get there directly by Métro, bus or taxi. Virtually nothing remains of the former **Bastille**, a 14th-century fortification that was long used as a royal prison, reserved principally for high-ranking citizens who had incurred the king's displeasure. These included such notables as Mirabeau, Voltaire (who was twice a guest), the mysterious "Man in the Iron Mask," and the notorious Marquis de Sade. The name "Bastille" gained its place in history on July 14, 1789, when a rioting mob stormed it in the mistaken belief that weapons were stored there. Finding none, they freed the seven remaining prisoners and created a political symbol that fueled the French Revolution.

Actually, if the king's bureaucracy had not been so slow there would have been no Bastille to storm, as Louis XVI had already approved plans to tear it down as an economy measure. Just a few months after the attack it was completely demolished to prevent it from falling into the hands of Revolutionary splinter groups. Today, its ground plan is marked out by paving stones in the square, which continues to be a rallying point for political demonstrations. The **July Column** in its center commemorates not the French Revolution, but the Parisians killed in the riots of July, 1830.

The area around the Bastille has long been a rough neighborhood, succumbing to gradual gentrification with a boating marina at the south end of the Canal St.-Martin and a controversial opera house, the **Opéra de la Bastille**, opened to a storm of criticism in 1989. *For afternoon tours,* ☎ *01-4001-1970. Adults 50FF, seniors, students, children 30FF.*

From here the route leads into the enchanting Marais district, once a marsh (hence the name), then an elegant residential zone, eventually nearly a slum, and now a restored—and very fashionable—bit of old Paris. In the 13th century the swamp was drained and members of the wealthier classes began building their impressive town houses *(hôtels particuliers)* there as a way of escaping the crowded conditions on the Île de la Cité. Reaching a climax of urban civilization during the 17th century, it gradually declined as society moved into the new suburbs to the west. The Revolution brought the final blow and the once-lovely houses fell into a state of dilapidation. Threatened by bulldozer redevelopment after World War II, the historical neighborhood of ancient houses and narrow streets was saved by preservation laws in the 1960s and is now among the most desirable residential areas in Paris, with an interesting and highly varied population.

Continue down Rue St.-Antoine and turn right into Rue de Birague, which opens through a passage into the incomparable **Place des Vosges** (2). Begun in 1605 by Henri IV as a set of town houses for himself and his aristocracy, it is the oldest intact square in Paris, and arguably the most beautiful. Alas, he was assassinated before its completion in 1612 and, in fact, no king ever lived there. Despite this, its original name was Place Royale, which was changed in 1800 in honor of the first *département* of France to pay its Revolutionary taxes.

All of the houses have street-level arcades, behind which lurk shops, restaurants, cafés and the like. Victor Hugo lived upstairs at Number 6 from 1833 to 1848, and his apartment is now the **Victor Hugo Museum**, where you can examine his numerous drawings, homemade furniture, and various memorabilia of the great author. ☎ *01-4272-1016. Open Tues.–Sun. except holidays, 10–5:40. Adults 27FF, students 19FF, under 18 free.*

Leave the square via Rue des Francs-Bourgeois and turn right on Rue de Sévigné. The **Carnavalet Museum** *(Musée de l'Historie de Paris)* (3) is housed in a much-altered 16th-century *hôtel particulier* that was the home of the witty hostess Madame de Sévigné from 1677 to 1696. The magnificent displays here cover the entire history of Paris from the Renaissance to the early 20th century. Far from being stuffy, the museum is alive with fascinating mementos of everyday life in a bygone age, including shop and tavern signs, models of the Bastille and the guillotine, Revolutionary propaganda, period furniture and room settings, and enough other items to keep you entranced for at least an hour. Don't miss it. ☎ *01-4272-2113. Open Tues.–Sun. except holidays, 10–5:40. Adults 30FF, students 20FF, under 18 free.*

Now follow the map to the 17th-century **Hôtel Salé**, which since 1985 has been home to the extremely popular:

*PICASSO MUSEUM (4), ☎ *01-4271-6315. Open Wed.–Mon. 9:30–6, closing at 5:30 in winter. Adults 30FF, youths 18–15 20FF. Cafeteria. Gift shop.*

When Pablo Picasso died in 1973 he left behind an enormous collection of paintings, sculptures, ceramics, drawings, graphics and the like covering all of the periods of his extraordinary career. A large selection of these were given to the French government in lieu of estate taxes, along with his private collection of works by other modern artists such as Cézanne, Renoir, Rousseau, Matisse, Braque and so on. All of these can be seen in a magnificent setting with explanations in English and an audio-visual introductory show.

There are two rather specialized museums nearby that might be of interest to you. One of these, the **National Archives** (5), with its entrance at 60 Rue des Francs-Bourgeois, contains the **Historical Museum of France**. Among the documents on display here are such treasures as the Edict of Nantes, the wills of Louis XIV and Napoleon, and a letter from Joan of Arc. ☎ *01-4027-6419. Open Mon. and Wed.–Fri., noon–5:45, and on weekends from 1:45–5:45. Adults 15FF, seniors, youths, and children 10FF.*

Close to this, at 60 Rue des Archives, is the splendid 17th-century **Hôtel Guénégaud** (6), home of the **Museum of Hunting** *(Musée de la Chasse et de la Nature)*. This well-restored mansion is worth a visit in itself, and as a bonus you get to see a superb collection of hunting weapons, paintings of the hunt by famous artists, stuffed animals, and much more.

The route now leads through an increasingly modernized area and turns south to the incredible:

*POMPIDOU CENTER *(Centre National d'Art et de Culture Georges Pompidou)* (7), ☎ 01-4478-1233, Internet: www.cnac-gp.fr. *Reopening in January 2000, after renovation. Cafeteria. Shops.*

Pompidou Center is often referred to as Beaubourg after the neighborhood it dominates. And dominate it certainly does. As a cultural institution this is pure theater, aimed at the widest possible audience. Everyone in Paris comes here to gawk at the immense structure of dazzling colors that looks more like an oil refinery than anything else, what with its inside-out construction of steel rods, ventilator shafts, pipes, and a huge plastic tube carrying escalators. Opened in 1977 to a storm of controversy, it has become one of the most popular attractions in Paris and has been recently renovated after more than twenty years of heavy use. The wide sloping piazza in front of the center is at least as much fun as the building itself, and is filled with pedestrians enjoying the antics of street musicians, mimes, jugglers, fire-eaters, acrobats and other struggling entertainers—along with the usual pickpockets.

Pompidou Center contains a variety of cultural institutions, the most important of which is the **National Museum of Modern Art**, installed on the third and fourth floors and reached by the external escalator. By putting all of the building's functional parts on the outside, an enormous clutter-free internal environment has been created, one that is ideal for the needs of changing art exhibitions. The museum's collections, frequently rearranged, cover the entire scope of modern art right up to the present day. Nearly all of the famous names are represented including a great many foreigners, especially Americans. All in all, a visit here is a delightful experience even if you have little interest in art.

Other parts of Pompidou Center are devoted to the **Public Information Library** with its more than one million books, photos, records, video tapes, periodicals and other documents; the **Industrial Creation Center** with exhibitions on contemporary design; and the **Cinémathèque**, which shows interesting films. Just outside the main building is the **Atelier Brancusi**, where works by the Romanian sculptor Constantin Brancusi are displayed in a reconstruction of his Paris studio. **IRCAM**, an organization for contemporary music, is located underground and is open for concerts only. Be sure to ride the escalator to the top of Pompidou Center for a stunning **view of Paris** and perhaps a drink or a bite to eat at the cafeteria.

Opening off the south end of Pompidou Center is a marvelous little square called Place **Igor Stravinsky**, where amusing mobile fountains by Jean Tinguely and Niki de St.-Phalle dance out the composer's creations. Getting too close to these can result in an unexpected shower, but you can always dry off at one of the outdoor cafés under the adjacent trees. Facing the south end of this is the 16th-century **Church of St.-Merri** (8), curiously built in the Flamboyant Gothic style at a time when the Renaissance was all the rage. Its interior, opening on Rue St.-Martin, is especially attractive with its 17th-century organ loft, 16th-century stained-glass windows, and a bell dating from 1331.

Now follow the map to the **Forum des Halles** (9), a neat solution to an unwanted hole in the ground. As the name suggests, this was the site of the late, lamented Les Halles—fondly remembered by all who knew Paris prior to 1969. The "Belly of Paris," as the area was then called, once throbbed with late-night activity as a wholesale food market, where fashionable people came for a bowl of onion soup after a night on the town. Alas, the markets are now located near Orly Airport and the charming 19th-century iron-and-glass pavilions are long gone. In their place a gigantic, deeply underground transportation center for RER commuter trains and the Métro was built, above which was The Hole *(Le Trou)*. Instead of filling this in, an amazing shopping center descends in levels around a sunken courtyard, bringing light, air, and outdoor cafés to the lower depths. Hundreds of shops, theaters, and restaurants operate in a futuristic environment, providing a delightful ambiance for commercial activities.

While there, you might want to visit the **Holographic Museum**, where strange three-dimensional moving images are created by lasers. *Located on Level (niveau) -1, it is open Tues.–Sat., 10:30–7, and on Sun. and Mon. 1–7.* On the same level is a branch of the famous **Grévin Waxworks Museum**, the Madame Tussaud's of France, which re-creates street scenes in Paris at the turn of the century.

Take only a few steps from the Forum and you are back in the past at the **Church of St.-Eustache** (10). Second in size only to Notre-Dame Cathedral among the churches of Paris, it was built between the 16th and 17th centuries and has a curious combination of Gothic form overlaid with Classical detailing. This was the parish church of the rich food merchants of Les Halles, whose immense wealth is evident throughout the entire majestic structure and particularly in its luxurious decoration. The proximity of St.-Eustache to the Louvre made it a favorite among the aristocracy. Louis XIV took his first communion here while still a child; Richelieu, Molière, and Madame de Pompadour were baptized here; and this was the setting for the funerals of Mirabeau, Rameau, and La Fontaine. Among the outstanding works of art is an early Rubens painting of the *Pilgrims af Emmaus,* a sculpture of the *Virgin* by Pigalle, and the tomb of Colbert by Le Brun—all near the northeast end. Note also the marvelous 17th-century stained-glass windows in the choir.

Amble through the gardens behind the Forum des Halles and follow Rue du Pont-Neuf down to the Seine. A short walk along the river brings you to the Louvre, whose enormous bulk totally dominates the neighborhood. Before examining it in more detail, however, it is best to continue on to the nearby **Palais Royal** (11). Built in 1634 by Cardinal Richelieu as his own palace, it was willed to Louis XIII, whose widow and young son, the future Louis XIV, lived there for a few years after the king's death in 1643, thus making it a royal palace. After that it was given to Louis XIV's brother and passed into the Orléans family, who added the apartment houses and shopping arcades around its park. In the late 18th century the entire complex became notorious as a center for Revolutionary activities and later as a den for gambling and prostitution. Cleaned up after the Restoration, the palace itself is now used as government offices and cannot be visited, but its often-overlooked **gardens** are a delightful little corner of Paris that should not be missed. Enter via a passageway on Rue de Valois and take a stroll through this enclave of tranquillity, then exit through more passageways onto Rue de Richelieu and turn left. At the intersection of Avenue de l'Opéra and Rue St.-Honoré stands the famous **Comédie-Française**, a 19th-century theater where French classical plays are still performed along with modern works.

Continue straight ahead and enter into the Louvre complex on Rue de Rivoli. Most of this former royal palace—the largest in Europe—is occupied by the world-renowned:

*****LOUVRE MUSEUM** (Musée du Louvre) (12),** ☎ 01-4020-5050, Internet: www.louvre.fr. Open Mon. and Wed., 9 a.m. to 9:45 p.m., Thurs.–Sun. 9–6. Closed certain holidays. Ticket sales end 45 minutes before closing. Permanent collections: Adults 45FF, under 18 free; 26FF after 3 p.m. and all day on Sun. Free to all on the first Sun. of the month. Tickets are valid for re-entry on the same day. Extra admission for temporary exhibitions. Combination ticket for both permanent and temporary exhibitions available. Guided tours (in English) depart from under the glass pyramid, at the Accueil des Groupes counter. Additional charge for tours: Adults 38FF, children 13–18 22FF, under 13 free. Acoustiguide recorded tours cost 30FF. Restaurant. Café. Shops.*

Although they may appear to have a certain sense of unity, the various sections of the palace actually evolved over many centuries, beginning in 1202 as a fortress inside what is now the **Square Court** (Cour Carrée) at the eastern end. Parts of this have been excavated and form an underground archaeological display on the history of the Louvre. The defensive bastion was converted into a palace during the 14th century by Charles V, the first king to reside in the Louvre. His successors disliked the place and avoided it (and Paris!), until François I began a reconstruction in the 16th century. Since then it has continued to grow as various kings and emperors added their own wings, while changing the look of the older ones. It became a public museum as early as 1793.

The latest—and most controversial—appendage was begun on the initiative of President Mitterand and opened in 1989 as the new **main entrance**. Externally, this is in the form of a giant **glass pyramid** designed by the American architect I.M. Pei, while its functional parts are decently buried beneath the central courtyard.

A visit to the Louvre Museum can be a formidable experience, best saved for another day. Even then, you will be able to see only a tiny fraction of the hundreds of thousands of works of art on display along the miles of corridors and galleries. **Guided tours** of the highlights are conducted in English throughout the day, or you can get a printed layout plan at the entrance and explore on your own. Three of the most popular attractions are Leonardo da Vinci's **Mona Lisa** *(La Joconde)*, the **Venus de Milo**, and the **Winged Victory of Samothrace**. You may expect to find huge mobs of tourists around these, but many of the other treasures are practically ignored and may be appreciated in peace.

From the glass pyramid you can look straight ahead for a fabulous **view** past Napoleon's Carrousel Triumphal Arch, the Egyptian Obelisk in the Place de la Concorde, the Champs-Élysées, and the distant Arc de Triomphe—all of which are in a perfectly straight line.

If you've sensibly put off visiting the Louvre Museum for another day, you might be interested in two other small museums in the northwest corner of the Louvre Palace. These are the **Museum of Decorative Arts** *(Musée des Arts Décoratifs)* (13) and the adjacent **Museum of Fashion and Textile** *(Musée de la Mode et du Textile)*. The first has marvelous room settings, furniture, household objects and the like from the Middle Ages right up to the present time, with an emphasis on contemporary styles, Art Deco, and Art Nouveau. The second concerns itself with the evolution of costume and present-day trends in fashion. ☎ *01-4455-5750. Both open Tues.–Fri. 11–6 and weekends 10–6, remaining open on Wed. until 9. Admission to both: Adults 30FF, youths 18–25 20FF.*

Now continue past the small **Arc de Triomphe du Carrousel**, which celebrates Napoleon's victories in 1805, and enter the **Tuileries** (14). These formal gardens, extending over half a mile along the Seine as far as the Place de la Concorde, are a favorite spot for Parisians and visitors alike. They were first laid out in the mid-16th century as part of the royal palace, but their present appearance dates from 1664, when the noted landscape gardener André Le Nôtre—who also created the magnificent gardens at Versailles—was commissioned to redesign them.

About midway between the two ponds, on either side of the central avenue, there are small outdoor cafés under the trees where you can stop for a drink or a snack. Turn right here and leave the park via steps leading to Rue de Castiglione. Continue straight ahead to **Place Vendôme** (15), a dignified square that speaks quietly of opulence and wealth. Designed by the renowned architect Jules Hardouin-Mansart in the late 17th century, it is home to such symbols of luxury as the Ritz Hotel, Cartiers, Boucheron, and Van Cleef & Arpels. In its center once stood a statue of Louis XIV that was destroyed during the Revolution, only to be replaced with a column commemorating Napoleon's victory at Austerlitz. As the political winds shifted, the emperor was knocked off his perch and Henri IV put in his place, followed by a gigantic fleur-de-lys. Napoleon, now in military uniform, regained the position and was again pulled down by an angry mob. The present statue of Napoleon dressed as Caesar dates from the late 19th century.

A short stroll up the Rue de la Paix brings you to the bustling intersection known as Place de l'Opéra, where you can meet your friends at the famed Café de la Paix. Everyone in the world seems to wind up here sooner or later.

The grandiose structure filling the north side of the square is the **Opéra** (16), built by the young architect Charles Garnier between 1861 and 1875 in a suitably theatrical style. Construction took so long because of the existence of an underground stream, whose grottoes gave birth to the legendary *Phantom of the Opera*. Yes, a chandelier did fall, in 1896, thus adding credence to that wonderfully spooky tale.

Inside, the Opéra, or Opéra Garnier as it is now known, is every bit as lavish as its exterior promises. The spectacular Grand Foyer, the Great Staircase, and the auditorium itself are about as richly decorated as is conceivably possible. Although the best way to see them is to attend a performance, you may visit the **Opéra Museum** in the west wing, which includes a look into the auditorium. *Museum:* ☎ *01-4742-0702. Open daily 10–noon and 2–5. Adults 30FF, seniors, students, and children 20FF, under 10 free.*

You have now reached the end of this walking tour, with convenient Métro stations located both in front of and behind the theater. In case you are continuing on, the next tour begins at the Chaussée d'Antin Métro Station, one block to the northeast.

North to Montmartre

After probing the historical sections of Paris on the previous three walking tours, you might want to try something a bit different. There are no important cultural sights along this amble through picturesque Montmartre, but there's a lot of fun to be had exploring what was once a great artists' quarter and what remains today a well-preserved remainder of Bohemian life in the *Belle Époque*.

Occupying the highest hill in Paris, Montmartre was only a simple country village when it was joined to the capital in 1860. The steepness of its narrow, twisted streets and the porous nature of its soil—riddled with countless tunnels of abandoned gypsum mines—have prevented any large-scale development, so its character remains refreshingly simple and down-to-earth. In contrast to this, the bawdy entertainment quarter at its base is a sea of neon signs, sleazy porno shops and dubious revues; attracting bus loads of tourists intent on having a naughty time.

Locals call the hill *La Butte Montmartre* or, more simply, just *La Butte* (The Mound). The name Montmartre probably derives from the Roman god Mercury, who might have had a temple there in ancient times. A more colorful explanation, originating in the 8th century, attributes it to the three martyrs who were beheaded there around AD 250. One of these, St.-Denis (Dionysius), the first Bishop of Paris, is said to have picked up his head and carried it to the northern suburb where his basilica stands today, expiring there no doubt from exhaustion.

Montmartre is still haunted by memories of the great artists who lived there between the 1880s and the end of World War I. Toulouse-Lautrec, Renoir, Van Gogh, Braque, Picasso, Utrillo—these are just some of the famous names. The present-day painters, although not nearly as talented, add a touch of color to the delightful Place du Tertre, while other sights along the tour include the notorious Pigalle district, the spectacular Sacré-Coeur Basilica, the only vineyards in Paris, and a few tiny but engrossing museums.

GETTING THERE:

If you are continuing on from the previous tour, you should take **bus** number 68 from the northeast corner of Rue de la Chaussée-d'Antin and Boulevard Haussmann, just beyond the Opéra. Get off at Place Blanche and begin the tour. You could also walk there, a slightly uphill distance of nearly one mile.

Those coming from another part of town can take the **Métro** directly to the Blanche stop. The area is also served by **bus** routes 30, 54, 68, and 74. By **taxi**, ask the driver for Place Blanche.

PRACTICALITIES:

Anytime is a good time to make this walk as there are no really important cultural attractions that might be closed. Montmartre is quite hilly, so wear comfortable shoes.

FOOD AND DRINK:

The numerous restaurants on and around Place du Tertre are oriented to the tourist trade, serving acceptable food at somewhat inflated prices. While many of the cafés are nice for a drink, you will be better off dining at:

UP TO PLACE DU TERTRE:

Au Clair de la Lune (9 Rue Poulbot, just south of Place du Tertre) A genuine atmosphere in a touristy area. ☎ 01-4258-9703. X: Sun., Mon. lunch. $$$

L'Oriental (76 Rue des Martyrs, 2 blocks northeast of Place Pigalle) North African cuisine. ☎ 01-4264-3980. X: Sun., Mon., Aug. $ and $$

Le Bateau-Lavoir (8 Rue Garreau, near Pl. Émile-Goudeau) An atmospheric, unpretentious old bistro. ☎ 01-4254-2312. X: Sat. lunch, Mon. $

BEYOND PLACE DU TERTRE:

A. Beauvilliers (52 Rue Lamarck, 3 blocks northwest of the Sacré-Coeur) Celebrated cuisine in lovely surroundings. Proper dress expected, for reservations ☎ 01-4254-5442. X: Sun., Mon. lunch, holidays. $$$

Poulbot Gourmet (39 Rue Lamarck, 2 blocks north of the Sacré-Coeur) A favorite with a loyal clientele. ☎ 01-4606-8600. X: Sun. $$ and $$$

Wepler (14 Place de Clichy) A big, bustling restaurant famous for its seafood. ☎ 01-4522-5324. $$

SUGGESTED TOUR:

Numbers in parentheses correspond to numbers on the map.

Begin your tour at **Place Blanche** (1), which can be reached directly by Métro to the Blanche stop. Those continuing on from the previous tour can take bus number 68 or walk up Rue de la Chaussée-d'Antin and Rue Blanche. This is the heart of Montmartre's entertainment district, at the foot of the hill. On the north side of the square is the famous **Moulin Rouge**, immortalized around the turn of the century by Toulouse-Lautrec's renderings of its can-can dancers. The cabaret is still going strong after a century of operation, still drawing bus loads of tourists beneath the turning vanes of its fake windmill.

A stroll down Boulevard de Clichy takes you past a number of seedy bars, porno shops, and assorted peep shows, all promoted by peculiar hustlers on the lookout for customers. You can avoid being pestered and still see all the sights by walking along the tree-lined strip in the center of the street. Along here is the **Museum of Eroticism** *(Musée de l'Érotisme)*, a sweeping survey of sexual fantasies, past and present. *72 Blvd. de Clichy.* ☎ *01- 4258-2873. Open daily 10 a.m. to 2 a.m. Adults 40FF.*

Place Pigalle (2), the infamous "Pig Alley" of the 1940s, is named for a famous 19th-century sculptor who specialized in religious art. It is somewhat ironic that this area has long been the raunchiest center of commercialized sex in Paris; ever since the last genuine artists fled to Montparnasse.

Things begin to look better after you turn left on Rue Houdon. Another left at the top of the street brings you into **Place des Abbesses**, whose rather quaint Métro stop is the one closest to the top of the hill. Continue on to **Place Émile-Goudeau** (3), often regarded as the birthplace of modern art. Several renowned painters, including Picasso, Juan Gris, Van Dongen, and Modigliani lived and worked in a house at Number 13 known as the *Bateau-Lavoir,* which burned down in 1970 and was replaced with new artists' studios.

The route now leads to the base of the famous **Funicular** (4) where, for the price of one Métro ticket, you can ride up the steep hill instead of making the long climb on foot.

Crowning the top—and visible from all over Paris—is the monumental **Sacré-Coeur Basilica** (5), a neo-Romanesque-Byzantine monstrosity that has become almost as much a symbol of Paris as the Eiffel Tower. Begun in 1876 as an act of contrition for the disastrous Franco-Prussian War and the bloody Commune uprisings of 1871, the church was not completed until 1910 and only consecrated in 1919. Prayers have been said here day and night, perpetually since 1885, without a break for even the wars. The enormous weight of its gleaming white stones, much too heavy for the hill to bear, is supported by underground columns to a depth of 100 feet. One of the largest bells in the world hangs in its north tower. Step inside for a look at the ornate mosaics, to visit the rather gloomy crypt, or perhaps to ascend the dome for a spectacular *panorama of Paris extending some 30 miles. ☎ *01-5341-8900. Church open daily 7 a.m. to 11 p.m. Dome open daily 9–6, 7 in summer, 15FF. Crypt open daily 9–6, 7 in summer, 15FF.* Actually, there is an excellent view from the terrace in front of the church, a popular gathering spot for tourists from all over the world.

A short stroll around the rear of the basilica leads to the ancient **Church of St.-Pierre-de-Montmartre** (6), all that remains of a 12th-century Benedictine abbey. Although much altered over the years, the interior of this modest church—the third-oldest in Paris—has some interesting columns once believed to be from a Roman temple dedicated to Mercury but which are more likely remnants of the 7th-century Merovingian church that previously occupied the site. There are also some attractive modern plaques depicting scenes of old Montmartre.

No visitor to Paris should miss seeing the adjacent **Place du Tertre** (7),

Paris
North to Montmartre

M = Métro Station

400 Yards

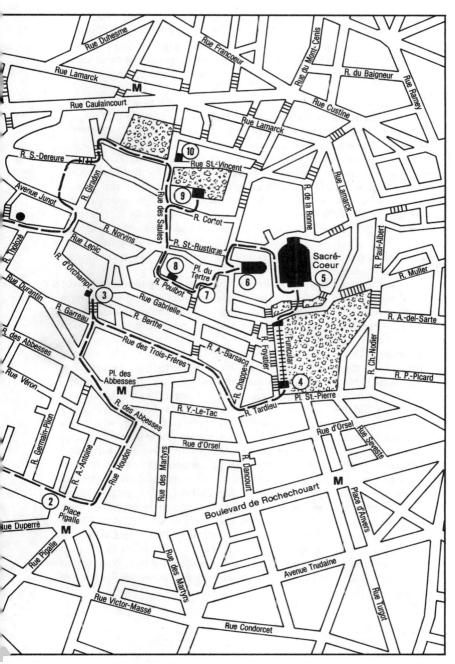

truly a scene right out of *La Bohéme,* or a painting by Utrillo. The artists whose easels surround the old village square may not be terribly talented, but their presence does stir memories of Montmartre during the *Belle Époque.* This effect is heightened by the period restaurants and cafés, with outdoor tables under the trees—a delicious place to linger over a drink.

Just a few steps to the south and you are on the tiny Rue Poulbot, home to the **Espace Montmartre Salvador Dali** (8), where some 330 dream-like works by the renowned surrealist artist are on display. ☎ *01-4264-4010. Open daily 10–6. Adults 40FF, seniors, students and children 25FF.*

Now continue around and follow Rue des Saules to Rue Cortot, where you will find the **Montmartre Museum** (9) in a delightful 17th-century house inhabited at different times by Renoir, Utrillo, Dufy and others. The displays here recall the Montmartre of old with mementos of the Bohemian life. ☎ *01-4606-6111. Open Tues.–Sun. 11–6. Adults 25FF, seniors and students 20FF.* Directly aside of the museum are the only remaining **vineyards** in Paris, whose white wines may not be very distinguished but are certainly a novelty. Their early-October harvest is always celebrated with great festivities.

Across the street from the bottom of the vineyards is another survivor from old Montmartre, the rustic **Lapin Agile Cabaret** (10). Still functioning after all those years, it was at one time the haunt of impoverished artists and now features folk music in a wonderfully crude atmosphere, open every night except Mondays.

From here the route snakes its way through colorful neighborhoods and turns down the winding Rue Lepic. The Montmartre hill was once dotted with dozens of windmills, of which only the remnants of a few remain. One of these, often painted by Renoir, Van Gogh and others, is the famous **Moulin de la Galette,** stuck on a slope between Rue Lepic and Avenue Junot. A bit farther down, at Number 54 Rue Lepic, is the house where Van Gogh shared lodging with his brother Theo before going south to Arles.

Turn right on Rue Joseph-de-Maistre and left on the busy Rue Caulaincourt. To the right is the **Montmartre Cemetery** (11), the final resting place of many famous painters, writers, composers, and actors. Among them are Emile Zola, Hector Berlioz, Alexandre Dumas, Edgar Degas, Jacques Offenbach, and the German poet Heinrich Heine. The main entrance is on the short Avenue Rachel, just north of Boulevard de Clichy.

The walk ends at the bustling intersection of **Place de Clichy** (12), where there is a Métro stop. If you would like to continue on to the next tour, you can take a bus back to the Opéra or walk there by following Rue de Clichy and Rue de la Chaussée-d'Antin, a slightly downhill distance of just under one mile.

From the Opéra to the Arc de Triomphe

With a few notable exceptions, the four previous walking tours have focused on the classical Paris of the past. Now it is time to explore today's busy international city of commerce and fashion. From the bustling shopping precincts near the Opéra to that grandest of promenades, the Champs-Élysées, this is the part of Paris that developed since the time of Napoleon.

By getting off to an early start, energetic walkers should be able to combine this tour with the previous one as there are few time-consuming attractions along the way. If you choose to do this, it will be better to start with the Montmartre tour first.

GETTING THERE:

The walking tour begins at the **Chaussée-d'Antin Métro Station**, only one block northeast of the Opéra and easily reached by Métro from anywhere in Paris. It is also served by **bus** routes 22, 26, 42, 52, 53, 66, 68, and 81. By **taxi**, just ask the driver for the Galeries Lafayette—Opéra.

PRACTICALITIES:

You can enjoy this walk at any time in good weather, but note that nearly all of the shops are closed on Sundays and that the museum in the Petit Palais—a relatively minor sight—is closed on Mondays and holidays except for special exhibitions.

FOOD AND DRINK:

The neighborhoods covered on this tour are exceptionally rich in restaurants, although prices may be a bit steeper than in other parts of town. Advance reservations and a thick wallet are nearly always necessary for the renowned temples of gastronomy near the Champs-Élysées, making them impractical choices for the purposes of this walk. You will be better off saving these treats for another day, and considering some of the following for an excellent lunch:

TO THE PLACE DE LA CONCORDE:

L'Ecluse Madeleine (15 Place de la Madeleine, by the church) This chic wine bar also serves light meals. ☎ 01-4265-3469. $$

Fauchon (26 Place de la Madeleine, behind the church) The fanciest food shop in Paris also offers gourmet specialties to be eaten at the counter. A unique experience. ☎ 01-4742-6011. X: Sun. $$

L'Ardoise (28 Rue du Mont-Thabor, 3 blocks northeast of Place de la Concorde) A great value in wonderful food, with limited selection. ☎ 01-4296-2818. X: Mon., Aug. $$

Restaurant Lescure (7 Rue de Mondovi, 2 blocks northeast of Place de la Concorde) A rustic country restaurant with traditional home cooking. ☎ 01-4260-1891. X: Sat., Sun. eve., Aug. $ and $$

NEAR THE CHAMPS-ÉLYSÉES:

Le Boeuf sur le Toit (34 Rue du Colisée, 2 blocks north of Rond-Point) Known for its fresh seafood in a charming 1930's atmosphere, with a piano bar. ☎ 01-5393-6555. $$ and $$$

Chez André (12 Rue Marbeuf, 3 blocks southwest of Rond-Point) This traditional bistro has been popular with the fashionable set for decades. ☎ 01-4720-5957. $$

Antoine's (31 Rue de Ponthieu, 2 blocks northwest of Rond-Point) A wide variety of sandwiches for a light lunch. ☎ 01-4289-4420. X: Sun. $

Lina's (8 Rue Marbeuf, 2 blocks west of Rond-Point) Excellent sandwiches, soups, salads, and the like. ☎ 0104723- 9233. $

Drugstore Champs-Élysées (133 Ave. des Champs-Élysées, a block southeast of the Arc de Triomphe) Light meals featuring salads, burgers, and the like. ☎ 01-4443-7900. $

There are a number of attractive outdoor cafés around Place de la Madeleine. Those along the Champs-Élysées are invariably overpriced, but the view might be worth the extra francs.

SUGGESTED TOUR:

Numbers in parentheses correspond to numbers on the map.

Directly facing the **Chausée-d'Antin Métro Station** (1) is the world-famous **Galeries Lafayette** department store, spread over three adjacent buildings. Go into the central (and largest) of these to marvel at the incredible glassed-in courtyard, and ride the escalators all the way up to the roof for a superb close-up view of Paris. An equally great store, just down the street, is **Au Printemps**, again located in three adjoining buildings. It, too, has a roof garden, in the "Havre Magasin." Both stores are usually open on Mondays through Saturdays, from 10 a.m. to 7 p.m., and both offer tax rebates *(détaxe)* for purchases taken out of the country. The details on this service change occasionally, so ask about the current procedures and minimums. Their English-speaking "welcome" personnel can also aid you in making purchases as well as provide general information.

Continue down Boulevard Haussmann and turn left on Rue Tronchet. This leads directly to the rear of the **Madeleine** (2), a church with both an extraordinary appearance and an amazing history. Begun in 1764 in the Baroque style, it was quickly altered to resemble the Panthéon, but never finished. Napoleon started to rebuild it as an imitation Greek temple dedicated to the glory of his Grand Army, then lost interest in the project. Following his downfall, the Parisians had no idea of what to do with this unfinished white elephant in their midst. Among the uses considered were a bank, a stock exchange, a parliament, a library, and a theater. In 1837 it almost became the first railway station in Paris, but it was really not large enough for that. Finally, all other ideas having failed, it was consecrated as the Church of St.-Mary Magdalen in 1842. It still looks like a bank. The richly decorated interior, although rather dark, is well worth a quick visit.

A number of luxury shops surround the Madeleine, notably that most sophisticated of delicatessens, Fauchon, where you can sample gourmet specialties on the spot at modest prices.

Stroll down the elegant **Rue Royale,** passing the Rue du Faubourg St.-Honoré—one of the world's most glamorous shopping streets—and the renowned *Belle Époque* restaurant, Maxims, where you can dine rather well for exorbitant sums. Opening in front of you is the largest and most impressive square in Paris, the **Place de la Concorde** (3). This was laid out during the reign of Louis XV to accommodate an equestrian statue of the king. With the Revolution, the statue was destroyed and a guillotine erected as the new center of attraction. The "Nation's Razor," as it was called, shaved off well over a thousand heads at this spot alone, including those of Louis XVI, Marie-Antoinette, Madame du Barry, Danton, and in the end Robespierre himself.

With the end of the Reign of Terror, the blood-soaked square was renamed Concorde and decorated with statues. In its center stands the **Egyptian Obelisk** from the 13th century BC, a gift from the Viceroy of Egypt in 1829. You might want to brave the constant car traffic to reach this for what is probably the most sweeping panoramic *view in all Paris.

The east side of the square is bordered by the gardens of the **Tuileries,** visited on one of the previous walking tours. Near the southwestern corner of this is the **Orangerie** (4), a small art museum specializing in paintings from the late Impressionists to the 1930s. Included in its collection are works by Monet, Renoir, Cézanne, Picasso and others. ☎ 01-4297-4816. *Presently closed for restoration, should reopen in mid-2001.* To the north of it stands the **Jeu de Paume,** formerly the home of a great Impressionist museum (since moved across the river to the Orsay) and now used for temporary exhibitions.

Stroll around to the west side of Place de la Concorde, where the **Champs-Élysées** begins its stately procession to the Arc de Triomphe. The entrance to what is arguably the most renowned avenue on Earth is flanked by the Marly Horses, two marvelous statuary groups of rearing horses transplanted from Louis XIV's château at Marly. From here to the Rond-Point the Champs-Élysées (meaning Elysian Fields) retains its 19th-century character, with English-style gardens on either side. Once a marshland, this area was drained and planted with rows of trees according

Paris
From the Opéra to
the Arc de Triomphe

M = Métro Station

500 Yards

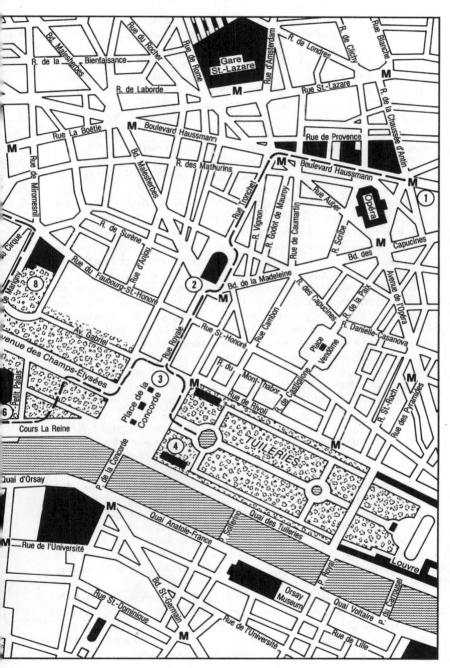

to the designs of Le Nôtre. In the 18th century an avenue was formed and extended to the top of the hill, but it remained undeveloped until well into the 19th century.

Turn left on a path past Ledoyen, once a country inn and for the last century a luxury restaurant known for its classic cuisine. A right on the Cours La Reine brings you to Avenue Winston Churchill and the **Pont Alexandre III** (5). This wildly flamboyant bridge, built in 1900 for the World Exhibition and named for a Russian czar, spans the Seine in a single leaping arch of cast steel. Every square inch of it is covered with exuberant decorations that speak volumes about turn-of-the-century optimism.

Another symbol of that age, and erected for the same exhibition, is the **Petit Palais** (6). Although architectural purists may quibble over its mixture of styles, it is indeed a handsome building and now houses the **Museum of Fine Arts of the City of Paris** *(Musée des Beaux-Arts de la Ville de Paris)*. All too often overlooked by visitors, the collections here range all the way from classical antiquity to early 20th-century art and include works by Delacroix, Corot, Monet, Cézanne, Redon, Bonnard, and many others. ☎ *01-4265-1273. Open Tues.–Sun., 10–5:40, closing at 8 on Thurs. Adults 30FF, students 25FF, under 18 free.*

Just across the street stands the much larger **Grand Palais** (7), again dating from the World Exhibition of 1900. Built of stone, glass, and steel, this immense structure is used primarily for temporary exhibitions and shows. Its west wing, opening on Avenue Franklin-D.-Roosevelt, houses the interesting **Palace of Discovery** *(Palais de la Découverte)*, a hands-on science museum where you can have lots of fun pushing buttons to make things work. There is also a planetarium with several heavenly shows a day. ☎ *01-4074-8000. Open Tues.–Sat., 9:30–6, Sun. and holidays 10–7. Adults 30FF, seniors, students, and children 20FF. Extra charge for planetarium.*

Continue up Avenue Winston Churchill, cross the Champs-Élysées, and follow Avenue de Marigny. An outdoor **stamp market** *(Marché aux Timbres)* is held on Thursdays, Saturdays, and Sundays, from 10 a.m. until evening, at the intersection of Avenue Gabriel. Beyond this, to the right, is the **Élysée Palace** (8), which you cannot visit as it is the official home of the French president and the multitude of heavily-armed guards just won't let you in. You can however, usually catch a glimpse through the gateway. Built in 1778, it was later home to Madame de Pompadour and then used by both Napoleon I, who signed his final abdication here, and his nephew, Napoleon III, who plotted his 1851 coup d'état within its walls. Recent presidents have often preferred to use it as an office only and to actually live elsewhere.

Turn left on that most elegant of shopping streets, the **Rue du Faubourg St.-Honoré**, where top designer names embellish the many boutiques. Another left on Avenue Franklin-D.-Roosevelt—one of six streets in Paris named for American presidents—brings you to the **Rond-Point** (9). From here on the Champs-Élysées completely changes its character from a shady green belt to a broad, bustling avenue of offices, shops, theaters, and sidewalk cafés as it gently climbs to the Arc de Triomphe. This is the great promenade of Paris, where everyone—native and tourist alike—wanders about to see and be seen. It is also where the massive parades are held, like the annual celebration on Bastille Day, July 14.

Some of the shopping arcades along the north side of the Champs-Élysées are well worth exploring. In them you will find a colorful variety of boutiques and cafés where you can window shop or have a drink. The most fashionable outdoor café, on the southeast corner at the intersection of Avenue George V, is **Fouquet's**—a bit expensive and snobbish but worth it for the truly Parisian experience. The main tourist information office for Paris is at Number 127, on the south side.

The summit is crowned by the magnificent ***Arc de Triomphe** (10), located in the center of Place Charles-de-Gaulle, an enormous circular hub still known to Parisians by its former name, *Place de l'Étoile*. From here, eleven other great avenues besides the Champs-Élysées radiate outwards to all points in Paris. The Arc de Triomphe was begun by Napoleon in 1806 to commemorate French military victories, but political changes and cost overruns delayed its completion until 1836. It is the largest triumphal arch in the world, and since 1920 has sheltered the **Tomb of the Unknown Soldier**, whose memory is rekindled each everting at 6:30 by an eternal fame.

You can safely reach the arch by using the underpass from the north side of the Champs-Élysées or the Avenue de la Grande-Armée, rather than risk your life in the ferocious traffic. Visits to its top platform may be made by elevator or steps. The ***sweeping panoramic view** from it is absolutely spectacular and makes the perfect climax to end your walking tours of Paris. ☎ *01-5537-7377. Open April–Sept., daily 9:30 a.m. to 10:30 p.m.; rest of year daily 10–6. Adults 40FF, youths 12–25 25FF, under 12 free.*

Additional Attractions in and around the City

This chapter has absolutely nothing to do with daytrips, but gives a brief description of the more outstanding attractions in and around Paris that were not covered on the five previous one-day walking tours. They are listed alphabetically and include the address, the *arrondissement* (district) number, the name of the nearest Métro or RER station(s), and the times of opening when appropriate.

WITHIN PARIS:

African and Oceanic Arts Museum *(Musée des Arts Africains et Océaniens)*—Situated at the edge of the Bois de Vincennes, this museum houses superb collections of native art, weapons, masks, pottery, jewelry, and similar artifacts from Africa, Oceania, and Australia. There is also a tropical aquarium with crocodiles. *293 Avenue Daumesnil, 12e, served by Métro to Porte Dorée. ☎ 01-4474-8480. Open Mon. and Wed.–Fri., 10–noon and 1:30–5:30; weekends 12:30–6. Adults 30FF, seniors and youths 18–24 20FF, under 18 free.*

Balzac Museum *(Maison de Balzac)*—The great author Honoré de Balzac lived in this charming country house from 1840 to 1847, escaping his creditors. It is filled with mementos of his life, manuscripts, and personal effects. *47 Rue Raynouard, 16e, reached by Métro to Passy or RER to Kennedy-Radio France. Open Tues.–Sun. 10–5:40, closed holidays. Adults 22FF, seniors, students, children 15FF.*

Bois de Boulogne—Once a royal hunting preserve, this 2,225-acre park is a favorite recreational area for Parisians. Among its many attractions are the **Lower Lake** *(Lac Inférieur)* where rowboats and bicycles can be rented, the **Upper Lake** *(Lac Supérieur)*, the **Pré Catelan** (a park-within-a-park with its famous Shakespeare Garden), the **Bagatelle** (a former estate with lovely gardens), and the **Jardin d'Acclimatation** (primarily a children's amusement park with a zoo and a miniature railway). In addition, there are two racetracks, waterfalls, the Municipal Flower Gardens, several restaurants, and enough other sights to keep you busy all day. *Located in the 16e*

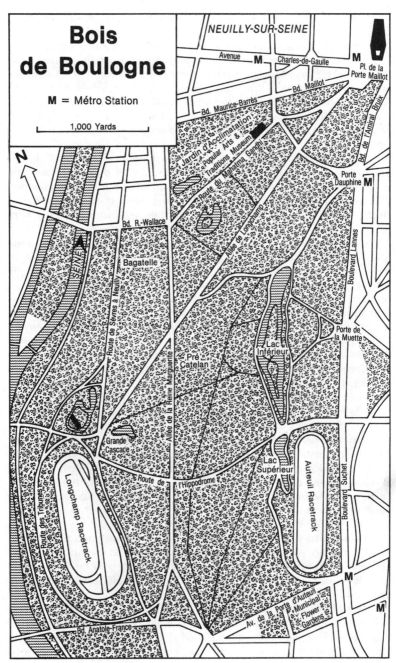

Bois de Boulogne

M = Métro Station

1,000 Yards

N

NEUILLY-SUR-SEINE

Avenue —M— Charles-de-Gaulle

M

Pl. de la
Porte Maillot

Bd. Maillot

Bd. Maurice-Barrès

Bd. de l'Amiral Bruix

Jardin d'Acclimatation
Popular Arts &
Traditions Museum

Route du Mahatma Gandhi

Porte
Dauphine M

Bd. R.-Wallace

SEINE

Bagatelle

Allée de Longchamp

Boulevard Lannes

Route de Sèvres à Neuilly

Porte de
la Muette

Lac
Inférieur

Pré
Catelan

Allée de la Reine Marguerite

Grande
Cascade

Route de   l'Hippodrome

Lac
Supérieur

Auteuil Racetrack

Boulevard Suchet

Longchamp Racetrack

Route des Tribunes

M

M

Bd. Anatole-France

Av. de la Porte d'Auteuil

Municipal
Flower
Gardens

arrondissement, it is best reached by Métro to Porte Maillot, Sablons, Porte Dauphine, or Porte d'Auteuil.

Botanical Gardens *(Jardin des Plantes)*—Much more than its name suggests, the Botanical Gardens also encompass a zoo, hothouses, and the **Natural History Museum.** Located in the 5e *arrondissement,* close to the Seine and Gare d'Austerlitz train station, it can be reached by Métro to Gare d'Austerlitz, Jussieu, or Monge. ☎ *01-4079-3000. Gardens open daily 7:30 a.m. to dusk. Zoo open daily, 9–5, 6 in summer. Garden free, charge for hothouses. Zoo: Adults 30FF, seniors and students 16–25 20FF, children 10FF.*

Buttes-Chaumont Park—This is the most unusual and possibly the most romantic park in Paris. Laid out over a former quarry, it has steep wooded paths and a lake with a rocky island whose summit is crowned with a temple. Set in the 19e *arrondissement,* its most convenient Métro stop is Buttes-Chaumont. *Open daily, until 11 p.m. in summer or 9 in winter.*

Catacombs—As Paris expanded in the 18th and 19th centuries, some of its cemeteries had to be emptied to make room for buildings. All of those generations of bones from millions of bodies were ghoulishly stacked in these abandoned underground quarries, where they have been on public view since 1874. During World War II the Catacombs served as a headquarters of the Resistance. A flashlight will be helpful for this macabre experience. *1 Place Denfert-Rochereau, 14e, served by Métro to Denfert-Rochereau. ☎ 01-4322-4763. Open Tues.–Fri. 2–4, and on weekends 9–11 and 2–4. Adults 33FF, students and children 22FF.*

Cernuschi Museum—Chinese art from prehistoric times all the way up to the present is the focus of this delightful little museum just east of the Monceau Park. *7 Avenue Vélasquez, 8e, reached by Métro to Villiers or Monceau. ☎ 01-4563-5075. Open Tues.–Sun. 10–5:30, closed hoidays. Adults 22FF, seniors, students and children 15FF.*

City Museum of Modern Art *(Musée d'Art Moderne de la Ville de Paris)*—An outstanding museum for art of the 20th century, this avant-garde institution specializes in Cubist, Fauve, and School of Paris paintings along with temporary exhibitions. *11 Avenue du Président-Wilson, 16e, close to the Métro stops Iéna and Alma-Marceau as well as the RER stop Pont de l'Alma. ☎ 01-5367-4000. Open Tues.–Fri. 10–5:30, weekends 10–6:45. Adults 30FF, seniors, students and children 20FF.*

Cognacq-Jay Museum—Both the fine and decorative arts of 18th-century Europe are well displayed in this elegant and intimate museum, the epitome of refined French taste. *8 Rue Elzévir, 3e, served by Métro to St.-Paul. ☎ 01-4027-0721. Open Tues.–Sun. 10–5:30. Adults 22FF, seniors, students and children 15FF.*

Flea Market *(Marché aux Puces)*—The largest flea market in Paris is held at Saint-Ouen, on the northern city limits. Walk under the elevated highway and turn left into an area filled with several thousand stalls selling all kinds of junk, some of which might actually be of value. You'll need to bargain, and you're up against expert dealers. Of course, you can come here just for the fun and not buy anything at all. Located on the edge of 18e arrondissement, it is easily reached by taking the Métro to Porte de Clignancourt and strolling north. The markets are open on Saturdays, Sundays, and Mondays only; from about 8 a.m. to perhaps 8 p.m.

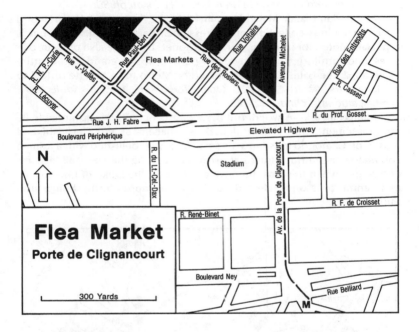

Gobelins Tapestry Factory *(Manufacture Nationale des Gobelins)*— Craftsmanship of the highest level can be witnessed in these government-owned workshops where works of art are woven with intricate care. The results, each taking years to finish, are for state use only and are never sold. *42 Avenue des Gobelins, 13e, served by Métro to Gobelins.* ☎ *01-4461-2169. Guided tours Tues., Wed., and Thurs.; 2 and 2:45 p.m. Adults 45FF, youths 7–24 25FF.*

Grévin Museum—A waxworks fantasy world where contemporary personalities compete with historical tableaux for your entertainment. Distorting mirrors, magic tricks, and strange environments add to the fun. *10 Boulevard Montmartre, 9e, reached by Métro to Richelieu-Drouot or Rue-Montmartre.* ☎ *01-4246-1326, Open daily 10–7. Adults 58FF, children 6–14 38FF.*

Guimet Museum *(Musée National des Arts Asiatiques—Guimet)*— Oriental art from all over the Far East is gathered together here to form one of the most outstanding museums of its kind in the world. *9 Place d'Iéna 16e, served by Métro to Iéna or RER to Pont de l'Alma. Open*

Wed.–Mon., 9:45–6. Admission charged.

Gustave Moreau Museum—The strange paintings of the great 19th-century symbolist artist are displayed in his former studio and home. *14 Rue de la Rochefoucault, 9e, take the Métro to Trinité.* ☎ *01-4874-3850. Open Mon. and Wed., 11–5:15, Thurs.–Sun. 10–12:45 and 2–5:15. Adults 22FF, seniors, students and children 15FF, 15FF for all on Sun.*

Marmottan-Claude Monet Museum—Famous throughout the art world for its marvelous collection of Impressionist paintings, this museum is especially noted for its major works by Monet. There are also objects, pictures, and furniture from many other periods in this grand 19th-century mansion. *2 Rue Louis-Boilly, 16e, served by Métro to La Muette or RER to Boulainvillers.* ☎ *01-4224-0702. Open Tues.–Sun. 10–5:30. Adults 40FF, seniors, students, children 25FF.*

Monceau Park—A wonderful oasis of greenery in the fashionable 8e arrondissement, this delightful park is adjacent to the Cernushi and Nissim de Camondo museums. Its small lake is embellished with a Roman colonnade and curious follies are scattered among the trees, all legacies of the time when this was the private garden of the Duke of Orléans. Its main entrance is on Boulevard de Courcelles, opposite the Métro stop Monceau.

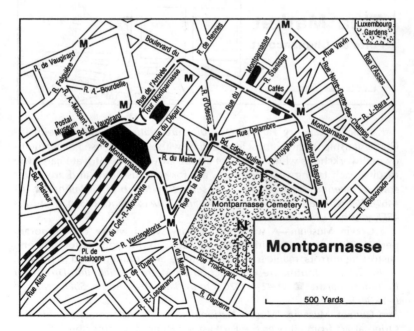

Montparnasse—The Montmartre of the Left Bank, Montparnasse has changed greatly since the days of Hemingway, Picasso, Cocteau,

Stravinsky, Chagall, Modigliani, Lenin, Trotsky, and other famous personalities who lived and worked here in the early 20th century. Some of the
atmosphere survives in the La Coupole and Le Sélect cafés on Boulevard
du Montparnasse, and around the nearby Montparnasse Cemetery, but
the area is noted today mostly for its modern office buildings and shopping centers. You can ascend the sleek 59-story **Tour Montparnsse** for a
spectacular view of the city. ☎ *01-4538-5256. Open daily 9:30 a.m.–11:30
p.m., closing at 10:30 p.m. from Oct.–March. Adults 46FF, seniors, students
and youths 15-20 35FF, 14 and under 30FF; a bit more for the open-air terrace.* The **Postal Museum** on nearby Boulevard de Vaugirard tells the story
of French communications from Roman times to the present, every day
except Sundays and major holidays. Another worthwhile stop is the
Montparnasse Cemetery, where you'll find the graves of many famous personalities. Located at the junction of the 6e, 14e, and 15e *arrondissements,*
Montparnasse is best served by the massive Métro stop Montparnasse-
Bienvenüe.

   Mosque of Paris—A 130-foot-high minaret towers over one of the most
impressive mosques in the world, a corner right out of the Middle East or
North Africa. Take your shoes off and join a guided tour, then relax at the
traditional Arab café. *Place du Puits-de-l'Ermité, 5e, reached by Métro to
Monge.* ☎ *01-4535- 9733. Visits daily except on Fri. or Muslim holidays,
9–noon and 2–6. Guided tours 15FF, 10FF for children and students.*

   Nissim de Camondo Museum—A sumptuous mansion decorated with
priceless objects in the 18th-century manner, this was one of the most luxurious homes in Paris. In 1936 it was presented to the nation by the Count
de Camondo in honor of his son Nissim, killed in World War I. *62 Rue de
Monceau, 8e, reached by Métro to Monceau.* ☎ *01-5389-0640. Open
Wed.–Sun. 10–5. Adults 27FF, seniors and under 25 18FF.*

   Père-Lachaise Cemetery—An enormous number of famous personalities, from the tragic 12th-century lovers Héloise and Abélard to rock star
Jim Morrison of the Doors, are buried in what is probably the most
famous cemetery in the world. You can get a map of their graves at the
entrance and explore some of the most interesting tombs anywhere. Be
sure to see the Federalists' Wall in the southeast corner, where in 1871 the
last 147 insurgents of the Paris Commune were lined up and shot, then
interred on the spot. It still has strong political overtones. Located in the
20e *arrondissement,* the main entrance is on Boulevard de Ménilmontant,
and the closest Métro stop is Père-Lachaise. *Open daily from 7:30 or 8:30
to 5 or 6, depending on the season.*

   Popular Arts and Traditions Museum—Everyday life in rural France
before the Industrial Revolution is explored in this exceptionally interesting museum near the northern end of the Bois de Boulogne. *6 Route de
Mahatma-Gandhi, 16e, reached by Mètro to Sablons.* ☎ *01-4417-6000.
Open Wed.–Mon. 9:45–5:15. Adults 25FF, seniors, youths 17FF, 17FF for all
on Sun.*

   St.-Martin Canal—Dug in the early 19th century, this commercial waterway with six locks links the Seine with a northern canal system and other rivers. It runs underground from the Place de la Bastille for about one mile to the north, then continues on the surface through strangely atmospheric and oddly romantic neighborhoods to La Villette, where it joins the St.-Denis and Ourcq canals. Boat rides are available from the marina at the Arsenal Basin near Place de la Bastille in the 12e *arrondissement,* reached by Métro to Bastille. Check the Paris tourist office for current information, then make reservations. Two companies offering enjoyable canal trips are: Canauxrama, ☎ 01-4239-1500, and Paris Canal Croisières, ☎ 01-4240-9697.

Sewers of Paris *(Les Égouts de Paris)*—Explore a sample section of the over 1,300 miles of sewer tunnels under Paris on these smelly but nevertheless popular tours that begin with an audiovisual presentation. This is an experience you will never forget. The tours depart from the corner of Quai d'Orsay and the Pont de l'Alma, 7e, reached by Métro to Alma-Marceau or RER to Pont de l'Alma. ☎ *01-4705-1029. Tours Sat.–Wed., 11–5, until 6 from May–Sept., closed during heavy rain. Adults 25FF, seniors, students, children 20FF.*

La Villette—Slaughterhouses once occupied this vast site in the northeast corner of Paris, bisected by industrial canals and bordered by an elevated highway. It has now been transformed into the pride of French technology by the **City of Science and Industry**, a gigantic high-tech, space-age, hands-on museum that celebrates the very latest in technological progress. Next to it is the **Géode**, an enormous sphere of stainless steel surrounded by water and containing the inevitable Omnimax projection theater. Some of the other features include a French Navy submarine and the Cinaxe, a small movie theater that bounces around with the screen action. The rest of the 125-acre site is laid out as a futuristic park dotted with exhibition halls, modernistic follies, and a huge space for concerts. The main entrance is on Avenue Corentin-Cariou, 19e, served by Métro to Porte de la Villette. ☎ *01-4005-1212, Internet: www.cite-sciences.fr. Open Tues.–Sat. 10–6, Sun. 10–7. Adults 50FF, seniors, students, children 35FF, under 7 free, 35FF for all on Sat. Extra charges for some features.*

Vincennes—Located in the 12e *arrondissement* near the southeast corner of Paris, the Bois de Vincennes park is similar to the Bois de Boulogne, although not as fashionable. Its two main features are the **Château de Vincennes**, a medieval castle, and the **Zoo de Paris**, the largest zoo in France. There are also several lakes, lovely gardens, and a Buddhist temple. The château and floral gardens are best reached by Métro to Château de Vincennes, while the zoo and the temple are served by Métro to Porte Dorée. *Château open daily except on holidays, 10–6, closing at 5 in winter.* ☎ *01-4808-3120. Long tours 32/21FF, short tours 25/15FF. Zoo open daily 9–6, closing at 5 in winter, a half-hour longer on Sun.* ☎ *01-4475-2010. Adults 40FF, seniors 30FF, students 10FF.*

JUST BEYOND PARIS:

In addition to the six attractions outlined below, there are several major daytrip destinations within the immediate area surrounding Paris. These are described in full detail in Section III, The Île-de-France, beginning on page 80.

Air and Space Museum *(Musée de l'Air et de l'Espace)*—Over 150 historic aircraft are displayed in six exhibition hairs at Le Bourget Airport just north of Paris, covering the history of aviation from its beginnings until the present. Audiovisual presentations describe the conquest of space, while you can inspect the first Concorde and an Ariane rocket on display outdoors. The museum may be reached by taking bus number 152 from the Porte de la Villette or bus number 350 from the Gare de l'Est or Gare du Nord. Get off a Musée de l'Air. By car, take the A-1 highway northeast to the Le Bourget exit. ☎ *01-4992-7199, Internet: www.mae.org. Open Tues.–Sun., 10–5, staying open until 6 from May–Oct. Adults 30FF, students and children 8–16 22FF.*

La Défense—The city of the future is here today, at least in part. Whether you like it is another matter. Begun in the 1960s and still incomplete, La Défense embodies the fondest aspirations of architects and city planners in a mixed commercial and residential center built on a gigantic elevated concrete platform, with streets below and pedestrians above. Walking along its open terraces provides a fabulous view of Paris, which is even better from the top of the 360-foot-high **Grande Arche**. There are also enough shopping centers and exhibition halls to keep you busy for a few hours, along with an IMAX theater, an automobile museum, and a sculpture garden. This "Manhattan-on-the-Seine" is best reached by taking the RER line A to the Grande-Arche-de-la-Défense stop. The RER connects with the Métro at several points, including Charles-de-Gaulle-Étoile. *Tourist information at Info Défense, 15 Pl. de la Défense,* ☎ *01-4774-8424.*

Disneyland Paris—Mickey Mouse has come to the suburbs of Paris, but he still speaks English. This little bit of America in the heart of France is extremely popular and offers a fun time for all but the most churlish of curmudgeons. Children, especially, will enjoy a day here. Take the RER line A4 to Marne-la-Vallée-Chessy, a quick 40-minute ride from Charles-de-Gaulle-Étoile. You can also board at La Défense, Auber, Châtelet-Les Halles, Gare de Lyon, or Nation. By car, take the A-4 highway to Exit 14, about 20 miles east of Paris. ☎ *01-6030-6030, Internet: www.disneyland paris.com. Open late June–early Sept., daily 9 a.m.–11 p.m.; rest of year, daily 10–6, until 8 on Sat. and some other days. Inclusive one-day entry: 220FF, 170FF for ages 3–11, with lower prices in winter.*

Malmaison—Napoléon and Josephine lived in this lovely château and, after their divorce, the empress continued to occupy it until her death in 1814. Still furnished as it was in those days, it makes for an interesting and very pleasant little excursion. To get there, take the RER line A to Rueil-Malmaison, then walk a short distance. ☎ *01-4129-0555. Open Mon. and Wed.–Fri., 9:30–12:30 and 1:30–5:45, weekends 10–6:30. Adults 32FF, seniors*

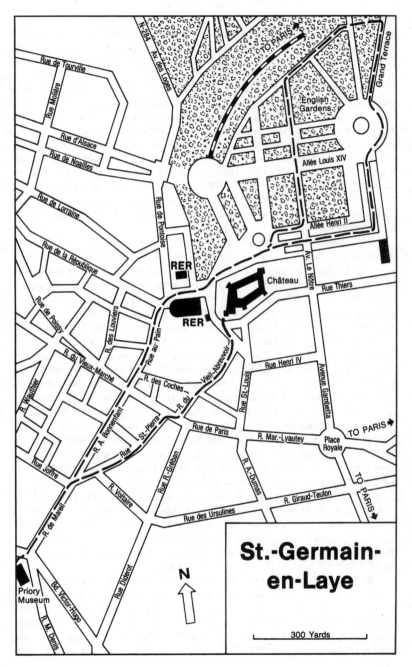

Rue de Tourville

Rue Molière

Rue d'Alsace

Rue de Noailles

Rue de Lorraine

Rue de la République

N-284 AV. des Loges

Rue de Pontoise

TO PARIS

Grand Terrace

English Gardens

Allée Louis XIV

Allée Henri II

RER

Château

Rue Thiers

Av. Le Nôtre

Rue de Poissy

R. des Louviers

Rue au Pain

RER

Vieil-Abreuvoir

Rue St.-Louis

R. du Vieux-Marché

R. des Coches

R. du

Rue Henri IV

Avenue Gambetta

R. Waurhier

R. A. Bonnefant

Rue St.-Pierre

Rue de Paris

R. Mar.-Lyautey

TO PARIS

Rue Joffre

R. Voltaire

Rue R.-Gréban

R. A.-Dumas

Place Royale

TO PARIS

R. de Mareil

R. Giraud-Teulon

Rue des Ursulines

Priory Museum

Bd. Victor-Hugo

Rue Diderot

R. M. Denis

N

St.-Germain-en-Laye

300 Yards

and students 12–25 21FF.

St.-Denis Basilica—The first major structure in the Gothic style, the Basilica of St.-Denis was the prototype for the great cathedrals of France. Begun in 1136 on the site of a 5th-century church, it served as the royal necropolis for nearly all of the kings of France, from Dagobert I in the 7th century until Louis XVIII in the 19th. During the Revolution the mausoleums were plundered and the bones thrown into a common grave beneath the crypt, but the tombs themselves had previously been removed for safekeeping and are now back in place, albeit empty. The historic basilica is located in the town of St.-Denis, just north of Paris. You can get there by taking the Métro to St.-Denis-Basilique. ☎ *01-4809-8384. Open April–Sept., daily 10–7, rest of year, daily 10–5; closing at noon on Sun. Admission charged.*

St.-Germain-en-Laye—This attractive old suburb is famous for its château—the birthplace of Louis XIV and other kings—and for its unusual Priory Museum. Set atop a hill overlooking Paris, the town also has a long terrace with magnificent views, and some beautiful English gardens. The **Château**, long a royal residence, was once home to the young Mary, Queen of Scots, and to the deposed King James II of England. It now houses the **National Antiquities Museum**, where artifacts from prehistoric times to the 8th century are exquisitely displayed. ☎ *01-3451-5365. Open Wed.–Mon., 9–5:15. Admission charged.* A short walk through town leads to the **Priory Museum** *(Musée du Prieuré)*. Located in the former home of the symbolist painter Maurice Denis, it displays his works along with those of Gauguin, Bonnard, Vuillard, and others. ☎ *01-3973-7787. Open Wed.–Fri., 10–12:30 and 2–5:30, weekends 10–12:30 and 2–6:30. Admission charged.* The easiest way to get there is by RER line A to St.-Germain-en-Laye.

Vaux-le-Vicomte—This fabulous château was in a way responsible for the building of Versailles. When young Louis XIV was entertained there by his finance minister, Fouquet, in 1661, he became enraged at the thought of a public servant living better than the king. Suspecting embezzlement, he had Fouquet thrown in jail and then employed the same architects to build an even greater palace for himself at Versailles. Restored to its original splendor, Vaux-le-Vicomte is located just east of Melun, on the way to Fontainebleau. There is fairly frequent train service from the Gare de Lyon in Paris to Melun, after which you will have to take a taxi to Vaux-le-Vicomte. By car, follow the N-6 to Melun, 34 miles southeast of Paris, then local roads. ☎ *01-6414-4190. Open daily mid-March to mid-Nov., 10–6. Adults 62FF, seniors, students, and children 49FF.*

Section III

DAYTRIPS FROM PARIS
THE ÎLE-DE-FRANCE

To explore the Île-de-France is to see the story of a great civilization unfold before your eyes, an experience no visitor to Paris should miss. This central region, without defined borders and existing in the mind almost as much as in reality, is the very heart and soul of France—the royal island from which a remarkable nation emerged.

Roughly speaking, the Île-de-France is the area within about a fifty-mile radius of Paris. A dense network of rail lines and highways provides easy access to its many attractions. The seven daytrip destinations that follow were chosen for both their high quality and for the broad variety of adventures they offer. Once having sampled these delights, you may want to try other places in the same region—such as St.-Denis, Compiègne, Vaux-le-Vicomte, Barbizon, Rambouillet, St.-Germain-en-Laye, Malmaison, or Beauvais. Some of these were briefly described in the previous chapter.

Paris is by far the most convenient base for one-day excursions into the Île-de-France, but those wishing to stay outside the city might consider nearby towns with both hotels and fast commuter service. Two excellent choices for this are Versailles and St.-Germain-en-Laye.

Because of the short distances involved, it is sometimes possible to visit two destinations in the same day, albeit at a rather hectic pace. Such pairings that work well in this region are: Versailles with Chartres, Fountainbleau with Moret-sur-Loing, and Chantilly with Senlis.

Those traveling by rail will note that several different train stations in Paris are used for the various trips. The map on page 15 shows the general location of these.

*Versailles

By far the most popular daytrip destination in France, Versailles embodies in stone the awesome will of Louis XIV, the "Sun King." A visit to this enormous place will tell you a great deal about the Age of Absolutism, for Louis XIV did not merely rule a country, he *was* the State.

Versailles was built, in effect, as the seat of government—a place where the king could keep his eye on the treacherous nobility. Begun in 1661, it took over fifty years to complete. Few structures on Earth can begin to match its splendor, with so much to see that attempting to do it all could lead to the visual equivalent of indigestion. A more sensible plan is to hit only the highlights of the château, the gardens, and the Trianons on the first visit; then plan on returning at some later date. The tour outlined here is limited to the most important features and—with a bit of rushing—could be done in half a day.

Energetic travelers making an early start will find it possible to combine this trip with one to Chartres, the subject of the next chapter.

GETTING THERE:

Trains on the RER commuter line C-5 leave very frequently from the underground Invalides Station in Paris, located on the left bank of the Seine just across the Alexandre III bridge. These take you to Versailles' Rive Gauche Station, a short stroll from the château, in under 30 minutes. There are also regular SNCF trains (railpasses valid) from Montparnasse and St.-Lazare stations in Paris that go to other stations in Versailles, just a bit farther from the château.

By car, Versailles is about 13 miles southwest of Paris via the A-13 Autoroute or the N-10 road.

PRACTICALITIES:

Good weather is necessary to appreciate the marvelous gardens at Versailles. Avoid coming on a Monday or major holiday, when the château is closed. Thursdays and Fridays are the least crowded.

The **tourist office,** ☎ 01-3950-3622, is located near the château at 7 Rue des Réservoirs, with a branch near the RER station.

FOOD AND DRINK:

Versailles has a number of fine restaurants, including:

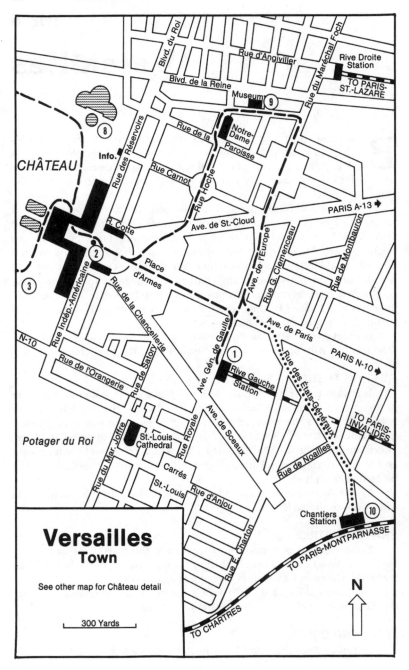

Versailles
Town

See other map for Château detail

300 Yards

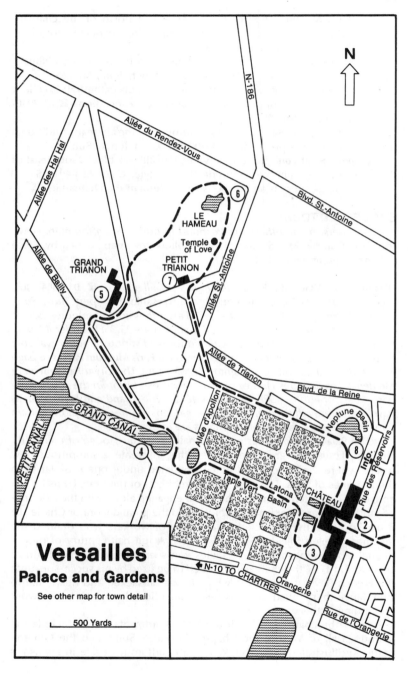

N

LE HAMEAU

Temple of Love

GRAND TRIANON

PETIT TRIANON

Allée du Rendez-Vous

N-186

Blvd. St-Antoine

Allée des Hai Hai

Allée de Bailly

Allée St-Antoine

Allée de Trianon

Blvd. de la Reine

GRAND CANAL

PETIT CANAL

Allée d'Apollon

Neptune Basin

Info.

Rue des Réservoirs

Tapis Vert

Latona Basin

CHÂTEAU

Rue de l'Orangerie

N-10 TO CHARTRES

Orangerie

Rue de l'Orangerie

Versailles
Palace and Gardens
See other map for town detail

500 Yards

Les Trois Marches (1 Blvd. de la Reine, just north of the château) Celebrated cuisine with excellent wines. Proper dress expected, for reservations ☎ 01-3950-1321. X: Aug. $$$ +

Rescatore (27 Av. de St.-Cloud, 2 blocks northeast of the château) Noted for its seafood. ☎ 01-3925-0634. X: Sat. lunch, Sun., Aug. $$$

Potager du Roy (1 Rue Mar.-Joffre, near St.-Louis cathedral) Excellent cuisine in simple surroundings. Very popular, for reservations ☎ 01-3950-3534. X: Sun. eve, Mon. $$

Le Falher (22 Rue Satory, 2 blocks southeast of the château) Traditional dishes at reasonable prices. ☎ 01-3950-5743. X: Sat. lunch, Sun. $$

Crêperie Saint-Louis (33 Rue du Vieux Versailles, 2 blocks southeast of the château) Crêpes in the traditional Breton style. ☎ 01-3953-4012. $

In addition, there is an inexpensive cafeteria in the château itself.

SUGGESTED TOUR:

Numbers in parentheses correspond to numbers on the map. Leave the **Rive Gauche RER Station** (1) and follow the map to nearby Place d'Armes, opening into the:

***PALACE OF VERSAILLES** (Château de Versailles) (2),* ☎ *01-3084-7400, recording 01-3084-7676, Internet: chateauversailles.fr. Open Tues.–Sun., 9–6:30, closing at 5:30 from Oct.–April. Last admission 30 minutes before closing. **State Apartments:** Adults 45FF, youths 18–25 35FF, under 18 free. Rental of audiotour device 30FF. Guided tours of various lengths available for an extra charge. Holders of the economical **Paris Museum Pass** (see page 27) avoid the lines and go straight to Entrance A2. The **Great Parliamentary Moments** (Les Grandes Heures du Parlement) exhibition in the south wing costs 20FF for adults, 15FF for youths 18–25. The **Grand and Petit Trianons** have a separate admission, below. The gardens are free, except on certain Sundays in season when the fountains are in operation.*

The Palace of Versailles was originally a hunting lodge of Louis XIII. His son, Louis XIV, greatly expanded this to create a sumptuous new palace where the court could be consolidated under one roof, far from the intrigues of Paris. The most noted architects of the time, Louis Le Vau and, later, Jules Hardouin-Mansart, were engaged along with the celebrated landscape gardener André Le Nôtre and the great decorator Charles Le Brun. Together they directed a vast army of workers who drained the marshes, leveled hills and moved forests. A full half-century of monumental labor went into the Versailles you see today. After the death of Louis XIV in 1715, the château continued to be used by his successors until the French Revolution, during which it was ransacked and nearly fell to ruin. Since then, much of it has been magnificently restored, with work continuing to this day.

Enter the château and visit the **State Apartments**, which include the famous ***Hall of Mirrors**, the Chapel, the King's Suite, and the Queen's Suite. An illustrated guide booklet or an audiotour device in English is available at the entrance, which is quite useful since you'll be wandering through on your own.

No visit to Versailles is complete without a stroll through the fabulous gardens. Begin with the **Parterres du Midi** (3), overlooking the **Orangerie**. Walk over to the Latona Basin and follow the Tapis Vert, a long green avenue between some enchanting hidden groves, to the **Grand Canal** (4), where boats may be hired.

Continue on to the **Grand Trianon** (5), a smaller château built in 1687 to avoid the formalities of court life. After the Revolution it was used by Napoleon and is furnished in the Empire style. *Open Tues.–Sun., 10–6:30, reduced hours from Oct.–April. Adults 25FF, 15FF after 3:30.*

Now follow the map to **Le Hameau** (6), a thoroughly delightful little hamlet where the unfortunate Marie-Antoinette played at being a peasant. Paths from here lead past the Temple of Love to the **Petit Trianon** (7), an elegant small château erected by Louis XV and later used by Marie-Antoinette. *Open Tues.–Sun., 10–6:30, reduced hours from Oct.–April. Adults 15FF, 10FF after 3:30.* Return to the main palace by way of the Neptune Basin (8).

Before heading back to Paris, you may want to explore a bit of the town of Versailles. An interesting short walk can be made by following the map past the Church of Notre-Dame to the pleasant **Lambinet Museum** (9), which specializes in 18th-century art. ☎ 01-3950-3032. *Open Tues. and Fri. 2–5, Wed.–Thurs. 1–6, weekends 2–6. Adults 25FF, seniors, students, children 15FF.* Those intrepid souls intent on continuing on to Chartres by rail should depart from Versailles' **Chantiers Station** (10).

*Chartres

Rising majestically above the Beauce Plain, the Cathedral of Chartres is one of the great legacies of the Middle Ages and the quintessential Gothic cathedral. Pilgrims and tourists from all over the world are drawn to it by the thousands, yet most overlook the charms of the town itself. And that's a pity—for Chartres is one of those rare French *villes* that kept its essentially medieval character intact.

It may seem surprising that a town as small as Chartres should possess one of the largest cathedrals on Earth. The place, however, appears to have a long history of religious significance. Ancient Druids probably worshiped at the well under the cathedral crypt. Later the capital of the Gallic Carnutes, it was called *Autricum* by the Romans, who built a temple on the same site. Early Christians replaced this with a basilica, saving the statue of the Roman goddess whom they took to be the Virgin. Five subsequent churches were built on the spot, culminating in the present l3th-century masterpiece. A precious relic believed to be a garment worn by the Virgin Mary, which has been in the cathedral since 876, is responsible for Chartres being a place of pilgrimage for over a thousand years.

GETTING THERE:

Trains leave Montparnasse Station in Paris fairly frequently for the one-hour trip to Chartres. Return service operates until late evening.

By car, Chartres is 55 miles southwest of Paris via the A-10 and A-11 Autoroutes. A slower but more interesting route is to take the N-10 through Versailles and Rambouillet.

PRACTICALITIES:

Try to visit Chartres in good weather, when sunshine illuminates the incredible stained-glass windows to best effect. The art museum is closed on Tuesdays and major holidays. The local **Tourist Information Office**, ☎ 02-3721-5000, is at the far end of the cathedral square. An Internet site to check is www.chartres.com. Chartres is in the Île-de-France region, and has a population of about 40,000.

FOOD AND DRINK:

Some good restaurant choices are:

La Vieille Maison (5 Rue au Lait, near the cathedral) Regional cuisine in an attractive old house. Proper dress expected, for reservations ☎ 02-3734-1067. X: Sun. eve., Mon. $$$

Café Serpente (2 Cloître Notre-Dame, facing the cathedral) An old-fashioned bistro. ☎ 02-3721-6881. $$

Buisson Ardent (10 Rue au Lait, near the cathedral) Good-value dining in an attractive setting. ☎ 02-3734-0466. X: late July, Mon., Tues. $$

La Reine de Saba (8 Cloître Notre-Dame, near the cathedral) Good-value traditional food in a casual setting. ☎ 02-3721-8916. $

SUGGESTED TOUR:

Numbers in parentheses correspond to numbers on the map. From the **train station** (1) you will have a clear view of the cathedral. Follow the map to:

*CHARTRES CATHEDRAL *(Cathédrale Notre-Dame)* (2–4), ☎ 02-3721-7502. *Open daily 7:30 a.m. to 7:15 p.m., except for Mass, weddings and funerals. Free, donation. Tower open 10–11:30 and 2–4, later in season, adults 25FF, youths 12–25 15FF. Crypt tours daily, fee 11FF.*

Much of the cathedral's fascinating **West Front** survives from an earlier 12th-century structure largely destroyed by fire in 1194. The two asymmetrical towers make a dramatic study in architectural evolution. On the right is the **Old Tower** *(Clocher Vieux)*, representing the fullest development of the Romanesque style. The **New Tower** *(Clocher Neuf)*, to the left, is capped with a 16th-century spire, a masterpiece of the Flamboyant Gothic. Between them stands the **Royal Portal**, three arched doorways from the 12th century. Look carefully at the stunning *Christ in Majesty* carving above the center door. The figures over the right portal depict the Nativity, while those on the left are of the Ascension.

Step inside to witness the true glory of Chartres Cathedral—its miraculous **stained-glass windows**. Almost all of these are original, mostly 13th-century with some dating from the 12th. Replacements account for less than six percent of the total 26,000 square feet, making this the largest collection of medieval glass in the world.

Guided tours of the interior are available—those in English being particularly good—or you can pick up a printed guide and explore on your own. Binoculars can be a great help for studying the Biblical stories depicted in the windows. Be sure to visit the **Treasury**, behind the choir, which displays the venerated garment thought to have been worn by the Virgin Mary.

A climb to the top of the **North Tower** will reward you with spectacular views. The entrance to this is by the door in the **North Transept** (3). Another sight not to be missed is the ancient **Crypt** of the original church, which can be visited on special guided tours only. These depart, oddly enough, from a souvenir shop called La Crypte in front of the **South Porch** (4).

Leave the cathedral and follow the map to the Rue des Écuyers. On

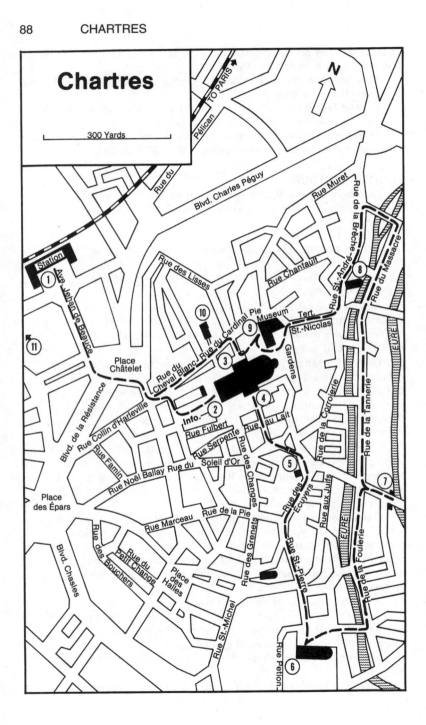

Chartres

300 Yards

the right, at Number 35, you will find a curious old house with a 16th-century turret staircase of carved oak known as the **Escalier de la Reine Berthe** (5). Continue on to the **Church of St.-Pierre** (6). If its great cathedral did not exist, Chartres would still be noted for this magnificent medieval church, whose flying buttresses and original stained glass are truly impressive.

Stroll over to the Eure River and cross it. There is a nice view of the cathedral from here. Turn left on Rue de la Foulerie and follow along to **Porte Guillaume** (7) to see what little remains of the old town walls. Return to the stream and walk along Rue de la Tannerie, passing several delightful old waterside buildings. Across the Eure stands the 12th-century **Église St.-André** (8), a Romanesque structure whose choir once spanned the water on a daring arch, long since destroyed.

Continue by following the map to the **Musée des Beaux-Arts** (9), reached via the steep Tertre Saint-Nicolas steps which open into lovely gardens. The museum, housed in the former Bishop's Palace, contains a superb collection of paintings (particularly those by Vlaminck), enamels, tapestries, furniture, and artifacts of regional history. ☎ *02-3736-4139. Open Mon. and Wed.–Sat. 10–noon and 2–5, Sun. 2–5. Closed on Tues. and holidays. Adults 10FF, seniors and students 5FF.*

Another attraction you may want to visit is the **Cellier de Loëns** (10) at Number 5 Rue du Cardinal Pie. This 13th-century cellar once stored tithes and is now the **International Stained-Glass Center** *(Centre International du Vitrail)*, offering rotating exhibits of the art that made Chartres famous. ☎ *02-3721-6572. Open daily 9:30–12:30 and 1:30–6, closed between exhibitions. Adults 20FF, seniors, students, children 12FF.*

Some visitors might also be interested in the **Conservatoire du Machinisme et des Pratiques Agricoles** *(Le Compa)* (11, off the map), an exhibition of farm machinery from early times to the present. It is housed in a 19th-century steam locomotive depot just west of the train station. *Open Sun.–Fri., 9–12:30 and 1:30–6.*

Trip 8

Fontainebleau

Haunted by memories of François I and Napoleon Bonaparte, the Château of Fontainebleau beguiles with its marvelously haphazard layout and intimate atmosphere. Many prefer it to Versailles. This was a real home for the rulers of France, from the 12th century right down to Napoleon III in the 19th.

The palace as it stands today is mostly the result of an extensive construction carried out in the 16th century by François I, the king most credited with bringing the Renaissance to France. Only the keep *(donjon)* in the Oval Court survives from the Middle Ages. Later kings, including Louis XIV, made frequent use of the château, drawn primarily by the sporting opportunities of the surrounding forest. Fontainebleau became the favorite residence of Napoleon I, who had it thoroughly redecorated. It was also the scene, in 1814, of his abdication and departure for Elba.

The Forest of Fontainebleau is exceptionally lovely with its wide variety of wild, natural beauty. Those with cars may want to pick up a map at the tourist office and go exploring, particularly to the charming village of Barbizon.

GETTING THERE:

Trains depart Gare de Lyon station in Paris frequently for Fontainebleau-Avon, less than 45 minutes away. These are met by a bus marked "Château," which goes to the palace. Return trains run until mid-evening.

By car, the fastest way is via the A-6 Autoroute, followed by the N-37 and N-7 roads. Fontainebleau is 40 miles southeast of Paris.

PRACTICALITIES:

Avoid coming on a Tuesday, when the château is closed. Pleasant weather will make a walk in the gardens more enjoyable. The local **Tourist Information Office**, ☎ 01-6074-9999, is at 4 Rue Royale, near the château. An Internet site to check is www.fontainebleau.fr.com. Fontainebleau is in the Île-de-France region, and has a population of about 16,000.

FOOD AND DRINK:

The town of Fontainebleau has a great many restaurants and cafés in all price ranges, particularly on and near Rue Grande and Place Général-de-Gaulle. Among the better choices are:

Aigle Noir (27 Place Napoléon-Bonaparte, near the tourist office) Excellent modern cuisine in the renowned hotel's Le Beauharnais restaurant. Proper dress expected, reservations advised, ☎ 01-6074-6000. Garden dining in season. $$$

La Table des Maréchaux (9 Rue Grande, near the tourist office) Indoor/outdoor dining at the Hôtel Napoléon, in a suitably napoleonic setting. ☎ 01-6039-5050. $$

Chez Arrighi (53 Rue de France, 2 blocks northwest of the château) Corsican dishes near Napoléon's palace. ☎ 01-6422-2943. X: Mon. $$

Croquembouche (43 Rue de France, 2 blocks northwest of the château) A wonderful value, especially at lunch. ☎ 01-6422-0157. X: Wed., Thurs. lunch, Aug. $ and $$

SUGGESTED TOUR:

Numbers in parentheses correspond to numbers on the map. The **Fontainebleau-Avon Train Station** (1) is nearly two miles from the palace. Get there by one of the frequent buses marked "Château" or on foot through the park.

*CHÂTEAU DE FONTAINEBLEAU (2), ☎ 01-6071-5060. *Open Wed.–Mon., 9:30–12:30 and 2–5, remaining open until 6 in July and Aug. From June to Sept. there is no midday closure. Closed Tues. and certain holidays. Last admission is one hour before closing time. Adults 35FF, youths 18–25 23FF, under 18 free. Sunday admission for adults is also 23FF. Chinese Museum is another 16FF, 12FF for youths. Gardens are free.*

Enter the château via the White Horse Courtyard, also known as the **Cour des Adieux**, where Napoléon I bid a tearful farewell to his troops in 1814 as he went into exile. You may stroll through the **Grand Apartments** at your own leisure, following a well-marked route. In order to understand what you're seeing, however, it will help to purchase an illustrated guide in English, available at the entrance. The most outstanding sights are the 16th-century ***Galerie François I**, the King's Staircase, the ***Ballroom**, the **Royal Apartments**, and **Napoléon's Apartments** *(Musée Napoléon Ier)*. There is also a **Chinese Museum** *(Musée Chinois)* on the ground floor where Empress Eugénie's collection of objects from the Far East are displayed, which involves a separate entrance fee. To see the more intimate **Petit Apartments** requires taking a guided tour.

Leave the château and follow the map through a passage in the south wing to an intriguing 16th-century grotto. This opens into the informal **Jardin Anglais** (English Gardens) (3) laid out by Napoléon. Continue on past the original spring, the **Fontaine Bliaud**, from which the name of the palace and town derives. Next to this is the Carp Pond with its delightful little island pavilion. Rowboats may be rented here.

You are now in the formal gardens, the Parterre designed for Louis XIV by the architect Le Vau, which offers marvelous views of the château. Stroll down to the **Cascades** (4) and look out over the Grand Canal, a cen-

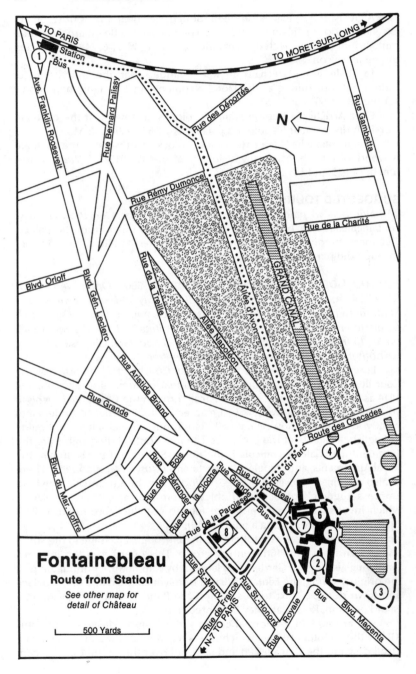

TO PARIS

Station

Bus

TO MORET-SUR-LOING

Ave. Franklin Roosevelt

Rue Bernard Palissy

Rue des Déportés

Rue Gambetta

N

Rue Rémy Dumonce

Rue de la Charité

Blvd. Orloff

Blvd. Gén. Leclerc

Rue de la Treille

Allée d'Avon

Allée Napoléon

GRAND CANAL

Rue Aristide Briand

Rue Grande

Route des Cascades

Blvd. du Mar. Joffre

Rue des Bois

Rue Béranger

Rue de la Cloche

Rue Grande

Rue du Château

Rue du Parc

Bus

Rue de la Paroisse

St-Merry

Rue St-Merry

Rue de France

N-7 TO PARIS

Rue St-Honoré

Rue Royale

Bus

Blvd. Magenta

Fontainebleau

Route from Station

*See other map for
detail of Château*

500 Yards

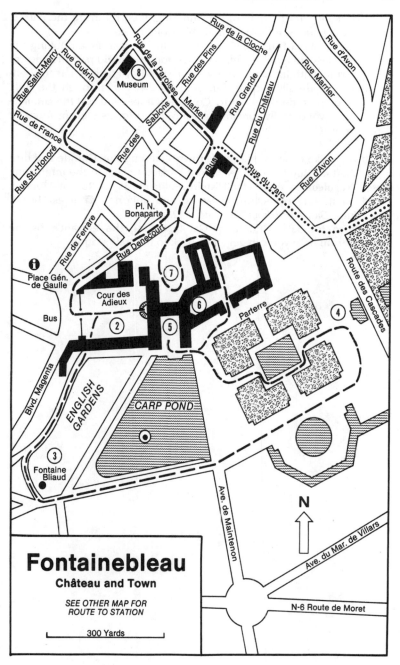

Fontainebleau
Château and Town

*SEE OTHER MAP FOR
ROUTE TO STATION*

300 Yards

ter of pageantry in the time of the Sun King, then return to the palace. Horse carriage rides are usually available along here.

The **Cour de la Fontaine** (5) is a beautiful courtyard overlooking the carp pond. Take an admiring glance, then follow around past the ancient **Oval Court** (6) with its 12th-century keep—used by François I as his bedroom. This is usually locked, but you can peek in through the grill. Continue on past the 17th-century Cour des Offices and visit the **Jardin de Diane** (7), a wonderfully romantic garden noted for its elegant fountain dating from 1603.

If you'd like to see some of the town, exit onto Rue Grande and turn right. A left on Rue Paroisse leads past a market place to the interesting **Musée Napoléonien d'Art et d'Histoire Militaire** (8) on Rue St.-Honoré, noted for its fine collection of swords and uniforms. ☎ *01-6074-6489. Open Tues.–Sat. 2–5. Adults 10FF, under 12 free.*

Return to Place Général-de-Gaulle, facing the entrance of the château. from here you can get a bus back to the train station.

Moret-sur-Loing

Although it has long been a favorite weekend retreat for Parisians, Moret-sur-Loing has yet to be discovered by foreign visitors. This deliciously picturesque old town on the meandering Loing River looks like a scene from an Impressionist painting, and in fact is one. The noted artist Alfred Sisley spent the latter years of his life here, immortalizing for all time its narrow streets, quaint church, delightful bridge, and charming watermills.

Moret was a strategically important border fortress as early as the 12th century, when it protected the Île-de-France from the counts of Champagne. Many of its original structures still exist, preserved amid a medieval atmosphere virtually unmatched elsewhere in the region.

A daytrip to Moret can be combined quite easily with one to Fontainebleau, just six miles away on the same rail line. If you are driving, you could visit Vaux-le-Vicomte, a fabulous château just outside Melun, instead. This is briefly described on page 79. Those going to Moret only will find that it makes a good afternoon trip.

GETTING THERE:

Trains leave Gare de Lyon station in Paris fairly frequently for Moret-Véneux-les-Sablons Station, usually stopping at Fontainebleau en route. The trip takes less than one hour. Return service operates until mid-evening. Although Moret is a very small town, it is also an important rail junction, with trains to and from Paris using different, widely spaced platforms. Be careful to note the correct one on the departure board.

By car, the quickest route is to follow the directions to Fontainebleau on page 90, then take the N-6 into Moret, which is about 48 miles southeast of Paris.

PRACTICALITIES:

Moret can be enjoyed at any time in good weather, particularly on weekends. *Son et Lumiére* spectacles are held on Saturday nights in summer—check the tourist office for details. The **tourist office**, ☎ 01-6070-4166, Internet: www.ville-moret-sur-loing.fr, is located on Place de Samois, next to the Porte de Samois.

FOOD AND DRINK:

There are a number of charming restaurants, mostly located near the bridge. Some choices are:

Auberge de la Palette (Av. Jean-Jaurès, on way to station) A well-recommended inn. ☎ 01-6070-5072. X: Tues. eve., Wed., early Apr., late Aug. $$

Rôtisserie du Bon Abri (90 Av. de Fontainebleau, in nearby Véneux-les-Sablons, not far from the train station) An excellent choice. ☎ 01-6070-5540. X: Sun. eve., Mon. $$

SUGGESTED TOUR:

Numbers in parentheses correspond to numbers on the map.

The **Moret-Véneux-les-Sablons Train Station** (1) is nearly a mile from the town proper. You could call for a taxi, although the walk is rather pleasant. Enter the Old Town through the 12th-century **Porte de Samois** gate (2), next to the tourist office. Continue down Rue Grande where, at Number 24, opposite the war memorial park, you will pass the house where Napoleon spent the last night on his return from Elba. Turn right into a passageway leading to a courtyard behind the town hall. Here stands the so-called **Maison François I** (3), a splendid Renaissance façade built in 1527 and later moved, stone by stone, to Paris, where it remained until 1956. It was then returned to Moret. Back on the Rue Grande there are two fine Renaissance houses at numbers 28 and 30.

Stroll straight ahead through the venerable 12th-century **Porte de Bourgogne** gate (4). From here a famous bridge spans the Loing River. Midstream, on either side, are two striking old mills, now private residences. Once across, make a left into the **park** (5) on the river's edge where you can enjoy the romantic view captured in Sisley's renowned painting, *The Bridge at Moret*, displayed in the Orsay Museum in Paris.

Follow the map past locks on the Burgundy Canal to the ***Georges Clemenceau Museum** *(La Grange Batelière)* (6). Designed as a retirement place by the eminent French premier shortly before his death, this intimate, very personal and extremely charming small house was occupied by his son until 1964. It is now open for escorted visits; confirm times with the tourist office or the site. ☎ *01-6070-5121. Usually open on weekends and holidays, from Palm Sunday through Sept., 2:30–6; and in Oct. and Nov. at 2 and 5. Tours 35FF.*

Return across the bridge and follow Rue de la Tannerie to the ancient **Castle Keep** *(Donjon)* (7) on Rue du Donjon. Built in 1128, it was used for several months as a prison for Nicolas Fouquet, Louis XIV's finance minister who amassed a great fortune at the State's expense.

At Number 9 Rue du Donjon is the **house** (8), where the artist Alfred Sisley spent the last years of his life. One of the pioneers of Impressionism, he showed little aptitude in promoting his work and died in poverty. Ironically, his paintings now hang in the world's greatest museums.

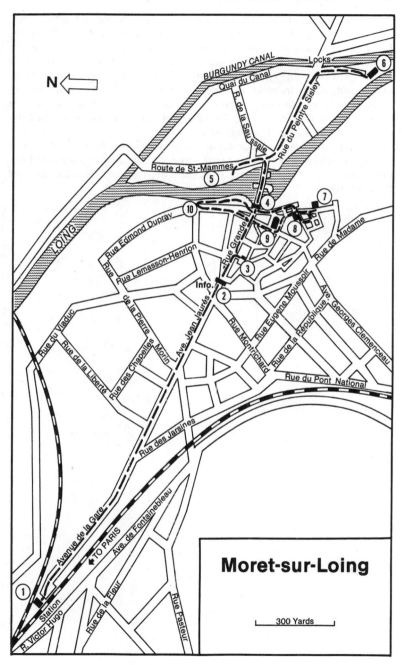

N

BURGUNDY CANAL   Locks
Quai du Canal
6
R. de la Saussaie
Rue du Peintre Sisley
Route de St.-Mammes
5
LOING
Rue Edmond Dupray
10
4
7
Rue Lemasson-Henrion
Rue
9
8
Rue de Madame
Rue Grande
3
Info.
2
Rue Eugene Moussoir
Ave. Jean Jaurès
de la Pierre Morin
Rue
Rue Montchard
Rue de la République
Ave. Georges Clemenceau
Rue du Viaduc
Rue de la Liberté
Rue des Chapelles
Rue du Pont National
Rue des Jarsines
Avenue de la Gare
TO PARIS
Ave. de Fontainebleau
1
Station
R. Victor Hugo
Rue de la Fleur
Rue Pasteur

Moret-sur-Loing

300 Yards

Stroll through the evocative narrow alleyways in the immediate area, then continue on to the magnificent Gothic **Church of Notre-Dame** (9). Begun in 1166 on a site consecrated by Thomas à Becket, the Archbishop of Canterbury, construction continued until the 15th century, when its Flamboyant porch was added. The church is quite interesting to visit—its flying buttresses dramatic in their upward surge. To the right of the church, in an old timbered house, nuns once sold their famous Sucres d'Orge, the barley-sugar specialty of Moret. The nuns are gone, but the candy is still available at several shops in town.

Follow the map via Rue Grande and make the first possible turn through an old building to the river's edge. Wander along to some **old fortifications** (10) that are now parts of houses, then return to Rue Grande and the station.

Provins

Another one of those intriguing medieval towns that somehow get overlooked by tourists, Provins can be a real charmer. Once the third-largest city in France (after Paris and Rouen), it is now a pleasant backwater with distant echoes of a long-ago past. This is a place for quiet contemplation far from the madding crowds, where vestiges of the early Middle Ages have survived intact.

The town's decline began as early as the 13th century. Before that, Provins was the capital of Brie, seat of the counts of Champagne and the site of major fairs famed throughout Europe. It has a curious connection with English history. During the 13th century it was ruled by Edmund, duke of Lancaster, who adopted as his own the famous red rose of Provins—later to become a symbol in the War of the Roses. Both the plague and the Hundred Years War took their toll, but it was perhaps the growing importance of nearby Paris that contributed most to the downfall of this once-great city.

Provins is built on two levels. The lower town *(Ville Basse)* is reawakening with renewed prosperity, while the upper town *(Ville Haute)*, perched high on a promontory overlooking the Brie plain, slumbers on amid ruined memories. Both have their fascinations, and both are covered on the suggested walking tour.

GETTING THERE:

Trains depart Gare de l'Est station in Paris in the morning for the 70-minute ride to Provins. Return service operates until early evening.

By car, it's the N-19 all the way to Provins, 53 miles southeast of Paris. A more complex but probably faster route is to leave Paris on the A-4, switching quickly to the N-4, then finally the D-231 into Provins.

PRACTICALITIES:

Good weather is essential for this largely outdoor trip. The famous Tour de César is open every day except Christmas and New Year's, but other attractions tend to operate only on weekends and holidays. The local **tourist office** can be reached at ☎ 01- 6460-2626, Internet: www.provins/net.

FOOD AND DRINK:

Provins offers a nice variety of restaurants along the walking route. Some suggestions are:

Au Vieux Remparts (3 Rue Couverte, in the upper town, near the Tour de César) Real country cooking in a charming atmosphere, indoors or out. ☎ 01-6408-9400. $$

Le Médiéval (6 Place Honoré de Balzac, in the lower town) A local favorite, with good-value lunches. ☎ 01-6400-0119. X: Sun. eve., Mon. $$

SUGGESTED TOUR:

Numbers in parentheses correspond to numbers on the map.

Leave the **train station** (1) and follow the map past several streams in the colorful lower town. The climb to the upper town is rather steep, but manageable and highly worthwhile. Once there, step into the **Jardin des Brébans** for a nice view, then stroll over to the *****Tour de César** (2). Dating from the 12th century, this massive octagonal tower was erected on the site of a Roman fortress and is still in magnificent condition. Its circular base was built by the English during the Hundred Years War as a platform for their artillery. Enter the tower and climb its narrow staircases, which get somewhat spooky as you ascend to the very top for a fantastic *****panorama** of the entire region. *Open April–Oct., daily 10–6; Nov.–March, daily 2–5. Adults 22FF, children 14FF.* At its base is a branch of the local tourist office, where you can get current information about the town's other offerings.

The **Church of St.-Quiriace** (3), equally ancient, is just a few steps away. Originally planned to be much larger, its choir, apse, and transepts were the only parts completed before the days of prosperity ran out for Provins. Its interior, however, is quite impressive and should not be missed. *Open weekends and holidays; otherwise see the tourist office for entry.*

Stroll over to the **Maison Romane** (4) on Rue du Palais. This partly 10th-century house now contains a small museum of local archaeology. *Usually open in the afternoons on Sundays and holidays during the season.* Return to the Tour de César and continue along the footpath at its base to Rue de l'Ormerie, following that to Place du Châtel.

The **Grange aux Dîmes** (5), a curious 12th-century tithe barn, now houses a collection of medieval artifacts in period room settings. In its basement is an entrance to a large network of underground passageways. *Open April–Aug., daily 10–6; Sept.–Oct., weekdays 2–6, weekends 10:30–6; Nov.–March, weekends and holidays 2–5. Adults 22FF, children 14FF.*

Now follow Rue de Jouy to the **Porte de Jouy** (6), a medieval gate in the still-extant town walls. Turn right and follow the inside of the ramparts for a short distance, then return and go through the gate. A left turn down a delightful country lane leads along the massive fortifications.

Re-enter the town through the 12th-century **Porte St.-Jean** (7), another fortified gate, and return on Rue St.-Jean to Place du Châtel. From here walk downhill on Rue St.-Thibault to the **Hôtel Dieu** (8). Once the palace of the countess of Champagne, this heavily reconstructed medieval building

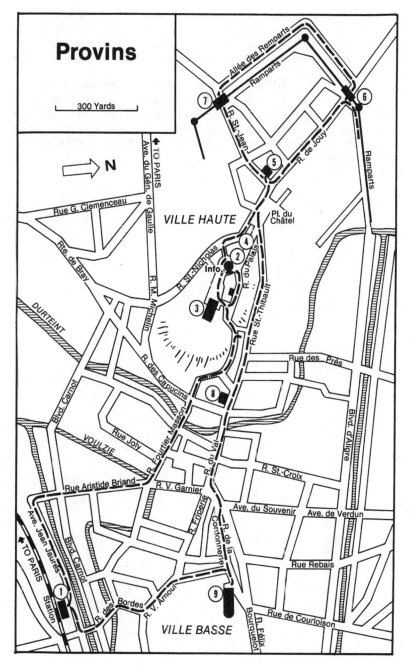

Provins

300 Yards

N

TO PARIS
Ave. du Gén. de Gaulle

Allée des Remparts
Ramparts

Rue G. Clemenceau

Rue de Bray

R. M. Michelin

DURTEINT

R. des Capucins

VILLE HAUTE

R. St-Nicholas

Info.

PL du Châtel

R. du Palais

R. de Jouy

Ramparts

R. St-Jean

Rue St-Thibault

Rue des Prés

Blvd. Carnot

VOULZIE

Rue Joly

R. Fourtier Masson

Blvd. d'Aligre

Rue Aristide Briand

R. V. Garnier

R. du Val

R. St.-Croix

Ave. du Souvenir   Ave. de Verdun

R. Friperie

R. de la Cordonnerie

Rue Rebais

TO PARIS
Ave. Jean Jaurès

Blvd. Carnot

Station

R. des Bordes

R. V. Arnoul

R. Félix Bourquelot

Rue de Courloison

VILLE BASSE

has an entrance to the mysterious, enigmatic subterranean passages *(Souterrains)* of Provins, some of which may date from the time of the Franks. *Open April–Oct., weekends and holidays 10:30–6, weekdays tours at 3 and 4; Nov.–March, weekends and holidays, tours at 2, 3, and 4. Adults 22FF, children 14FF.*

You have now returned to the lower town. Stroll along Rue du Val and Rue de la Cordonnerie to the **Church of St.-Ayoul** (9), once the center of a cult around which the Ville Basse developed. Destroyed by fire in the 12th century, the church was soon rebuilt and features some truly outstanding sculptures along with other works of art. From here it is a short walk back to the station.

Chantilly

The Île-de-France region is justly renowned for its many splendid châteaux. Some of these, especially Versailles, are monumental in scope while others, such as Fontainebleau, leave the visitor endowed with an immensely satisfying sense of history. For sheer beauty, however, the dream-like Château of Chantilly is by far the most outstanding. Many even consider it to be the loveliest in all France. This is surely reason enough to make the easy daytrip, but Chantilly gilds the lily with yet more sumptuous attractions. There are enchanted gardens, a magnificent forest, one of the nation's best art museums, stables that resemble a palace, a world-famous racetrack, a great horse training center and—of course— the delicious whipped cream and black lace for which the town is noted.

Chantilly has an illustrious history going back to a Roman named *Cantilius.* The present château—actually two separate châteaux joined by a common entrance—is the fifth on the same site. Its larger part, the impossibly romantic Grand Château, is a late-19th-century pastiche while the older Petit Château dates from the 16th century. It was here that a well-known event (or story!) occurred in 1671, when Louis XIV came calling for a three-day visit—along with five thousand of his retainers. The greatest chef in France at the time, François Vatel, was employed at the château and had to feed all those hungry mouths on virtually no notice. Things went wrong and finally, when the promised fish failed to arrive in time, the overwrought Vatel ended it all with a sword thrust through his body.

GETTING THERE:

Trains leave Nord Station in Paris almost hourly for the 30-minute ride to Chantilly. Return service operates until early evening.

By car, leave Paris on the A-1 Autoroute, switching to the N-I near St.-Denis and then to the N-16. Chantilly is about 25 miles north of Paris.

PRACTICALITIES:

Good weather is essential for a visit to Chantilly. Avoid coming on a Tuesday, when nearly everything is closed. The local **tourist information office,** ☎ 03-4457-0858, is at 60 Avenue du Maréchal-Joffre, between the train station and the town. Bicycles may be rented nearby. Chantilly has a population of about 11,000.

FOOD AND DRINK:
There are several good restaurants between the train station and the château. Some choices are:
Auberge le Lion d'Or (44 Rue du Connétable, near the Grandes Ecuries) Part of a conveniently-located inn. ☎ 03-4457-9231. $$
Maison Mandarin (62 Rue du Connétable, near the Grandes Ecuries) Chinese cuisine at reasonable prices. ☎ 03-4457-0029. X: Sun. eve., Mon. $ and $$
Capitainerie (in the château) A self-service cafeteria for light lunches. ☎ 03-4457-1589. X: Tues. $

SUGGESTED TOUR:
Numbers in parentheses correspond to numbers on the map.

Leave the **train station** (1) and follow the map to the **Hippodrome** (racetrack) (2), where the prestigious Prix de Diane and Prix du Jockey Club races are run on the first and second Sundays of June. This beautifully situated course has been attracting Paris society since 1836. Continue on to the:

*CHÂTEAU DE CHANTILLY (3), ☎ 03-4462-6262. *Open March–Oct., Wed.–Mon., 10–6; Nov.–Feb., Wed.–Mon., 10:30–12:45 and 2–5. Last entry 45 minutes before closing. Park open every day. Château and park: Adults 39FF, children 12–17 34FF, under 12 12FF. Park only: 17FF, children 10FF.*

Chantilly's magnificent château rises from the middle of a tiny lake like a fantastic scene from a fairy tale. As a special treat, you can opt to combine the admission fee with a ride in ***l'Aérophile**, the largest balloon in the world, which carries 30 people at a time for a thrilling overview of the estate. This fanciful flight is reasonably priced and operates from April to November. Alternatively, you can ride on the **Hydrophile**, an electric boat on the Grand Canal. Advance reservations are possible; ☎ 03-4457-3535. Adults 49FF, students 43FF, children 28FF.

Cross the bridge and enter the **Musée Condé**, a museum that occupies the entire château. The sumptuous collection of art, along with the estate, was bequeathed to the Institut de France in 1897 by its last owner, the Duke of Aumale, fifth son of Louis-Philippe, the last king of France. A guide booklet in English is available at the entrance.

The rooms to your right, in the **Grand Château**, contain the picture galleries and may be seen at your own leisure. Laid out in a charming 19th-century style, the walls are covered from top to bottom with an amazingly good collection of canvases. To see the rest of the château you will have to take a guided tour, included in the admission price. Don't miss the private apartments in the **Petit Château**, especially the Chapel and the Library, whose greatest treasure is the **Trés Riches Heures du Duc de Berry*, one of the greatest masterpieces of the Middle Ages. Because of its fragile condition, this is rarely exhibited, but copies are on display.

Leave the château and walk straight ahead into the park. Once in the

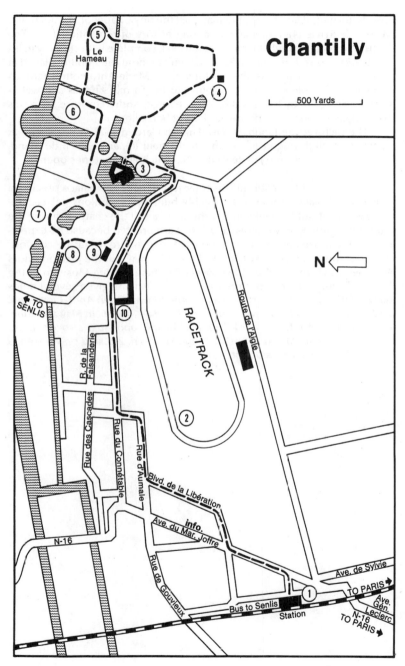

Chantilly

500 Yards

N

Le Hameau

RACETRACK

Route de l'Aigle

R. de la Faisanderie

Rue des Cascades

Rue du Connétable

Rue d'Aumale

Blvd. de la Libération

info.

Ave. du Mar. Joffre

Rue de Gouvieux

N-16

TO SENLIS

Ave. de Sylvie

TO PARIS

Ave. Gén. Leclerc

N-16 TO PARIS

Bus to Senlis

Station

woods, turn right and follow the map past the tiny Chapel of St. Paul to the **Maison de Sylvie** (4), a house with a long history of romantic affairs. The paths now lead through an enchanted forest, complete with statuary in little clearing, to **Le Hameau** (5), a rustic hamlet where the nobility played at being peasants. This was the prototype for Marie-Antoinette's famous hameau at Versailles. Continue around to the formal **gardens** and **waterways** (6) designed by that great landscape artist, André Le Nôtre, who was also largely responsible for the gardens at Versailles.

The picturesque **Jardin Anglais** (English Gardens) (7) come as a great contrast. Stroll through them to the **Île d'Amour** (8), an idyllic little island, then continue on to the **Jeu de Paume** (9), which is sometimes open.

One last sight remains at Chantilly, just outside the palace precincts. This is the **Grandes Écuries** (10), a stable built like a fabulous palace. The story is told about the Duke of Bourbon, owner of the château during the early 18th century, having this luxurious barn erected because he expected to be reincarnated as a horse and wanted to assure his future comfort. Whether this event actually occurred is not known, but the posh interiors are open to visitors as the **Musée Vivant du Cheval** (Living Museum of the Horse). Demonstrations of dressage, a great treat, are given several times daily. ☎ *03-4457-1313, Internet: www.emroll.fr/mvc. Open April–Oct., Mon. and Tues.–Fri., 10:30–5:30, weekends and holiday, 10:30–6. In May and June, it's also open on Tues., 10:30–5:30, and in July and Aug. also on Tues., 2–5:30. From Nov.–March, open Mon. and Wed.–Fri. 2–5, and on weekends 10:30–5:30. Adults 50FF, students 45FF.*

Senlis

Permeated with a distinctly medieval atmosphere, Senlis has almost totally escaped the turmoil of history. Its ancient, twisting lanes remain largely as they were during the Middle Ages, when the long line of French royalty began there in 987 with the election of Hugues Capet as the first true king of France. Senlis was old even then, having been built on the foundations of a Gallo-Roman settlement.

The town continued as a seat of kings, at least on a part-time basis, until the reign of Henri IV in the 16th century. After that, royalty no longer came and Senlis entered a peaceful period, interrupted only now and then by a few wars, the French Revolution, and a close brush with destruction at the hands of invading Germans in 1914.

Much of the town's fascinating past is still intact, steeped in an aura of charm and ready to be enjoyed today. You may want to combine this visit with one to nearby Chantilly, quite easily done by getting off to an early start.

GETTING THERE:

Trains depart Nord Station in Paris almost hourly for the 30-minute ride to Chantilly, where you change to a bus for Senlis. The distance is only five miles. Upon arrival at the Senlis bus station, check the posted schedule of return buses to Chantilly, from which trains to Paris operate until early evening.

By car, take the A-1 Autoroute north from Paris to the Senlis exit, a distance of 32 miles.

PRACTICALITIES:

Avoid coming on a Tuesday or on a Wednesday morning, when the ancient Royal Palace and the museums are closed. The local **tourist office,** ☎ 03-4453-0640, is located on Place du Parvis-Notre-Dame, in front of the cathedral. Ask them about horse-drawn carriage rides through town.

FOOD AND DRINK:

Senlis has a fair selection of restaurants, including:

Hostellerie de la Porte Bellon (51 Rue Bellon, near the bus station) A country inn with a charming restaurant. ☎ 03- 4453-0305. $$

Bourgois Gentilhomme (3 Place de la Halle, a block east of the Town

Hall) Inventive cuisine. ☎ 03-4453-1322. X: Sun. eve., Mon. $$

Vieille Auberge (8 Rue du Long-Filet, a block southeast of the Town Hall) Reasonably priced dining, indoors or out. ☎ 03- 4460-9550. X: Sun. eve. $$

SUGGESTED TOUR:

Numbers in parentheses correspond to numbers on the map.

Leave the **bus station** (1) and follow the map to the **Jardin du Roi** (2), a lovely park built along the remains of the original Gallo-Roman fortifications.

Retrace your steps and turn right on Rue de Villevert to Place du Parvis. This engaging little square facing the cathedral is home to the small but charming **Musée de l'Hôtel de Vermandois** (3), housed in a 17th-century mansion. Displays here range from art to local history, with an emphasis on the cathedral. *Open Wed. 2–6, Thurs.–Mon. 10–noon and 2–6. Closes at 5 in winter. Nominal charge.*

The 12th-century **Cathedral of Notre-Dame** (4) is one of the earliest Gothic structures in France. Although rather small, it is both handsome and interesting. Examine the carvings over the main portal, which relate to the life of the Virgin, then enter through the splendid south transept, added after a disastrous 16th-century fire. The interior, altered many times throughout the centuries, is noted for its exceptionally beautiful balcony running above the side aisles.

Stroll over to what remains of the **Château Royal** (5), a complex of ancient buildings that were once a principal residence for the early kings of France, particularly during the Merovingian and Carolingian eras. The last king to use the castle was Henri II, while still a 16th-century prince. Following that, the château deteriorated badly and was finally ruined during the Revolution. Enough has survived, however, to be of interest. Against the city wall, on the north side of the grounds, stands the foundations of the original keep.

Also within the castle precincts is the intriguing **Museum of the Hunt** *(Musée de la Vénerie),* located in the 18th-century Priory of St.-Maurice. Displays of this most royal of sports include costumes, artifacts, paintings and literally thousands of antlers. It may be seen only on guided tours, which begin hourly with an audiovisual show in an adjacent building. Tickets are sold at the entrance to the Château Royal, along with the tickets to the grounds alone—take your choice. ☎ *03-4453-0080. Both the castle ruins and the museum are open daily except on Tues. and on Wed. mornings, 10–noon and 2–6 p.m., closing an hour earlier during the winter season. Adults 15FF.*

From here, a delightful walk can be made following the map along colorful old streets and through the ancient **Fausse Porte** (6), a remnant of the original walls. Continue on to the 15th-century **Town Hall** *(Hôtel de Ville)* (7) on Place Henri IV. It is possible to take a side trip to the relics of a **Gallo-Roman Amphitheater** *(Arènes)* (8) unearthed in 1863, but this must

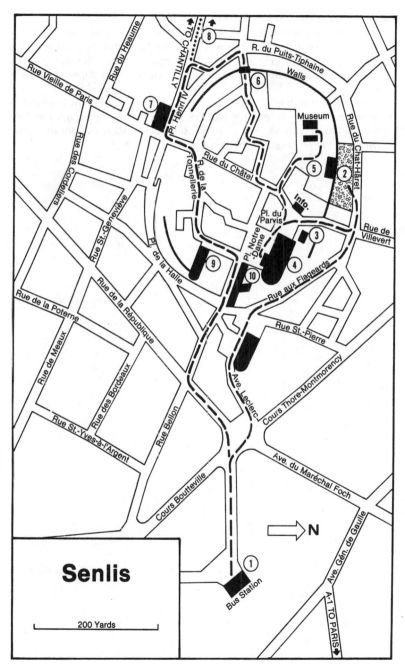

Senlis

200 Yards

be arranged in advance with the tourist office.

Return to the cathedral via Rue de la Tonnellerie and Rue St.-Frambourg. Along the way you will pass the 12th-century **Church of St.-Frambourg** (9), restored in 1977 by the Hungarian pianist Georges Cziffra as a concert hall and small museum of local archaeology. *Open weekends from 3–6:30.*

The former **Bishop's Palace** (10), next to the cathedral, now houses the **Museum of Art**, which features paintings from the 17th through the 20th centuries along with ancient archaeological finds. *Its hours are the same as those of the Museum of the Hunt, above.*

Section IV

DAYTRIPS FROM PARIS
NORMANDY AND THE NORTH

Normandy, an ancient province lying between the Île-de-France and the English Channel, is truly a land apart. Molded by its unique history, it offers an amazingly wide variety of sights ranging from some of the prettiest countryside in Europe to dynamic cities, from quaint fishing villages to luxurious seaside resorts. Although the distances are fairly great, an efficient transportation network brings many of its best attractions within comfortable daytrip range of Paris.

Throughout its often turbulent history, Normandy has been a battleground—a place conquered and re-conquered by forces outside the mainstream of the French experience. At various times it was held by the Celts, the Romans, the Germanic tribes and, most important of all, the Norsemen—Vikings from Scandinavia—who in the 9th century settled this land for good, thus accounting for the preponderance of tall, blue-eyed Normans today. It was their renowned leader, William the Conqueror, who defeated the English near Hastings in 1066—an event that forever changed the course of European history. As a result, much of our own heritage derives from Norman tradition.

During most of the Middle Ages, Normandy was at best only marginally under the control of French kings. For long periods it was ruled by the English, and its semi-autonomy ended only with the French Revolution. In the 20th century the Germans again occupied the land, being driven out by the Battle of Normandy in 1944.

*Giverny and Vernon: The Monet Gardens

B orn in 1840, the celebrated French painter Claude Monet was one of the founding fathers of Impressionism and a vital force in the modern art movement it led to. After a long period of ridicule and poverty, his talent finally received broad public recognition. Now fairly prosperous, Monet in 1883 created for himself and his family a lovely home surrounded by lush gardens near the Seine, in the tiny hamlet of Giverny. It was in this serene environment that his greatest works were achieved.

Following Monet's death in 1926, the property deteriorated badly until 1966, when it was willed to the *Institut de France* by his son Michel. Generous donations, primarily from the United States, have made possible a stunning restoration of this extraordinary place. Ever since its public opening in 1980 as the Claude Monet Foundation, the gardens—along with his remarkably charming house and cavernous studio—have become an extremely popular daytrip destination, indeed a pilgrimage, for art lovers and tourists alike.

Organized bus tours to Giverny are offered by several firms in Paris, which are certainly a convenient way to reach this secluded spot. They have the disadvantage, however, of limiting the amount of time you can spend savoring its enchanting atmosphere. They also overlook nearby Vernon, an ancient town of considerable charm, worthy of a trip in itself.

GETTING THERE:

Trains depart St.-Lazare Station in Paris several times daily for Vernon, less than an hour away. From here take a taxi (or infrequent bus) the three-mile distance to Giverny. It's also possible to walk or rent a bicycle at the Vernon station or elsewhere in Vernon. Return trains run until early evening.

By car, take the A-13 Autoroute to the Bonnières-Vernon exit, then the N-15 into Vernon, cross the Seine and follow signs to the Monet Museum. It is about 50 miles northwest of Paris.

PRACTICALITIES:

The Monet gardens and house are open from April through October, daily except Mondays. Avoid coming on a rainy day. The **Tourist**

Information Office in Vernon, ☎ 02-3251-3960, is at 36 Rue Carnot near the church. A helpful Internet site is: www.giverny.org.

FOOD AND DRINK:

Some good places for lunch in Giverny and Vernon are:

Les Jardins de Giverny (Rt. D-5, near the Monet Foundation) Creative cuisine in a traditional country restaurant. ☎ 02-3221-6080 for reservations. X: Sun. eve., Mon., Feb. $$ and $$$

Les Fleurs (71 Rue Carnot, near the Archives Tower in Vernon) A local favorite and a good value. ☎ 02-3251-1680. X: Sun. eve., Mon. $$

Les Nymphea (at the Monet Foundation) A self-service cafeteria for visitors. X: Mon. $

SUGGESTED TOUR:

Numbers in parentheses correspond to numbers on the map.

From the **Vernon Train Station** (1) you can take a taxi or bus to the *Musée Monet* in Giverny, a trip of nearly three miles. Walking is also possible by following the map, or you can rent a bicycle at the station.

*MUSÉE CLAUDE MONET (2), ☎ 02-3251-2821. *Open April–Oct., Tues.–Sun. 10–6. Admissions to house and gardens: Adults 35FF, students 25FF, children 7–12 20FF, under 7 free. Gift shop. Cafeteria.*

Visits at the Claude Monet Foundation in Giverny begin in the huge **Water Lily Studio**, built in 1916 to accommodate large canvases. The paintings on the wall are, of course, copies; the originals being in leading museums.

Stroll over to the painstakingly restored **house**, surfaced in pink crushed brick with green doors and shutters. Its exquisite interior, looking like the pages from a fashionable architectural magazine, is perhaps a bit too tidy for the home of an artist, but very beautiful nonetheless. It was here that Monet entertained his closest friends, including the French premier Georges Clemenceau and fellow artists Renoir, Degas, Rodin, and Cézanne, among others.

The **Clos Normand Garden**, facing the house, is totally French in concept. Monet Loved gardens, and as his fortunes improved he employed several gardeners to maintain them. From here, a tunnel leads under the public road to the famous **Water Garden** (3), which he created by diverting a nearby stream. This part of the property exudes a distinctly Oriental aura. Much of it seems familiar, especially the wisteria-entwined Japanese Bridge, a subject for many of his best-known paintings, around which clusters of water lilies float on the pond.

While there, you may want to visit the nearby **American Impressionist Museum** just down the road at 99 Rue Claude Monet. Works by leading American Impressionist painters who were influenced by Monet may be seen during the same time that the gardens are open. ☎ *02-3251-9465.*

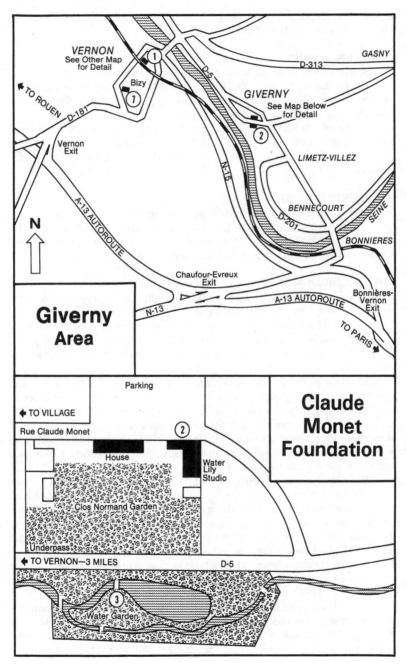

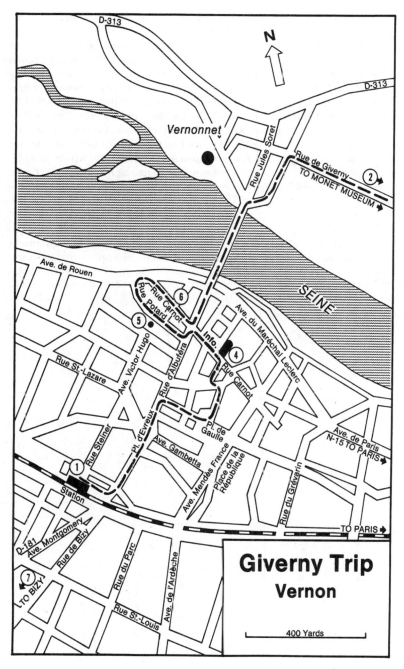

Giverny Trip

Vernon

400 Yards

Open April–Oct., Tues.–Sun., 10–6. Adults 35FF, seniors, teachers, students 20FF, ages 12–18 20FF, children 7–12 15FF.

Returning to **Vernon**, you will have a beautiful view from its bridge of the town, the Seine and the woods beyond. Visit the 12th-century **Church of Notre-Dame** (4), noted for its splendid west-front rose window and lavish interior. In the immediate vicinity stand a number of medieval half-timbered houses, lending atmosphere to this ancient settlement founded by Rollo, the first duke of Normandy, in the 9th century. Stroll along Rue Carnot and Rue Potard. The **Archives Tower** (5) is all that remains of a massive castle built in 1123 by King Henry I of England. Closeby, in another venerable building, is the **Poulain Municipal Museum** (6), which proudly displays two paintings by Monet along with items of local interest. *Open Tues.–Fri. 11–1 and 2–5:30, weekends 2–6. From Nov.–March it is open only in the afternoon.*

NEARBY SIGHT:

The **Château of Bizy** (7), an 18th-century mansion set in a charming park, may also be visited. Its interior contains many superb pieces in the Empire style along with Napoleonic souvenirs. To get there, follow the D-181 for one mile southwest of Vernon. *Open Apr.–Oct., Tues.–Sun. 10–12 and 2–6; Nov. and Feb.–March, weekends only, 2–5. Closed Dec. and Jan.*

Rouen

One of the best-preserved medieval cities in all of Europe, Rouen is also a thriving modern commercial center. This unusual combination of past and present results from a deliberate decision on the part of local government to strip away decades of "modernization" in the old part of town and restore its ancient features. At the same time, cars were banned from many of the streets, creating an unusually pleasant—and very beguiling—pedestrian shopping zone. If ever there was a city designed to be explored on foot, Rouen is it.

Over two thousand years ago, Rouen was already in existence as a Celtic encampment on the banks of the Seine. This evolved into a market town known as *Ratuma* to the Gauls and later as *Rotomagus* to the Romans. Its real history, however, begins with an invasion by the Vikings from Scandinavia, who made 't the capital of their Norman duchy in 972. The brilliant Norse leader Rollo established an able administration that did much to develop the local economy. His linear descendant, William the Bastard, known to history as the Conqueror, defeated the English near Hastings in 1066 and became king of England, bringing Norman civilization to that island country.

Centuries later it was the English who invaded Normandy. During the Hundred Years War a strange leader arose among the French, Joan of Arc, who persuaded the king to allow her to lead troops in battle. Eventually she was captured by the Burgundians and sold to the English, who brought her to Rouen in 1431 for a mockery of a trial—after which she was allegedly burned at the stake in the town's market place.

In the years that followed the re-establishment of French rule, Rouen blossomed into a beautiful and prosperous city with many fine Renaissance buildings. Although it suffered badly during the 16th-century Wars of Religion and again during World War II, it has today regained its place as one of the great cities of France.

GETTING THERE:

Trains leave St.-Lazare Station in Paris frequently for Rouen's Rive Droite Station, a trip of about 70 minutes. Return service operates until mid-evening.

By car, Rouen is 86 miles northwest of Paris via the A-13 Autoroute.

PRACTICALITIES:

Rouen may be enjoyed in any season, but avoid coming on a Tuesday or holiday if you plan on visiting any of the major museums. The local **Tourist Information Office**, ☎ 02-3208-3240, is in front of the cathedral. A useful Internet site is: www.mairie-rouen.fr. Rouen is the Normandie region, and has a population of about 105,000.

FOOD AND DRINK:

The city offers an extraordinarily wide range of excellent restaurants, many of which specialize in the rich, highly caloric Norman cuisine. Some good choices are:

Le Beffroy (15 Rue du Beffroy, 2 blocks east of the Fine Arts Museum) Norman and modern cuisine in a fashionable restaurant. For reservations ☎ 02-3571-5527. X: Sun. eve. and Tues. $$$

La Couronne (31 Place du Vieux-Marché) Norman specialties, especially duck, in a 14th-century house. Proper dress expected, for reservations ☎ 02-3571-4090. $$$

La Réverbère (5 Place de la République, 3 blocks southeast of the cathedral) A broad selection of well-prepared cuisine in a simple setting. ☎ 02-3507-0314. X: Sun., Aug. $$

Les P'tits Parapluies (46 Rue Bourg-l'Abbé, 2 blocks north of St.-Ouen) A stylish restaurant with innovative cooking. ☎ 02- 3588-5526. X: Sun., Mon., Aug. $$

La Vieille Auberge (37 Rue St.-Etienne-des-Tonneliers, 3 blocks south of the Great Clock) An exceptional value. ☎ 02- 3570-5665. X: Mon. $

Les Flandres (5 Rue des Bons-Enfants, 3 blocks southwest of the Fine Arts Museum) Simple and very popular, with good steaks. ☎ 02-3598-4516. X: Sat. eve., Sun., Aug. $

La Tarte Tatin (99 Rue de la Vicomté, 1 block southeast of Place du Vieux-Marché) An outstanding crêperie. ☎ 02-3589-3573. X: Sun. $

Gourmand'grain (3 Rue du Petit Salut, a block southwest of the cathedral) Healthy vegetarian lunches. ☎ 02-3598-1574. X: Sun., Mon. $

SUGGESTED TOUR:

Numbers in parentheses correspond to numbers on the map.

Follow the map from Rouen's **Rive Droite Train Station** (1) to Place de la Cathédrale, where the tourist office is housed in an elegant 16th-century Renaissance building. Along the way you will pass many examples of old half-timbered houses that have been put to modern use while still retaining the town's medieval atmosphere. Be sure to visit the:

*CATHEDRAL OF NOTRE-DAME (2). *Open daily 8 a.m. to 7 p.m., closing at 6 on Sun. Limited access on Sun. morning during Mass.*

Rouen's great cathedral, one of the finest Gothic structures in existence, is familiar to art lovers as the subject for a series of Impressionist paintings by Monet that captured its spirit under changing atmospheric conditions. Its **west front** displays at a glance the entire history of Gothic cathedral construction. The base of the left tower dates from the early 12th century and, along with two doors, is the only portion of the church that survived the devastating fire of 1200. On the right is the so-called **Butter Tower** *(Tour de Beurre)*, supposedly financed by the sale of indulgences allowing the faithful to eat butter during Lent. This Flamboyant structure was erected in the 15th century. The next hundred years saw the addition of the central portal and the rose window. Construction continued through the 19th century, when the delicate open-ironwork spire, the tallest in France, was completed.

A stroll through the cathedral's majestic interior is impressive. Note in particular the **Booksellers' Staircase**, in the north transept, and the **tombs** of several historical figures, including those of Rollo, the first duke of Normandy, and Richard the Lionheart, king of England. Guided tours are conducted through the fascinating 11th-century **crypt** and the ambulatory, several times daily during the summer season, and on weekends and some holidays the rest of the year.

Walk down Rue du Gros-Horloge, a pedestrians-only shopping street of well-preserved houses, many of them half-timbered. The *Gros-Horloge (Great Clock) (3), a famous symbol of Rouen, was relocated here in 1527. Its adjoining 14th-century Belfry may once again be climbed at certain times after renovations are completed in 2000. ☎ 02-3571-2840. Splendid views of the old city make the climb very worthwhile.

Stroll over to the magnificent **Palais de Justice** (4), one of the great civic structures of Europe. Originally built in the 16th century and later modified, its Gothic façade becomes increasingly Flamboyant as it rises above the ground floor. Excavations in the courtyard have unearthed an underground 12th-century synagogue or yeshiva, which can be seen by arrangement with the tourist office.

On May 30th, 1431, Joan of Arc was, according to legend, burned at the stake in Rouen's **Place du Vieux-Marché** (Market Place) (5), the next stop on the walking tour. Some historians now question whether this really happened. In any case, a huge cross now marks the spot where she supposedly met her fiery end. The strikingly contemporary **Église Sainte-Jeanne-d'Arc**, adjacent to this, was consecrated in 1979 and contains a large area of marvelous 16th-century stained-glass windows from a previous church on the site. Also in the square is a modern covered marketplace, several inviting outdoor cafés, and the tiny but fascinating **Musée Jeanne-d'Arc** (6), a somewhat kitschy waxworks crammed with re-created scenes from the life of the Maid of Orléans. ☎ 02-3588-0270. *Open May to mid-Sept., daily 9:30–6:30; rest of year Tues.–Sun., 10–noon and 2–6:30. Adults 24FF, students and children 12FF.*

Another nearby sight that might be of interest is the **Maison Natale de Corneille** (7) at Number 4 Rue de la Pie, where the famous French playwright Pierre Corneille was born in 1606 and where he lived most of his

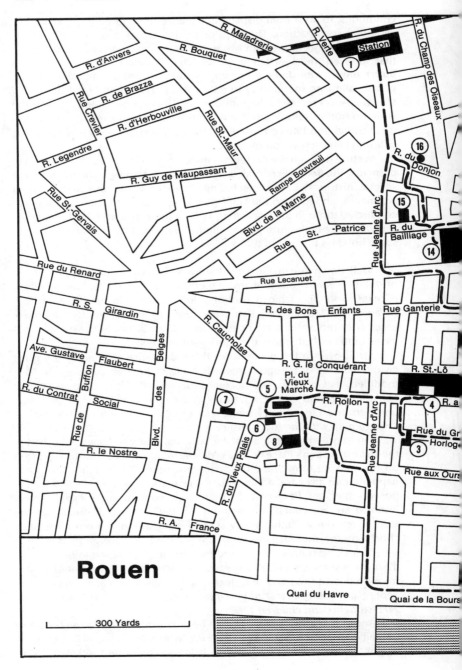

Rouen

300 Yards

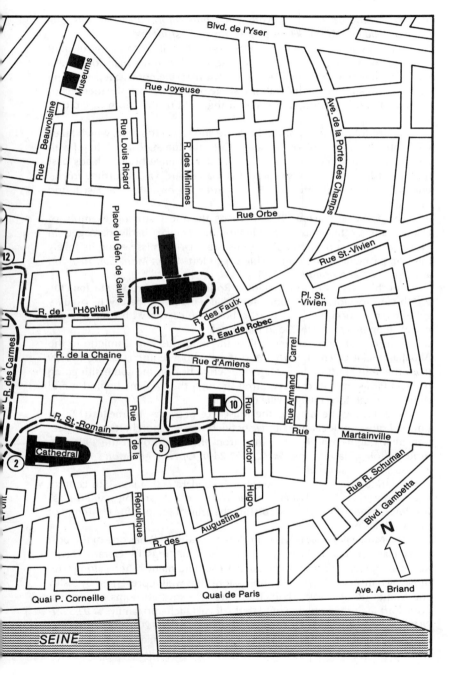

life. ☎ 02-3571-6392. *Open Wed. 2–6, Thurs.–Mon. 10–noon and 2–6. Closed holidays. Adults 5FF, free for seniors and students.*

It is only a few steps to the Place de la Pucelle, site of the elegant **Hôtel de Bourgtheroulde** (8). This sumptuous 16th-century mansion, now a bank, combines Gothic with early Renaissance elements. Step into the courtyard to admire the decorations, some of which depict the meeting of François I and England's Henry VIII at the Field of the Cloth of Gold in 1520.

Return to the cathedral via the route shown on the map, which takes you along the right bank of the Seine. Colorful Rue St.-Romain, lined with picturesque half-timbered medieval and Renaissance houses, leads past the **Archbishop's Palace.** It was here that Joan of Arc was, according to legend, sentenced to death and, 25 years after the execution, at last found innocent.

The **Église St-Maclou** (9) is perhaps the most striking example of Flamboyant Gothic church architecture in France. Badly damaged in World War II, it is now completely restored. Don't miss seeing its lovely interior, particularly the remarkable organ loft. *Open Mon.–Sat. 10–noon and 2–6, Sun. and holidays 3–5:30.*

Another absolute "must" sight in Rouen is the ***Aître St.-Maclou** (10), a 16th-century cloister that once served as a plague cemetery. Its ossuary galleries, now occupied by an art school, are carved with exceptionally macabre figures of death. Go in for a peek.

Return to the church and follow the gorgeous Rue Damiette to the **Abbatiale Saint-Ouen** (11). This enormous abbey church, dating mostly from the 14th century, replaces earlier churches on the same site going back as far as the 7th century. Stroll through the gardens behind it and return through the **Hôtel de Ville** (City Hall).

Now follow the map to the **Musée Le Secq des Tournelles** (12), an unusual museum located in a desanctified former church. Its vast collection of wrought-iron objects dating from the 3rd through the 19th centuries is totally fascinating. ☎ 02-3571-2840. *Open Wed.–Mon., 10–1 and 2–6. Adults 13FF students 9FF.*

Continue on to the nearby **Église St.-Godard** (13), a late-15th-century church noted for its unusual wooden roof and outstanding stained-glass windows, especially the one depicting the Tree of Jesse at the choir end of the south aisle.

The **Musée des Beaux-Arts** (Fine Arts Museum) (14) has one of the best provincial collections in France. There are paintings by Gérard David, Rubens, Ingres, Delacroix, Velázquez, Corot and many others, along with those by native-son Géricault. Impressionism is well represented by Sisley and Monet (Rouen Cathedral). There are also several rooms of contemporary art including one devoted to the local Duchamp family. ☎ 02-3571-2840. *Open Wed.–Mon., 10–6. Closed holidays. Adults 20FF, students 13FF.*

Now amble over to the splendid **Musée de Céramique** (15), an exhibition of lovely ceramics located in a former mansion just one block away.

The specialty here is 16th- to 19th-century faïence produced locally. ☎ 02-3507-3174. *Open Wed.–Mon., 10–1 and 2–6. Closed holidays. Adults 13FF, students 9FF.*

Before leaving Rouen, it would be fitting to visit the **Tour Jeanne-d'Arc** (16) on Rue du Donjon near the train station. This former keep is all that remains of a 13th-century castle, and is the place where the Maid of Orléans was supposedly confronted with the instruments of torture. You can climb to its top for a nice view. ☎ 02-3598-1621. *Open Wed.–Mon., 10–noon and 2–5. Adults 10FF, students free.*

Caen

J ust enough of old Caen survived the terrible devastation of World War II to make it an attractive daytrip destination. The three monumental structures associated with William the Conqueror remained miraculously intact while the rest of the city has been largely rebuilt in the contemporary mold, with broad boulevards, pedestrian malls, and open green spaces.

Caen had virtually no history before Duke William of Normandy, also known as "the Bastard" and "the Conqueror," made it his capital and favorite residence in the 11th century. During the years that followed it developed into both a seaport and a university town, sometimes under English rule. World War II brought ferocious destruction—over three-quarters of the city lay in total ruin after a lengthy battle beginning in June of 1944. Many of its citizens found shelter in the important historical structures, which were spared by the Allies after receiving this information from the Resistance. What has emerged since then is an unusually pleasant, if not very dramatic, city where modern architecture has blended in well with what remains of the past.

GETTING THERE:

Trains depart St.-Lazare Station in Paris almost hourly for the two-hour run to Caen. Return service operates until mid-evening.

By car, it's the A-13 Autoroute all the way. Caen is 150 miles west of Paris.

PRACTICALITIES:

Good weather is important for this largely outdoor trip. The two museums are closed on Tuesdays and major holidays. The local **tourist office**, phone ☎ 02-3127-1414, is located on Place St.-Pierre, near the castle.

FOOD AND DRINK:

Some choice restaurants are:

La Bourride (15 Rue Vagueux, a block east of the château entrance) Imaginative variations on classic Norman cuisine. Proper dress expected, reservations essential, ☎ 02-3193-5076. X: Sun. Eve, Mon., late Aug. $$$

Le Dauphin (29 Rue Gemare, 2 blocks southwest of the château)

Traditional Norman cuisine with a light touch. ☎ 02- 3186-2226. X: Sat. Lunch. $$ and $$$

Poêle d'Or (7 Rue Laplace, 3 blocks southeast of St.-Jean Church) An exceptional value. ☎ 02-3185-3986. X: Sat., Sun. eve. $

Alcide (1 Place Courtonne, at the north end of the Old Port) Good dining at modest prices. ☎ 02-3144-1806. X: Sat. $

La Petite Auberge (17 Rue des Equipes-d'Urgence, a block north of the Church of St. Jean) Norman cuisine on a budget. ☎ 02-3186-4330. X: Sun. eve., Mon. $

Tongasoa (7 Rue du Vaugueux, a block east of the château entrance) North African dishes. ☎ 02-3143-8715. X: Sun. lunch. $

In addition, there are a number of restaurants and cafés of all descriptions in the shopping zone between Place St.-Pierre and Place de la République, as well as in the old Vaugueux quarter east of the château.

SUGGESTED TOUR:

Numbers in parentheses correspond to numbers on the map.

The **train station** (1) is nearly a mile from Place St.-Pierre, the center of town. You could take a bus or taxi there, although the walk is both level and very pleasant. Along the way you will pass the remarkable **Church of St.-Jean** (2), a 15th-century Flamboyant Gothic structure whose unfinished west tower tilts ever so slightly.

Continue on to Place St.-Pierre. The tourist office occupies a splendid 16th-century mansion, the **Hôtel d'Escoville**, whose richly decorated courtyard should be seen. This feeling of luxury, a reflection of Caen's prosperous past, is mirrored in the **Church of St.-Pierre** (3). Its ornate, almost lush interior is among the most outstanding in Normandy.

The enormous **Castle** (4) begun by William the Conqueror still dominates the city. Stroll up to the massive ramparts, built between the 12th and 15th centuries, cross the moat and climb up on the fortifications for a stunning view of Caen. Little remains of the original structures within the walls, most of them having been replaced with later buildings. The most recent addition to the castle is the:

*FINE ARTS MUSEUM *(Musée des Beaux-Arts)* (5), ☎ 02-3185-2863. *Open Wed.–Mon., 10–6. Adults 25FF, students 15FF. Free to all on Wed. Cafeteria.*

This splendid museum's discreet contemporary architecture harmonizes with its ancient surroundings, while its superb collections are exceptionally well lit and displayed. They were begun in the early 19th century when both the Revolution and the Napoleonic conquests made large quantities of great art, formerly belonging to the Church and aristocracy as well as to foreign countries, available to public institutions. Artists represented include Van der Weyden, Breughel, Tintoretto, Poussin, Rubens, Van Dyck, Tiepolo and Géricault, among many others.

Amble over past the 12th-century **St.-Georges Church** to the **Normandy**

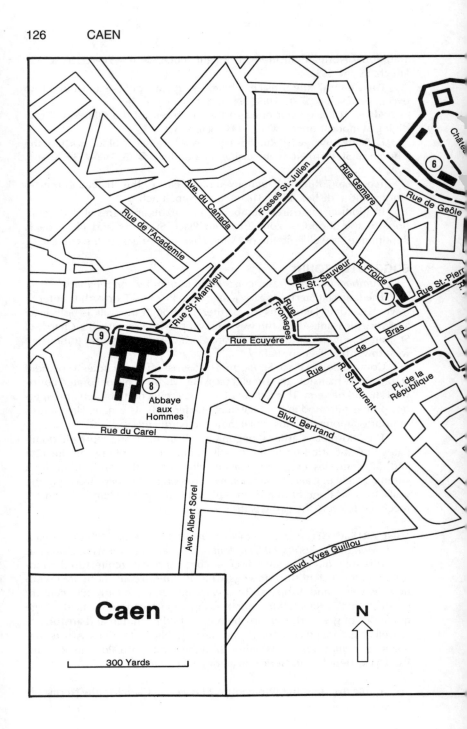

Caen

300 Yards

N

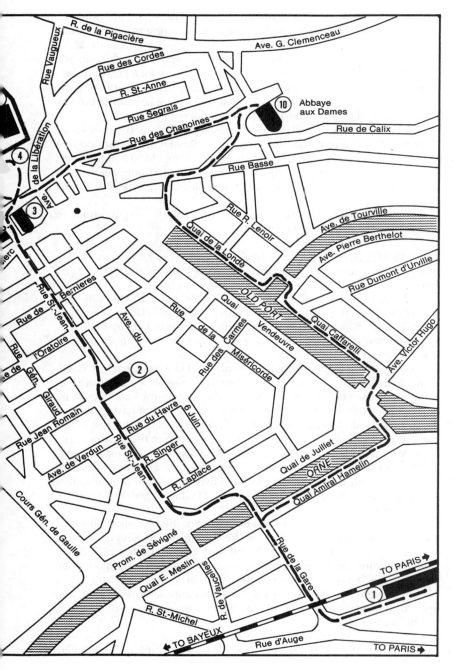

Museum (6), also within the castle precincts. Displays here are primarily concerned with local everyday life, particularly during the last century, and with regional arts and crafts along with the archaeological finds. ☎ 02-3186-0624. *Open Wed.–Mon., 9:30–12:30 and 2–6. Adults 10FF, students 5FF.*

Wander around to the rear of the castle enclosure for a look at the so-called Exchequer House—a rare example of early 12th-century domestic architecture—and at the ruins of an equally old square keep, both built by Henry I, king of England and son of the Conqueror.

Now follow the map to the interesting Gothic and Renaissance **Church of St.-Sauveur** (7) and the picturesque Rue Froide. Return on Rue St.-Pierre, passing the **Musée de la Poste** in one of the oldest half-timbered houses left on that street, and turn down Rue Hamon, continuing through a modern pedestrian shopping district with pleasant cafés to Place de la République.

From here the map leads the way through a colorful neighborhood to Caen's premier attraction, the famous:

*ABBAYE AUX HOMMES (Men's Abbey) (8), ☎ *02-3130-4281. Tours daily at 9:30, 11, 2:30, and 4; 10FF. Church open daily 8:15–noon and 2–7:30. Entry free.*

The abbey's conventual buildings now incorporate the City Hall *(Hôtel de Ville)*, the esplanade in front of which provides a marvelous sight for sore eyes. Interesting guided tours of the old abbey buildings, reconstructed in the 18th century, depart four times a day from the City Hall entrance.

Walk around to the rear of the complex and visit the **Church of St.-Étienne** (9), the original church of the abbey. This magnificent structure was founded in the 11th century by William the Conqueror—an illegitimate son of Duke Robert the Devil—as penance for the sin of having married his distant cousin Matilda. Not that the lady was willing—she had in fact made it perfectly clear that she would rather be a nun than marry a bastard. William, feeling his oats, dragged her by the hair and beat her into submission. Both were excommunicated as a result, and later reinstated by the Pope only after promising to build two abbeys and four hospitals. The union actually turned out well, with Matilda becoming queen of England in 1068.

Step inside to visit William's **tomb**, in front of the high altar. His burial was as tempestuous as his life. When he died in 1087 at Rouen, his heirs made a mad scramble for the spoils and neglected his body, which rotted for days before being ignominiously put in the grave after payment of an extortion fee. It did not lie there in peace, either. During the 16th century his bones were scattered by rebellious Protestants, later recovered, and again dispersed during the Revolution. Some parts of it may still be there, but no one is sure.

Return to the castle area via Rue St.-Mauvieu and Fossés St.-Julien, then follow the map to the **Abbaye aux Dames** (10), the other abbey founded as a result of the illicit marriage. Its **Church of La Trinité** is more richly ornamented than its male counterpart and has an interesting 11th-century **crypt**, which can be reached from the south transept. Matilda was buried here, in the choir, and like that of her husband William, her tomb was desecrated during the Wars of Religion and again in the Revolution. The church is closed between noon and 2 p.m. Its conventual buildings have been restored and may be visited at set times.

The suggested route back to the train station, shown on the map, takes you past the **Old Port** *(Bassin St.-Pierre)*, connected to the sea via the Orne River and a canal. It is now used for pleasure craft, with larger ships docking at the new harbor to the east.

ADDITIONAL SIGHT:

Located in the northwest corner of the city, the thoughtful ***Mémorial—A Museum for Peace** was opened in 1988. Using the most advanced techniques to document the quest for peace in this century, the museum leads visitors through an historic journey from 1918 to the present, in a variety of languages, with audiovisual shows, weapons displays, and related material. A gallery of Nobel Prize winners is located in a former Nazi command post, under the main building. There is a Garden of Remembrance, a gift shop, and a cafeteria. You can get there by bus 17 from near the tourist office, or follow signs for about 1.5 miles northwest of the castle. ☎ *02-3106-0644, Internet: www.unicaen.fr/collectivite/ memorial. Open daily, 9 a.m. to 7 p.m., closing at 8 p.m. in summer and 6 p.m. in winter. Adults 72FF, students 63FF, WWII veterans free.*

Bayeux

One of the greatest chronicles of the Middle Ages—the famous "Bayeux Tapestry"—is an incredibly lucid history lesson embroidered in cloth. You have surely seen reproductions of it, but to experience the real thing you will have to come to Bayeux, a thoroughly delightful town that is well worth the trip.

Known as the cradle of the Norman dynasty, the town has roots going back much further than the Viking invasions. In Gallo-Roman times it was called *Augustodurum,* and became a bishopric as early as the 4th century. Rollo the Dane, a progenitor of William the Conqueror, married the daughter of the town's ruler early in the 10th century, thus creating the line that gave England some of its most notorious kings. The Norse language continued to be spoken here long after the rest of Normandy adopted French culture, an early sign of Bayeux's stubborn resistance to change. Centuries later, in June of 1944, it was the first town to be liberated by the Allies during the Battle of Normandy, and miraculously suffered no damage.

Bayeux today remains a remarkably well-preserved medieval town whose narrow streets and ancient buildings continue to enchant thousands of visitors. Although well geared to the modern tourist trade, it seems to be amazingly unaffected by it.

GETTING THERE:

Trains (marked for Cherbourg) leave St.-Lazare Station in Paris several times in the morning for Bayeux, a run of about 2.5 hours. Return service operates until early evening. Check the schedules carefully.

By car, take the A-13 Autoroute to Caen, then the N-13 into Bayeux, 167 miles west of Paris.

PRACTICALITIES:

Bayeux's major attractions are open daily. Good weather will make the trip more enjoyable. The local **tourist office,** ☎ 02-3151-2828, Internet: www.bayeux-tourism.com, is located in the former Covered Fish Market, 2 blocks north of William the Conqueror Center.

FOOD AND DRINK:

As an important tourist center, Bayeux has restaurants and cafés in all price ranges. Some of the better choices are:

Lion d'Or (71 Rue St.-Jean, a block east of the watermill) A famous old inn serving superb Norman dishes since 1770. ☎ 02- 3192-0690. X: Late Dec. to mid-Jan. $$

Les 4 Saisons (in the Hotel Luxembourg, 25 Rue des Bouchers, 4 blocks northwest of the tourist office) A small hotel with good food. ☎ 02-3192-0004. $$

La Marmite (in the Hotel Brunville, 9 Rue Genas-Duhomme, 4 blocks northwest of the tourist office) Dining in a small hotel. ☎ 02-3121-1800. $

La Petit Normand (35 Rue Larcher, 1 block north of the tourist office) A good value in traditional Norman cuisine. ☎ 02-31-22-88-66. X: Sun. eve., Wed. eve. $

L'Amaryllis (32 Rue St.-Patrice, 5 blocks northwest of the cathedral) A bit out of the way, but an excellent value. ☎ 02- 3122-4794. X: Sun. eve., Mon. $

SUGGESTED TOUR:

Numbers in parentheses correspond to numbers on the map. Leave the **train station** (1) and follow the map to the:

***WILLIAM THE CONQUEROR CENTER** (Centre Guillaume le Conquérant)* (2), ☎ 02-3151-2550. *Open May to mid-Sept., daily 9–6; rest of year, daily 9:30–12:30 and 2–6. Closed Christmas and New Year's Day. Joint ticket with Baron Gérard Museum and Hôtel du Doyen, below: Adults 38FF, students 15FF, under 10 free. Rental of earphone device 5FF. Gift shop.*

Located in a courtyard just off Rue de Nesmond, this where the world-famous *Bayeux Tapestry, one of the greatest legacies of the Middle Ages, is displayed. Also known as *La Tapisserie de la Reine Mathilde*, it has long been the subject of two popular misconceptions. First, this is not a tapestry at all, but actually an embroidery on linen. Second, it was almost certainly not made by Queen Matilda herself since the style strongly suggests Saxon craftsmanship, and was probably commissioned by William's half-brother, Bishop Odon of Bayeux, as a decoration for his cathedral. That it survived at all is a miracle. In 1792, when Revolutionary zealots were stripping the churches bare, an observant army officer rescued it from the ignominious fate of being used as a wagon tarpaulin. Seeing its propaganda value, Napoleon had it widely exhibited to drum up support for his planned invasion of England.

The 231-foot-long 11th-century embroidery resembles nothing so much as a gigantic comic strip, and would not look out of place in our Sunday newspapers. Its 58 scenes graphically depict the events leading up to the Norman Conquest of 1066, as well as the Battle of Hastings itself— one of the major turning points in the annals of Western civilization. Of course, the story is seen through Norman eyes; victors do have a way of controlling history.

Be sure to rent one of the earphone devices, which give an engrossing blow-by-blow account in English of the entire complex saga. Without this it is very difficult to understand. You can move along at your own

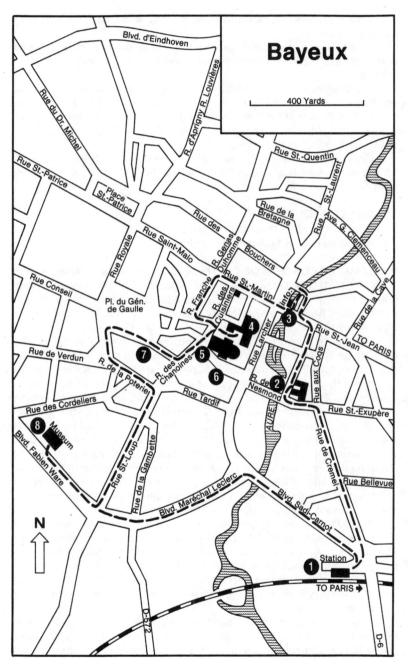

Bayeux

400 Yards

Blvd. d'Eindhoven
Rue du Dr. Michel
R. d'Aprigny
R. Louvières
Rue St.-Quentin
Rue St.-Patrice
Place St.-Patrice
Rue des
Rue de la Bretagne
St.-Laurent
Ave. G. Clemenceau
Rue Royale
Rue Saint-Malo
R. Genas
Bouchers
R. Duhomme
Rue St.-Martin
Rue Conseil
R. Franche
R. des Cuisiniers
Into
Rue de la Cave
Pl. du Gén. de Gaulle
Rue Larcher
Rue St.-Jean
TO PARIS
Rue de Verdun
R. de la Poterie
R. des Chanoines
Rue aux Coqs
R. de Nesmond
Rue des Cordeliers
Rue Tardif
AURE
Rue St.-Exupère
Museum
Blvd. Fabien Ware
Rue St.-Loup
Rue de la Gambette
Blvd. Maréchal Leclerc
Blvd. Sadi-Carnot
Rue de Cremel
Rue Bellevue

N

Station

TO PARIS ➡

D-512

D-6

pace, taking plenty of time to absorb it all.

Continue on through the grounds of an ancient hospital and follow the map to the Aure stream. Walk along the water's edge past a charming **old mill** for a truly gorgeous view with the cathedral's towers rising in the background. The former **Covered Fish Market** (3), now serving as a cultural center and home to the local Tourist information Office, is at the corner of Rue St.-Jean. Turn right on Rue St.-Martin and left on Rue des Cuisiniers.

The walking route now takes you through a picturesque neighborhood to the **Baron Gérard Museum** (4), in the former Bishop's Palace, which displays a fascinating collection of local ceramics and lace along with faïence from Rouen, furniture and paintings. The latter includes several Italian Primitives, Flemish and French works. ☎ *02-3192-1421. Open June to mid-Sept., daily 9–7, rest of year, daily 10–12:30 and 2–6. Joint ticket with Bayeux Tapestry, above.*

Next to this stands the very impressive **Cathedral of Notre-Dame** (5). Parts of it date from the 11th century, when the cathedral was consecrated by Bishop Odon in the presence of the Conqueror. Most of the original church was destroyed in 1105 by William's son, Henry I *(Beauclerc)* of England, and rebuilt in later centuries. The carvings above the west front doors depict the Passion and the Last Judgement, while those in the south transept tell the story of Thomas à Becket's murder in Canterbury Cathedral. Step inside for a look at the magnificent interior and to visit the 11th-century crypt.

Just south of the cathedral is the **Hôtel du Doyen** (6), the former bishops' palace, which now houses both the **Diocesan Museum of Religious Art** and the **Lace Conservatory** *(Conservatoire de la Dentelle)*. The latter is especially interesting as it allows you to watch some of France's best lace makers at work preserving an ancient craft for future generations to enjoy. ☎ *02-3151-6050. Open July–Sept., 9–7; rest of year, daily 10–12:30 and 2–6. Joint admission with Bayeux Tapestry, above.*

Now follow the route on the map to the **Memorial Museum General de Gaulle** (7), a celebration of the five visits the great wartime leader and later president of France made to Bayeux. ☎ *02-3192-4555. Open mid-March to mid-Nov., daily 9:30–12:30 and 2–6:30. Adults 10FF.* Just beyond this is Place du Général de Gaulle, a charming square where the general made his first speech on liberated soil in June of 1944.

Continue on to the **Memorial Museum of the Battle of Normandy** (8). This modern structure, surrounded by armor from the participating nations, commemorates the D-Day landings with intriguing displays of the soldiers' lives throughout the conflict. Little touches like cigarette packages and newspaper clippings make the human drama an unforgettable experience. Don't miss seeing this. ☎ *02-3192-9341. Open May to mid-Sept., daily 9:30–6:30; rest of year, daily 10–12:30 and 2–6. Adults 31FF, students 15FF, under 10 free. The British Military Cemetery is nearby.*

Trip 17

Deauville and Trouville

A ristocratic Deauville is Normandy's most elegant seaside resort, while its more down-to-earth neighbor Trouville possesses a charm distinctly its own. A daytrip here in the high season offers a chance to watch the Beautiful People at play. Things quiet down during the rest of the year, but enough activity remains to make the trip interesting.

Trouville is an old resort along the Normandy coast, with a popularity dating from the 1830s, when sea bathing first came into vogue. The court of Napoleon III flocked here, as did a number of famous writers and artists—especially the Impressionists. Its Belle Époque atmosphere lingers on amid the unspoiled ambiance of the simple fishing port it once was.

Just across the narrow Touques River, Deauville was developed by speculators in the mid-19th century as an elitist watering place for the smart set, who were presumably tired of plebeian Trouville. Sometimes called the "Twenty-first arrondissement of Paris," its aura of chic sophistication has remained pretty much intact to this day.

This trip can easily be combined in the same day with one to the utterly delightful fishing village of Honfleur, described in the next chapter.

GETTING THERE:

Trains for Trouville-Deauville depart St.-Lazare Station in Paris several times in the morning. Check at the information office as a change at Lisieux may be necessary and schedule variations are common. Travel time averages about two hours. Return service runs until early evening.

By car, Deauville is 129 miles northwest of Paris via the A-13 Autoroute.

PRACTICALITIES:

Deauville's high season lasts from June until September, with less activity during the months before and after this. Crowds are at their maximum on weekends. Trouville can be enjoyed any time during the warm season, provided the weather is good. Its art museum is closed on Tuesdays, on weekdays between Easter and mid-June, and completely between October and March.

The **tourist office in Deauville**, ☎ 02-3114-4000, is located on Place Mairie, two blocks from the Casino. Its counterpart in **Trouville** is at 32

Boulevard Fernand-Moureaux, near the bridge, ☎ 02-3114-6071. An Internet site to try is: www.normandy-tourism.org.

FOOD AND DRINK:

Most restaurants in Deauville and Trouville specialize in seafood, and many have outdoor café tables. Some excellent choices are:

Ciro's (Promenade des Planches in Deauville, right on the beach) The place to see and be seen. ☎ 02-3114-3131 for reservations. $$$

Le Spinnaker (52 Rue Mirabeau, Deauville, 3 blocks west of the station) Exceptional seasonal cuisine, with a light touch. ☎ 02-3188-2440 for reservations. X: Mon. except in Aug. $$$

La Petite Auberge (7 Rue Carnot, Trouville, 2 blocks northeast of the casino) A good value, so reserve by ☎ 02- 3188-1107. X: Tues., Wed. $$

Carmen (24 Rue Carnot, Trouville, 2 blocks northeast of the casino) Dining in a small hotel. ☎ 02-3188-3543. X: Mon. eve., Tues., except summer. $ and $$

Crêperie des Bains (8 Rue des Bains, Trouville, 3 blocks southeast of the casino) Full meals, salads, and crêpes, indoors or out. ☎ 02-3188-7615. X: Tues. and Wed. off season. $

SUGGESTED TOUR:

Numbers in parentheses correspond to numbers on the map.

Leave the **Trouville-Deauville Train Station** (1), which is shared by both towns, and follow the map past the Floating Basin and the Deauville tourist office to the **Casino de Deauville** (2). Games of chance offered here include roulette, blackjack, la boule, 325 slot machines, and horse track betting; all in a setting that recalls the splendor of the last century.

Wander around the opulent shops that fill the neighborhood, then stroll down Rue Gontaut-Biron to the Promenade des Planches, a wooden boardwalk where the famous and the infamous come to see and be seen. Follow this to the marina development of **Port Deauville** (3). A walk out on the breakwater will reward you with some marvelous views.

Return to the Planches and follow the elegant Boulevard Eugène-Cornuché to the yacht basin, where a tiny **pedestrian ferry** *(Bac Piétons)* (4) crosses the harbor to Trouville. At times of low tide a small footbridge is swung across the river in its place.

Trouville's **Casino Louisiane Follies** (5), built in 1912 in the grand Belle Époque manner, still reflects the days when such notables as Marcel Proust frequented the town—before high society drifted across the river to posher Deauville. Now billing itself as Europe's first thematic casino, it offers roulette, blackjack, stud poker, craps, boule, billiards, and 200 slot machines.

Once again, there is a Promenade des Planches. Stroll along this or on the beach, passing the **Trouville Aquarium and Reptile House**, then follow the map to the **Municipal Museum** (6) in Villa Montebello on Rue

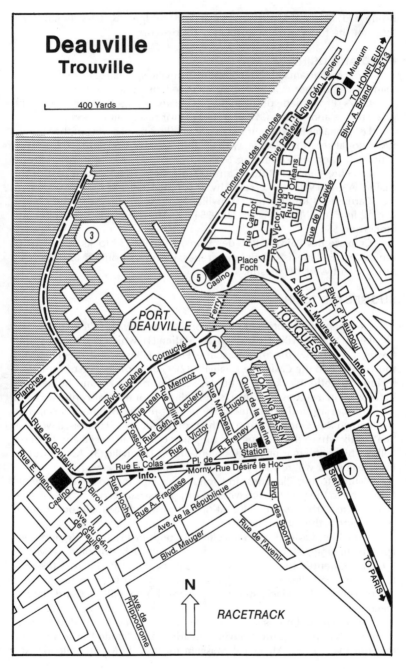

Deauville
Trouville

400 Yards

Général-Leclerc. Paintings by the early Impressionist Eugène Boudin and others, exhibited here, have captured the spirit of Trouville during its halcyon years. ☎ *02-3181-1626. Open in summer, Wed.–Mon., 2:15–6:15, and on weekends only from Easter to mid-June.*

Return via rues Pasteur, de la Chapelle and Victor-Hugo to the Old Town. Unlike Deauville, Trouville exists in its own right as a fishing village and remains active all year round. Much of the charming bustle can be enjoyed along its riverside quay, the Boulevard Fernand-Moureaux. From here, the **Pont des Belges** (7) leads across the river to the train station.

Honfleur

I f a contest were held to determine the loveliest fishing port in France, Honfleur would certainly be among the top contenders. Its old harbor is so astonishingly picturesque that it defies description. The wonder of it all is that this is not just a tourist attraction but a hard-working port that somehow escaped the march of time. Perhaps this is because Le Havre, just across the bay, has long ago captured the heavy shipping industry, and also simply because Honfleur has no beach to speak of.

Located at the mouth of the Seine estuary, Honfleur was an important port ever since the 14th century, falling into English hands on several occasions. It was from here that Samuel Champlain set sail for the New World in the early 17th century, a voyage that resulted in the founding of Québec as a French colony. Later, during the 19th century, it became popular with artists, particularly with the followers of locally-born Eugène Boudin, including Jongkind and Monet. The attraction still holds, as can be seen by the number of easels lined up along the old port on a nice day.

This trip can be combined in the same day with one to Deauville and Trouville, described in the previous chapter.

GETTING THERE:

Trains depart St.-Lazare Station in Paris several times in the morning for Trouville-Deauville. From there, transfer to a local bus for the nine-mile ride to Honfleur. You could also take a taxi. Return trains operate until early evening.

There are also buses to and from Lisieux or Évreux, both of which have train service to Paris. Check the schedules carefully.

By car, take the A-13 Autoroute to the Beuzeville exit, then the D-22 and D-580 into Honfleur—which is 120 miles northwest of Paris.

PRACTICALITIES:

Honfleur may be visited at any time in good weather, but note that the art museum is closed on Tuesdays and major holidays, and that some attractions are either closed or have limited hours during the off season. The local **tourist office**, ☎ 02-3189-2330, is at 9 Rue de la Ville, 2 blocks southeast of La Lieutenance.

FOOD AND DRINK:

L'Assiette Gourmande (2 Quai des Passagers, at the north end of the Avant Port) Honfleur's best restaurant, with creative cuisine. ☎ 02-3189-2488. X: Mon. except in July-Aug. $$ and $$$

L'Absinthe (10 Quai de la Quarantaine, by the Avant Port) Noted for its seafood. Dress properly and reserve, ☎ 02- 3189-3900. X: mid-Nov. to mid-Dec. $$

L'Ancrage (12 Rue Montpensier, just south of the Old Port) Superb Norman cuisine. Reserve. ☎ 02-3189-0070. X: Tues. eve. except July–Aug., Wed. $$

Hostellerie Lechat (3 Place Ste.-Catherine, near the church) Seafood specialties in a small inn. ☎ 02-3114-4949. X: Wed. & Thurs. off-season. $$

Au P'tit Mareyeur (4 Rue Haute, 2 blocks north of Ste.-Catherine Church) A good value. ☎ 02-3198-8423. X: Mon. eve., Tues. $$

SUGGESTED TOUR:

Numbers in parentheses correspond to numbers on the map.

The **bus stop** (1) is on Place de la Porte-de-Rouen. Stroll over to the exceedingly picturesque ***Old Port** (Vieux Bassin)* (2), whose quays are lined with quaint houses of wood and slate. The present tidal basin was begun in the 17th century to accommodate the growing maritime development of Honfleur; other harbors being added in the 19th century.

Just a few steps away, the former Church of St.-Étienne, dating from the 14th and 15th centuries, now houses the **Maritime Museum** *(Musée de la Marine)* (3). Displays here are concerned with the town's illustrious maritime past, going back as far as Gallo-Roman times. ☎ *02-3189-1412. Open Apr.–Sept., Tues.–Sun. 10–noon and 2–6; Oct., Dec. and mid-Feb.–March, Mon.–Fri. 2–6 and weekends 10–noon and 2–6. Adults 15FF, students 10FF.*

Next to this, on Rue de la Prison, the small **Museum of Ethnography and Folk Art** (4) features reproductions of local room interiors. Open same time as Maritime Museum, above. Same ticket applies.

Continue around the tiny street, little changed since the 16th century. All about you are the ancient slate-roofed houses that recall life in a small Norman town many centuries ago. Back at the quay, make a right to Place de l'Hôtel-de-Ville, a spot favored by amateur painters trying to recapture scenes made famous by the Impressionists of the 19th century.

Beyond the tidal locks lies **La Lieutenance** (5), a jumble of 16th-century buildings that was once home to the governor of Honfleur. Part of the 13th-century town walls, the Porte de Caen, is incorporated in the side overlooking the square. On your right is the Avant Port, anchorage of the town's fishing fleet.

Follow the map to the **Church of Ste.-Catherine** (6), a very strange sight in this part of Europe. It may well remind you more of Norway than Normandy. Built completely of wood by 15th-century shipwrights immediately after the Hundred Years War, this double-naved masterpiece has withstood five centuries of continued threat from fire and decay. Its inte-

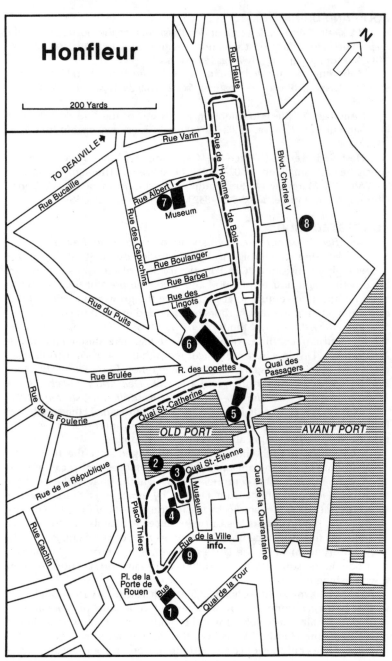

Honfleur

200 Yards

N

TO DEAUVILLE

Rue Bucaille

Rue des Capuchins

Rue du Puits

Rue de la Foulerie

Rue Brulée

Rue de la République

Rue Cachin

Place Thiers

Pl. de la Porte de Rouen

Bus

Rue Varin

Rue Albert I

Museum

Rue Boulanger

Rue Barbel

Rue des Lingots

R. des Logettes

Quai St-Catherine

OLD PORT

Quai St-Étienne

Museum

Rue de la Ville
info.

Quai de la Tour

Rue Haute

Rue de l'Homme de Bois

Blvd. Charles V

Quai des Passagers

AVANT PORT

Quai de la Quarantaine

rior is astonishing. Just opposite the church is its detached **Bell Tower**, also built of wood around the same time. A visit inside will only take a few moments and is quite interesting. ☎ *02-3189-5400. Open mid-March to Sept., Wed.–Mon., 10–noon and 2–6; rest of year, Mon. and Wed.–Fri., 2:30–5 and weekends 10–noon and 3:30–5. Joint admission with Boudin Museum, below: Adults 30FF, students 25FF.*

Continue on to the ***Eugène Boudin Museum** (7). A native of Honfleur, Boudin provided the original inspiration for the Impressionist painters, especially for his friends Jongkind and Monet. Outstanding works by these and other artists, as well as 20th-century painters such as Villon and Dufy, are very well displayed in a contemporary setting. *Open same times as the Bell Tower, above. Same ticket applies.*

Now follow the map to the charming Rue Haute, along which at number 90 is the birthplace in 1866 of the composer Erik Satie. His life is celebrated at the nearby **Maison de Satie** (8), a fanciful multi-sensory experience complete with strange images and appropriate music. *67 Blvd. Charles V,* ☎ *02-3189-1111. Open July–Aug., Wed.–Mon., 10–7; rest of year Wed.–Mon., 10:30–6. Adults 30FF, seniors and students 20FF.*

Return to the Old Port and stroll around it to Place Thiers. The **Rue de la Ville** (9) has two interesting 17th-century salt houses. From here it is only a few steps to the bus stop.

Amiens

Relatively few tourists venture into the often-bleak industrial north of France. This region does, however, have some outstanding attractions that make interesting daytrip destinations for experienced travelers in search of the unusual. By far the best of these is Amiens, an ancient riverside city that boasts the largest—and the most perfect—cathedral in all of France. The easy journey there provides an opportunity to experience yet another facet of this complex nation, and to see some sights unique to this town alone.

Throughout much of its long and turbulent history, Amiens was a battlefield lying in the path of invading armies. Once the capital of the Celtic Ambiani tribe, it was subjugated by Julius Caesar in the 1st century BC and again by the 9th-century Normans. During the Franco-Prussian War of 1870 Amiens was occupied by German forces, who returned in World War I and left it largely destroyed. The Second World War brought enormous losses as sixty percent of the city was reduced to rubble. Somehow, through all of this, the magnificent cathedral—along with a few other architectural gems—managed to survive unscathed. Postwar reconstruction has added a few interesting structures, while current restorations in the medieval quarter and city center are making the town attractive once again.

GETTING THERE:

Trains bound for Amiens leave Nord Station in Paris several times in the morning, the trip taking a little over one hour. Return service operates until mid-evening.

By car, Amiens is 92 miles north of Paris via the A-1 Autoroute and the D-934 and N-29 roads. There is a somewhat shorter route taking the A-16 Autoroute.

PRACTICALITIES:

Amiens may be visited at any time, noting that the Picardy museum is closed on Mondays. The local **tourist office**, ☎ 03-2271-6050, is located at 6 bis Rue Dusevel, a block southwest of the cathedral. Ask them about tours and boat trips in the famous Hortillonnages.

FOOD AND DRINK:

You can dine very well at moderate prices in Amiens. Some good restaurant choices are:

Les Marissons (68 Rue des Marissons, 3 blocks northeast of the cathedral, across the river) Inventive cuisine in a converted 15th-century workshop. ☎ 03-2292-9666. X: Sat. lunch, Sun. $$

La Couronne (64 Rue St.-Leu, 1 block north of St.-Leu Church) Straightforward cuisine at good prices. ☎ 03-2291-8857. X: Sat., Sun. eve. $$

Le T'chiot Zinc (18 Rue de Noyon, west of the Tour Perret) Both local and Cambodian cuisine, and a good value. ☎ 03-2291- 4379. X: Sun., Mon. lunch. $

La Mangeoire (3 Rue des Sergents, 2 blocks southwest of the cathedral) An atmospheric crêperie. ☎ 03-2291-1128. X: Sun., Mon. $

SUGGESTED TOUR:

Numbers in parentheses correspond to numbers on the map.

Leave the **train station** (1) and amble over to the **Tour Perret** (2), a curious 26-story mini-skyscraper of truly inspired ugliness. At the time of its construction in 1952 it ranked as the tallest office building in Europe. The route now leads through a busy shopping district, passing the beautiful façade of an 18th-century theater. Turn right into the Passage du Logis du Roi, where you will see the 16th-century brick-and-stone Logis du Roi alongside a fine Renaissance façade. Opposite this stands the imposing 19th-century Palace of Justice. Continue on to the:

*CATHEDRAL OF NOTRE-DAME (3). *Open April–Sept., daily 8:30 a.m. to 7 p.m.; rest of year 8:30–noon and 2–5 or 6.*

Amiens' cathedral is regarded by many to be the most perfect example of a pure Gothic structure on Earth. Its richly carved ***West Front** merits a long and careful examination, especially the 13th-century statue of Christ and the superb relief of the Last Judgement; both by the central doorway. The two towers flanking the rose window, of unequal height, are later additions. Amiens Cathedral was begun in 1220 and pretty much completed in record time, thus accounting for the truly remarkable architectural unity. A reflection of the town's medieval prosperity, it is the largest cathedral in France.

Step inside to witness its astonishing proportions and noble use of space. Of particular note are the 16th-century **choir stalls**, whose oak carvings depict both religious and secular life, the latter often satirically. Stroll around the ambulatory and admire the marvelous choir screen. The cathedral's greatest treasure, however, is the purported head of John the Baptist, the authenticity of which remains in doubt.

Walk around to the rear of the cathedral, then visit the **Art and Regional History Museum** (4) in a superb 17th-century mansion, the Hôtel

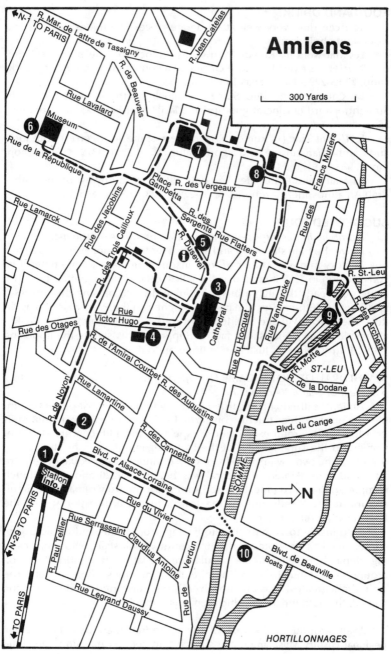

Amiens

300 Yards

N-1 TO PARIS

R. Mar. de Lattre de Tassigny

R. Jean Catelas

Rue Lavalard

R. de Beauvais

Museum

Rue de la République

Rue Lamarck

R. des Jacobins

R. des Trois Cailloux

Place Gambetta

R. des Vergeaux

R. des Sergents

Rue Flatters

R. Duseval

Francs Muriers

R. des

R. St-Leu

Rue Vanmarcke

R. des Archers

Rue des Otages

Rue Victor Hugo

Cathedral

Rue du Hocquet

R.R. Motte

ST.-LEU

R. de l'Amiral Courbet

R. des Augustins

R. de Noyon

Rue Lamartine

R. des Cannettes

R. de la Dodane

Blvd. du Cange

SOMME

N

Station Info.

Blvd. d'Alsace-Lorraine

Rue du Vivier

Rue Serrassaint

Claudius Antoine

Rue de Verdun

Blvd. de Beauville

Boats

N-29 TO PARIS

R. Paul Teller

Rue Legrand Daussy

HORTILLONNAGES

TO PARIS

de Berny. The furniture and room settings are quite interesting, as are items relating to the author Jules Verne, who lived most of his life in Amiens. ☎ *03-2297-1400. Open Sundays in summer, 10–12:30 and 2–6; other times on request. Adults 10FF, under 18 free.*

Return to the cathedral and stroll down Rue Dusvel, stopping at the **Tourist Information Office** (5) to ask about boat trips in the Hortillonnages, an interesting experience unique to Amiens, which are available at specific times from April to October.

Now follow the map to the **Picardy Museum** (6), which boasts an excellent collection of art focusing on the 18th-century French style, particularly paintings by Quentin de la Tour and Fragonard. Also featured is a great exhibit of sculptures on the ground floor, along with representative works of the Flemish and Dutch schools, other European masters, and modern art. Beneath it all is a display of archaeological exhibits. ☎ *03-2297-1400. Open Tues.–Sun., 10–12:30 and 2–6. Adults 20FF, children 10FF.*

Return to Place Gambetta and turn left to the 17th-century **City Hall** *(Hôtel de Ville)* (7). A right here leads past the 16th-century Bailliage (note the dormer windows and Renaissance façade), the equally-old square **Bell Tower** *(Beffroi),* and the nearby market hall. Just beyond is the **Church of St.-Germain** (8), built in the flamboyant Gothic style.

The medieval **St.-Leu Quarter** (9), cut through with numerous canals, still exudes an aura of the Middle Ages. Much of this area had become quite seedy, but recent efforts at gentrification, including the restoration of many fine old houses, are yielding results. Stroll through its evocative, narrow streets with their shops, galleries, cafés, and restaurants, noting in particular the picturesque 15th-century **Church of St.-Leu.**

From here you can return to the station following the route on the map. Along the way, be sure to make a little side trip to the extraordinary ***Hortillonnages** (10), a curious area of market gardens surrounded by irrigation canals, which have been cultivated since the Middle Ages. To get more than a fleeting glimpse of them requires exploring by boat. Current information about this is available at the tourist office.

Section V

DAYTRIPS FROM PARIS

CHAMPAGNE, BURGUNDY AND BEYOND

Wine lovers in particular will savor the five delicious daytrips in this section. Each destination offers a golden opportunity to sample some of France's best vintages right in their own region and return to your Paris base the same evening. But you don't really need a passion for liquid treasures to enjoy the area; even teetotalers will delight in its captivating old towns.

The Champagne district, where all of the world's true champagnes are made, centers on the ancient historical city of Reims. Once you've seen that, you may want to visit other places in the area. Épernay is an especially good choice for its champagne cellars alone, although the town itself is almost without interest.

Throughout most of its long history, Burgundy *(Bourgogne)* has been a land apart; one whose borders remain vague and undefined. Not until the 15th century was it absorbed into France. Much of its colorful past is still highly visible in Auxerre, Dijon and Beaune, the three daytrip destinations chosen to best represent this ancient wine region. Travelers with more time may want to stay over for a few days and explore some of its other attractions, such as Sens, Vézelay, Autun, Nevers or Cluny.

And beyond? That's Lyon—which makes no wine of its own but as the gastronomic capital of France certainly consumes enough; so much so that in fact it is reputed to lie at the junction of not two but three rivers—the Rhône, the Saône, and the Beaujolais.

Reims
(Rheims)

W orld renowned for its magnificent cathedral, traditionally the coronation site for the kings of France, Reims is also one of the two leading centers of the champagne trade. What better place could there possibly be to sample the bubbly while exploring an intriguing old city?

Reims' grandiose and often turbulent history goes back over two thousand years. Its name derives from a Celtic tribe, the Remi, who lived there long before the Romans changed it to *Durocortorum*. Clovis, king of the Franks, was baptized in a predecessor of its cathedral in AD 498, which resulted in the conversion of the Franks to Christianity. Since then, practically every French king received his crown in Reims, the last being Charles X in 1825.

During World War I the city found itself in the middle of a battle zone, being subjected to intense bombardment for four long years. Miraculously, the splendid 13th-century cathedral survived, wounded but still intact, although three-quarters of Reims was reduced to rubble. The Second World War brought some destruction as well, along with another place in history. It was here that the unconditional surrender of the Third Reich was signed in 1945, putting an end to that terrible conflict.

Postwar reconstruction and the restoration of ancient monuments has made Reims once again the fascinating place that it was in the past. Often spelled as "Rheims," the city's name is pronounced as *"Rrans,"* more or less rhyming with *dance*.

It is possible to combine a visit to Reims with one to nearby Épernay, the other major champagne producer, as they are both on the same rail line. The only sights to see there are the champagne caves, which are world-famous and absolutely first-rate. Ask the tourist office at 7 Avenue de Champagne in Épernay for details.

GETTING THERE:

Trains depart Gare de l'Est station in Paris several times in the morning for the 90-minute run to Reims. Some require a change at Épernay. Return service operates until mid-evening.

By car, Reims is 88 miles northeast of Paris on the A-4 Autoroute.

PRACTICALITIES:

Reims may be enjoyed at any time, but note that several museums are closed on Mondays or Tuesdays, plus major holidays. Some of the champagne cellars are closed on certain days, and several require advance reservations. The local **tourist office**, ☎ 03-2677-4525, Internet: www.ville-reims.com, is located at 2 Rue Guillaume-de-Machault, to the left of the cathedral. Ask them about visits to the champagne cellars.

FOOD AND DRINK:

Being a major wine center, Reims offers an extraordinarily high level of cuisine. Some choice restaurants are:

Boyer "Les Crayéres" (64 Blvd. Henry Vasnier, 4 blocks east of the St. Remi Basilica, near the champagne caves) One of the very best restaurants in France, with prices to match. Proper dress expected, reservations essential, ☎ 03-2682-8080. X: Mon., Tues. lunch. $$$ +

Au Petit Comptoir (17 Rue de Mars, 2 blocks south of the Mars Gate) A smart, old-fashioned bistro with contemporary cuisine. ☎ 03-2640-5858. X: Sat. lunch, Sun. $$

Le Vigneron (Place Paul-Jamot, 3 blocks east of the cathedral) Traditional old-fashioned cuisine of the region. ☎ 03-2679-8686 to reserve. X: Sat. lunch, Sun. $$

Le Continental (95 Place Drouet-d'Erlon, across from the train station) Good cuisine at fair prices. ☎ 03-2647-0147. $$

Le Bon Moine (14 Rue des Capucins, a block west of the Art Museum) A small inn with good, inexpensive lunches. ☎ 03- 2647-3364. X: Sun. $

Boeuf ou Salade? (41 Place Drouet-d'Erlon, 4 blocks west of the art museum) Inexpensive light meals, vegetarian and otherwise. ☎ 03-2640-4422. $

SUGGESTED TOUR:

Numbers in parentheses correspond to numbers on the map. Leave the **train station** (1) and follow the map to the:

*CATHEDRAL OF NOTRE-DAME (2), *Open daily 7:30 a.m. to 7:30 p.m. Closed during services. Free, donation. Tower visits in season: Adults 25FF, youths 12–25 15FF.*

Nearly all of the kings of France were crowned here following the baptism of Clovis, king of the Franks, in 498. The present cathedral, along with those of Paris, Chartres, and Amiens, is a perfect example of the French Gothic style's golden age. It was begun in 1211 and essentially completed within a century, thus accounting for its remarkable stylistic unity.

The richly decorated **West Front** with its three deeply recessed doorways recalls Biblical stories in carved stone. Its central portal is dedicated to the Virgin, while the right doorway, flanked by the prophets, represents the Last Judgement. Perhaps the most famous symbol of Reims is the enigmatic ***Smiling Angel** in the left doorway, easily worth the small effort of singling out.

Step inside to admire the **stained-glass windows**, some of which are 13th-century originals. Of particular note is the fabulous rose window in the west end. There are also some wonderful modern stained-glass windows by the artist Mare Chagall in the Lady Chapel, installed in 1974.

Leave the cathedral and stroll around to the rear to witness the almost weightless elegance of its flying buttresses. Next to it is the former **Archbishop's Palace** *(Palais du Tau)* (3), once the residence of the king during coronations and now a museum of the cathedral's treasures. Enter from the cathedral. ☎ *03-2647-8179. Open mid-March to mid-Nov., daily 9:30–12:30 and 2–5 or 6; rest of year daily 10:30–noon and 2–5. Adults 32FF, youths 12–25 21FF.*

The ***Museum of Fine Arts** (Musée des Beaux-Arts)* (4) is located in a former abbey just two blocks from the cathedral. Its collections include an outstanding series of 16th-century portrait drawings by both Lucas Cranach the Elder and his son, the Younger. Among the other treasures are two cycles of medieval tapestries and wall hangings, no less than 26 landscapes by Corot, and a marvelous gathering of 19th- and early-20th-century French paintings. ☎ *03-2647-2844. Open Wed.-Mon., 10-noon and 2-6. Closed major holidays. Adults 10FF. Students, children free.*

Now follow the map to the **Basilica of St.-Remi** (5) on Rue Simon. This is the oldest church in Reims, dating from the first half of the 11th century. Much of it is in the Romanesque style, while the huge 12th-century choir makes a transition into the early Gothic. Behind the altar lies the reconstructed tomb of Saint Remi, a 5th-century archbishop who established the importance of Reims by baptizing Clovis as a Christian here.

Adjoining the church on the north side is its former abbey, now housing the city's **Archaeological Museum** *(Musée Abbaye St.-Remi)*. Displays here include fascinating artifacts from prehistoric times to the late Middle Ages, along with notable tapestries illustrating the life of Saint Remi. ☎ *03-2685-2336. Open Mon.–Fri., 2–6:30, weekends 2–7, closed major holidays. Adults 10FF, students and children free.*

Now for a real treat—the famous **champagne cellars**, many of which are located in this part of town. Some that you may like to visit are:

Veuve Clicquot-Posardin (6). These caves date from Gallo-Roman times and may be seen by appointment, ☎ *03-2689-5441, Internet: www.veuveclicquot.fr.*

Pommery (7). An elegant and fascinating tour through ancient pits below the city. ☎ *03-2661-6255. Open April–Oct., daily, 10–5:30, otherwise by appointment. Adults 40FF, students 20FF.*

Taittinger (8). A somewhat spooky amble in the crypts of a former abbey. ☎ *03-2685-8433, Internet: www.taittinger.fr. Open March–Nov., Mon.–Fri. 9:30–noon and 2–4:30, weekends 9–11 and 2–5; rest of year Mon.–Fri. only. Tours 20FF.*

Piper-Heidsieck (9). A self-guided tour in a little car, with a tasting. ☎

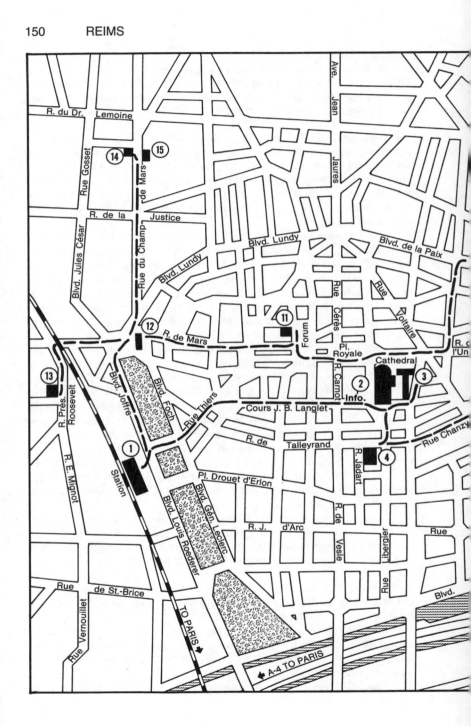

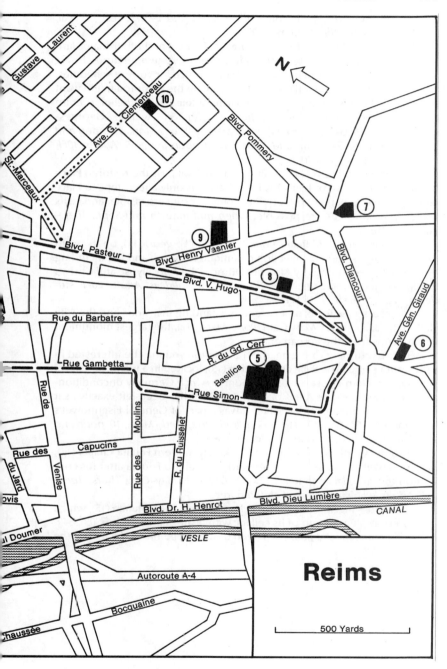

Reims

500 Yards

03-2684-4344. Open March–Nov., daily 9–11:45 and 2–5:15; rest of year, Thurs.–Mon., same times. Tours 35FF.

Visits are usually conducted in English, French, and other major languages. A jacket or sweater is helpful as the cave temperatures hover around the 50°F mark. Check with the tourist office for current schedules. Return to the cathedral area via the route on the map. You might want to make a little side trip to the **French Automobile Museum** *(Centre Historique de l'Automobile Française)* (10) on Avenue Georges-Clemenceau. ☎ *03-2682-8384. Open April–Nov., Wed.–Mon., 10–noon and 2–6; Dec.–March, Sat.–Sun. and holidays, 10–noon and 2–5. Adults 30FF, children 10–18 20FF, 6–9 10FF.*

Continuing on beyond the cathedral, you will pass the restored **Place Royale** with its statue of Louis XV. From here it is only a few steps to **Place du Forum**, where parts of the original Roman Forum are visible, and visits to its Cryptoporticus are possible. *Open mid-June to mid-Sept., Tues.–Sun., 2–5. Free.*

The **Museum of Old Reims** *(Musée-Hôtel le Vergeur)* (11), on its north side, displays a splendid collection of antique furniture and art, including a noted set of engravings by Albrecht Dürer of the Apocalypse and Christ's Passion. *Open Tues.–Sun., 2–6. Closed major holidays. Adults 20FF, students 15FF, children 11–16 5FF.*

The route now leads past several outstanding mansions and the City Hall to the 3rd-century **Mars Gate** *(Porte Mars)* (12), the largest monument left in Reims from the Roman era.

Before returning to the nearby train station you may be interested in a few other sights. The **Salle de Reddition** (13), located in a technical school at 12 Rue Franklin-Roosevelt, is the room in which Germany unconditionally surrendered to the Allies on May 7, 1945. It has been left exactly as it was on that momentous day, when it was a part of General Eisenhower's headquarters. ☎ *03-2647-8419. Open April–Nov., Wed.–Mon., 10–noon and 2–6. Adults 10FF, students and children free.*

Another worthwhile sight is the strikingly modern **Foujita Chapel** (14), designed by the Japanese artist Léonard-Tsugouharu Foujita after his conversion to Catholicism in Reims. ☎ *03-2640-0696. May–Oct., Thurs.–Tues., 2–6. Adults 10FF, students and children free.*

Just across the street is another champagne house, **Mumm** (15), which also offers a splendid tour of its cellars, with tastings included. ☎ *03-2649-5970. Open March–Oct., daily 9–11 and 2–5; reduced times the rest of the year. Tours 20FF.*

Auxerre

You won't find a great many tourists in Auxerre, but that's their loss. This marvelously atmospheric holdover from the Middle Ages is the capital of lower Burgundy and the center of the Chablis wine growing region. The town, as you approach it along the banks of the Yonne River, makes an exceptionally handsome sight with its church spires piercing the skyline above a huddle of ancient houses.

Inhabited since Celtic times, Auxerre was later a Roman fortress called *Autessiodurum,* from which its name derives. The town, converted to Christianity, became the seat of a bishop as early as the 3rd century, and later an important scholastic center. Its medieval heart is today one of the best-preserved in France—an exceptionally attractive place where you can enjoy strolling around the winding, narrow lanes and exploring its picturesque old structures in peace. Auxerre, incidentally, is pronounced *"Ausserre."*

GETTING THERE:

Trains leave Gare de Lyon station in Paris several times in the morning for Auxerre's St.-Gervais Station, less than two hours away. Some of these require a change at Laroche-Migennes. Return service operates until early evening.

By car, take the A-6 Autoroute and enter Auxerre on the N-6 road. The town is 105 miles southeast of Paris.

PRACTICALITIES:

A trip to Auxerre can be made at almost any time, but avoid coming on a Tuesday or holiday, when its major attractions are closed. The local **tourist office,** ☎ 03-8652-0619, Internet: www.ipoint.fr/auxerre, is located along the Quai de la République, by the river, below the cathedral.

FOOD AND DRINK:

Some good restaurants are listed below. Naturally, you will probably want to sip genuine Chablis, the local wine.

Restaurant Maxime (5 Quai de la Marine, by the river below the cathedral) Excellent food in a nice waterside location. ☎ 03-8652-0441. X: Sun. off season. $$$

Le Jardin Gourmand (56 Blvd. Vauban, 3 blocks northwest of the

Chapel of the Nuns) Superb cuisine at a fair price. ☎ 03- 8651-5352. X: Tues., Wed. $$

Salamandre (84 Rue de Paris, 2 blocks west of the cathedral) Good-value menus. ☎ 03-8652-8787. X: Sat. lunch, Sun. $$

De Seignelay (2 Rue du Pont, near the Church of St.-Pierre) A great value in a small hotel. ☎ 03-8652-0348. X: Mon. $

SUGGESTED TOUR:

Numbers in parentheses correspond to numbers on the map. Leave the **train station** (1) and follow the map to the Yonne River, from which you get a splendid view of the old town. A right here leads to a footbridge. Cross this and, passing the tourist office, walk uphill to the:

CATHEDRAL OF ST.-ÉTIENNE (2). *Open Palm Sunday to All Saints' Day, Mon.–Sat. 9–noon and 2–6, Sun. and holidays 2–6. Rest of year, Mon.–Sat. 9–noon and 2–6. From July–Sept. it remains open over the noon break. Free, donation. Crypt: 10FF. Treasury: 10FF. Organ recitals in summer, Sun. at 5 p.m.*

The Cathedral of St.-Étienne is a remarkable structure in the Flamboyant Gothic style, begun in the 13th century but not completed until the 16th. This was the scene, in 1422, of a fateful meeting in which the English and the Burgundians plotted against the French. In 1429 it was visited by a disguised Joan of Arc on her way to meet the dauphin at Chinon. After defeating the English at Orléans she returned here with Charles VII en route to his coronation at Reims. Another historical event took place in front of the cathedral in 1815 when Napoleon, returning from exile, conspired with Marshal Ney against Louis XVIII, for which Ney was later shot.

The cathedral's interior features some very fine medieval stained-glass windows along with an admirable Gothic choir. Be sure to visit its 11th-century *crypt, the sole remaining part of an earlier cathedral on the same site. There you will see the famous *Christ on Horseback* fresco, the only one of its kind in the world. Other sights in the church include its treasury of illuminated manuscripts and the north tower.

Now carefully follow the map through a maze of ancient streets to **Place St.-Nicolas** (3), a delightful square in the old marine quarter. Continue on past a handsome 16th-century half-timbered house to the **Abbey of St.-Germain** (4), founded in the 6th century by Queen Clothilde, wife of Clovis, above the tomb of Auxerre's 5th-century bishop and native son, Saint Germain. Rebuilt in later years, the church itself is of minor interest, but the *crypts are another story. Some of these date from as early as the 5th century. The 9th-century Carolingian chambers contain several fabulous frescoes, among the very earliest yet discovered in France, depicting the martyrdom of Saint Stephen. In the Merovingian part of the crypt there are some oak beams that are over 1,100 years old. The abbey complex also includes a **Museum of Archaeology and Fine Arts**, which

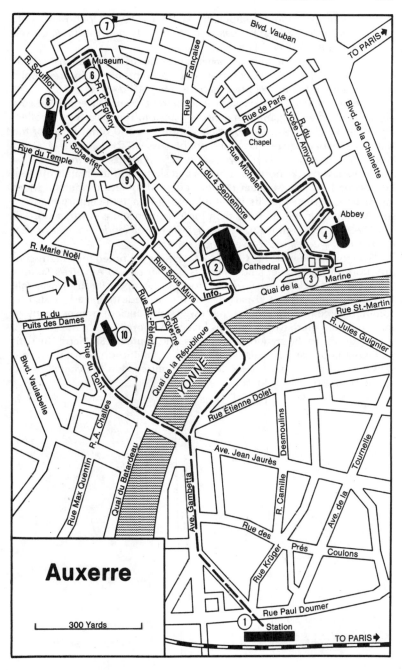

Auxerre

300 Yards

makes a visit even more compelling. ☎ *03-8651-0974. Open May–Sept., Wed.–Mon., 9:45–6:30; rest of year, Wed.–Mon., 9:45–noon and 2–6. Closed holidays. Adults 22FF, children under 16 free.*

Continue on to the former **Chapel of the Nuns of the Visitation** (5) at 100 Rue de Paris, where contemporary wooden polychrome sculptures depict the Massacre of the Innocents. *Open July–Aug., Wed.–Sun., 2–6.*

Rue de Paris and Rue d'Eglény lead to the **Leblanc-Duvernoy Museum** (6), installed in an elegant 18th-century mansion. The magnificent collection of Beauvais tapestries, porcelains, furniture, and other items of the 18th-century decorative arts should not be missed. ☎ *03-8651-0974. Open Wed.–Mon., 2–6. Closed holidays. Adults 12FF, students, children free.*

Just a few blocks northwest of this and slightly off the map is the **Paul Bert Natural History Museum** (7), located at 5 Boulevard Vauban. More interesting, perhaps, for its beautiful setting in a 19th-century mansion surrounded by lovely grounds than for its contents, it is worth a stop. ☎ *03-8672-9640. Open July–Aug., Mon.–Fri. 10–6, weekends 2–6; rest of year Mon.–Fri. 10–noon and 2–6, weekends 2–6. Free.*

The route goes past the **Church of St.-Eusèbe** (8), noted for its 12th-century Romanesque tower, and winds its way around to Auxerre's famous 15th-century **Clock Tower** *(Tour de l'Horloge)* (9), opposite the Town Hall. This delightfully animated part of town, now pedestrianized, is also its commercial center. All around the tower stand ancient houses, many of them half-timbered, which serve as luxurious shops.

Returning to the station, you will pass the **Church of St.-Pierre** (10) with its highly impressive Renaissance façade. Continue on downhill to the Paul-Bert Bridge for a last look at Auxerre mirrored in the waters of the Yonne before returning to Paris.

*Dijon

There is a lot to see in Dijon—if you can just tear yourself away from the pleasures of the table long enough to feast the eyes as well as the palate. Long renowned as the region's gastronomic center, this ancient city is also the traditional capital of Burgundy. Its rulers left behind a rich heritage that today makes it a veritable treasury of the arts. Dijon is an exceedingly likeable place, and an eminently walkable one as well.

Originally a Roman encampment on the military road linking Lyon with Mainz, *Divio*, as Dijon was then known, became the capital of the Burgundian kingdom during the Dark Ages, only to be destroyed by fire in 1137. The late 12th century saw its reconstruction as a fortified city, while the Cathedral of St.-Bénigne was begun a hundred years later.

Philip the Bold, son of King John II of France, inherited Burgundy in 1364, thus starting the powerful line of Valois dukes whose loyalty to the Kingdom of France wavered with each succeeding generation. During this time Burgundy was greatly expanded, making Dijon in effect the capital of much of what is now the Netherlands, Belgium, Alsace and Lorraine as well as the present region of *Bourgogne*. This enormous growth coincided with the beginning of the Renaissance, attracting many leading artists to Dijon, where there was both work and money. The golden days came to an end in 1477 when Duke Charles the Bold was killed fighting Louis XI, thus reunifying Burgundy with France.

GETTING THERE:

Trains for Dijon leave Gare de Lyon station in Paris fairly frequently. The speedy TGVs (reservations required) make the run in about 100 minutes; others take about 2.5 hours. Return service operates until mid-evening.

By car, Dijon is 195 miles southeast of Paris via the A-6 Autoroute. This may be a bit too far for a daytrip, although Dijon makes an excellent stopover en route between Paris and the Riviera.

PRACTICALITIES:

Most of the major sights are closed on Tuesdays and some holidays. The local **Tourist Information Office, ☎** 03-8044-1144, Internet: www.ot-dijon.fr, is at Place Darcy. Dijon is in the Bourgogne region, and has a population of about 146,000.

FOOD AND DRINK:

The overall quality of dining in Dijon is exceptionally high, with such local specialties as *boeuf bourguignon* and *coq au vin* being international favorites. The city is also famous for its mustard, a jar of which makes a nice souvenir. Some outstanding restaurants located on or near the suggested walking route are:

Le Chapeau Rouge (5 Rue Michelet, a block east of the cathedral) Serious classic dining in a tranquil setting. For reservations ☎ 03-8030-2810. $$$

La Toison d'Or *(Les Oenophiles)* (18 Rue Ste.-Anne, 5 blocks southwest of the Palace of the Dukes) In an old mansion, with ancient wine caves and a museum. A unique experience, dress well and reserve. ☎ 03-8030-7352. X: Sun. $$

La Porte Guillaume (in the Hôtel du Nord on Place Darcy) An old traditional establishment. ☎ 03-8030-5858. $$

Bistrot des Halles (10 Rue Bannelier, 3 blocks north of Pl. François Rude) Good value for a quality lunch. ☎ 03-8049-9415. X: Sun. eve. $ and $$

Brasserie Foch (1 bis Ave. Maréchal Foch, between the station and the tourist office) Inexpensive meals at a recommended brasserie. ☎ 03-8041-2793. X: Sun. $

L'Entresol (27 Rue Musette, 2 blocks northwest of Place François Rude) An upstairs source for healthy vegetarian dishes. ☎ 03-8030-1510. X: Sun. $

SUGGESTED TOUR:

Numbers in parentheses correspond to numbers on the map.

Leave the **train station** (l) and follow the map to **Place Darcy** (2), an attractive square with a tourist office, a small park and an 18th-century triumphal arch. Continue on Rue de la Liberté past the venerable **Grey Poupon** mustard store—which has an exhibit of antique jars on display—to **Place François Rude** (3). In the center of this lively square there is a fountain that once ran with new wine at harvest time, topped by a statue of a naked youth treading the grapes. The **Central Market** *(Les Halles),* two blocks north of this, bustles with activity on Tuesday, Friday and Saturday mornings.

Follow the narrow Rue des Forges past several exquisite old houses, the most notable being the 15th-century **Hôtel Morel-Sauvegrain** at Number 56; the 13th-century exchange—much restored—at Number 40; and the **Maison Milsand,** dating from 1561, at Number 38.

A left at Place Notre-Dame leads to the ***Eglise de Notre-Dame** (4), a unique jewel of 13th-century Gothic church architecture. Its façade is literally covered with hideous gargoyles, while from the roof rises the Jacquemart, a mechanical chiming clock that Philip the Bold brought back as war booty from the Flemish town of Courtrai in 1389. Be sure to visit the remarkably harmonious interior, noted for its ancient stained-glass windows and an 11th-century Black Virgin carved in wood.

Stroll around to the rear of the church on Rue de la Chouette. At Number 8 you will pass the **Hôtel de Vogüé**, a lovely residence in the Renaissance style dating from 1614. Make a left into Rue Verrerie, and the next right on Rue Chaudronnerie, followed by another right on Rue Vannerie—a short walk taking you down three very picturesque streets lined with medieval buildings. At the end you will come to the **Église St.-Michel** (5), a curious mixture of Gothic and Renaissance styles built during the 15th, 16th and 17th centuries.

The major attraction in Dijon, besides its food and wine, is the ***Palais des Ducs de Bourgogne** (6). Begun in the 14th century, the Palace of the Dukes of Burgundy was continually enlarged and modified until the 19th, with much of its classical façade designed by Louis XIV's architect, Jules Hardouin-Mansart of Versailles fame. This enormous complex of structures now houses both the **Hôtel de Ville** (City Hall), which may be strolled through, and the world-famous:

*FINE ARTS MUSEUM (*Musée des Beaux-Arts*) (6), ☎ 03-8074-5270. *Open Wed.–Mon., 10–6; some sections closed from noon–1:30. Adults 22FF, seniors, students under 25, children 10FF. The bargain Carte d'Accès aux Musées card covers all of Dijon's major museums for only a bit more, and is sold here.*

The entrance to the museum, one of the best in France, is on Place de la Ste.-Chapelle. Allow plenty of time for a visit—an hour at the very least—and carefully study the posted layout maps as it is quite easy to get disoriented and risk missing some of its best treasures. These include the ducal kitchens, the **tombs** of Philip the Bold and John the Fearless; Italian, Swiss, Flemish and German as well as French paintings and sculptures; and, of course, the outstanding galleries of modern and regional art.

Now stroll into Place des Ducs-de-Bourgogne, a charming square facing the original parts of the palace. A portal at the corner leads back into the palace complex, from which you can climb up the **Tour Philippe-le-Bon** (7) for an excellent view of the city, the mountains beyond and the beginnings of the Burgundy wine district. It is a steep 150 feet to the top of this 15th-century tower, but well worth the effort.

Follow the map through the elegant Place de la Libération to the **Musée Magnin** (8), housed in a fine 17th-century mansion, the Hôtel Lantin on Rue des Bons-Enfants. Step inside to view a sumptuous collection of paintings displayed in the gorgeous environment of original room settings reflecting period bourgeois life. ☎ 03-8067-1110. *Open Tues.–Sun., 10–noon and 2–6. Adults 18FF, students and children 12FF.*

Continue on past the Palais de Justice and turn right on Rue Amiral Roussin. The route now leads through a colorful old part of town to the **Cathedral of St.-Bénigne** (9), a 13th-century example of the Burgundian Gothic style. You can make an interesting visit to its unusual circular **crypt**, dating from 1002 with some 9th-century segments, which survives from an

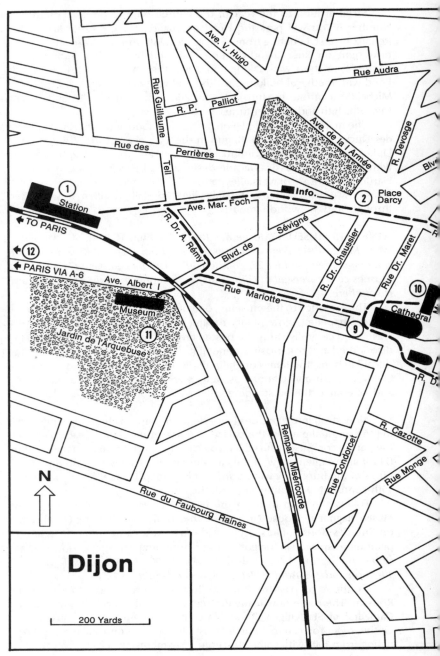

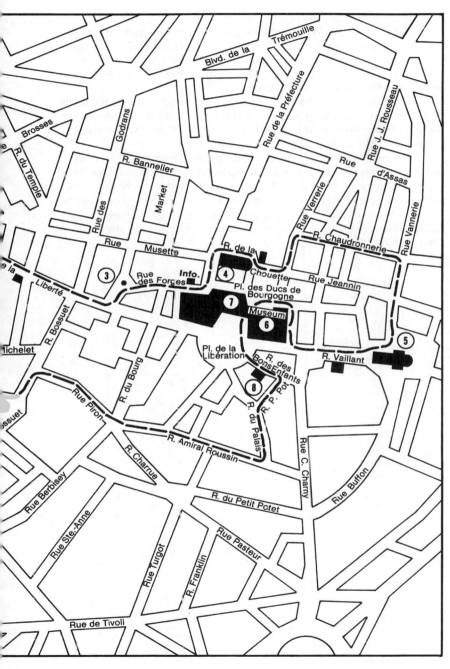

Blvd. de la Trémouille

Rue de la Préfecture

Brosses

R. du Temple

Godrans

R. Bannelier

Rue J. J. Rousseau

Rue d'Assas

Rue des

Market

Rue Verrerie

Rue Vannerie

Rue

Musette

R. de la

R. Chaudronnerie

Liberté

Rue des Forces

Info.

Chouette

Rue Jeannin

③

④

Pl. des Ducs de Bourgogne

R. Bossuet

⑦

Museum

⑥

⑤

Michelet

Pl. de la Libération

R. des Bons Enfants

R. Vaillant

ssuet

Rue Piron

R. du Bourg

⑧

R. du Palais

R. Charrue

R. Amiral Roussin

Rue C. Charny

Rue Buffon

Rue Berbisey

R. du Petit Potet

Rue Ste-Anne

Rue Turgot

R. Franklin

Rue Pasteur

Rue de Tivoli

earlier basilica on the same site.

Next to this is the **Musée Archéologique** (10), housed in the dormitory of a former Benedictine abbey. Displays here include some fascinating Gallo-Roman and medieval artifacts. ☎ 03-8030-8854. *Open June–Sept., Wed.–Mon., 10–8; rest of year Wed.–Mon., 9–noon and 2–6. Adults 14FF, students and children free. Free to all on Sun.*

On the way back to the train station you may want to stop at the **Jardin de l'Arquebuse** (11), a large and very lovely garden which also houses the **Natural History Museum.** ☎ *03-8076-8276. Open Mon.–Fri., 9–noon and 2–6; closed Tues. mornings. Adults 14FF, students 7FF.*

Those with a bit more time can make a short excursion of less than a mile to the famous **Chartreuse de Champmol** (12, off the map). Originally the burial place of the dukes of Burgundy, this 14th-century monastery was destroyed in the Revolution and the site is now occupied by a mental hospital. Some of its fabulous sculptures by the noted medieval master Claus Sluter are still there, and deserve to be seen by anyone interested in the art of the Middle Ages.

Beaune

Beaune is a mecca for wine lovers the world over, and long the center of Burgundy's liquid trade. Its major sight, the 15th-century Hôtel-Dieu, is surely one of the most extraordinary medieval structures in France, or in all of Europe for that matter. Visitors by the thousands are also attracted to its numerous *caves*, where the wines of Burgundy can be sampled in congenial surroundings.

Wine was not always Beaune's sole *raison d'être*. The 14th-century ramparts, still more or less complete, enclose a remarkably well-preserved town that dates from the time of the ancient Gauls. It remained an important political center of the duchy long after the dukes themselves moved to Dijon, with a strategic location between the once-powerful strongholds of warring nobles. All of this changed in the 17th century, when the local citizens finally turned their full attention to wine. That happy development has brought about a prosperity lasting to this day. Beaune (pronounced *Bone*) is indeed a joyful place to visit.

GETTING THERE:

Trains depart Gare de Lyon station in Paris frequently for Dijon, with the TGV types making the run in about 100 minutes. From there take a connecting local to Beaune, a trip of 22 minutes. There is also frequent bus service between the two towns. Some TGV trains run directly from Paris to Beaune, but at rather odd hours. Return service operates until early evening.

By car, Beaune is 196 miles southeast of Paris on the A-6 Autoroute. A daytrip by car is rather impractical, but the town makes an excellent stopover for those driving between Paris and Provence or the Riviera.

PRACTICALITIES:

Beaune may be enjoyed at any time. Even if it is raining, the underground *caves* stay dry—at least as far as precipitation is concerned. The local **tourist office,** ☎ 03- 8026-2130, is next to the Hôtel-Dieu. Be sure to ask them for current information concerning visits to the wine *caves* and, if you can stay longer, wine tours by bus or hot-air balloon.

FOOD AND DRINK:

As an important tourist attraction, Beaune offers a great many restaurants and cafés in all price ranges. Some particularly good choices are:

Relais de Saulx (6 Rue Louis-Véry, a block west of the Hôtel-Dieu) Burgundian cuisine in a lovely rustic setting. Reservations needed, ☎ 03-8022-0135. X: Sun., Mon. lunch. $$ and $$$

Auberge St.-Vincent (Place de la Halle, near the tourist office) Traditional dishes in an ancient house. ☎ 03-8022-4234. X: Wed. in winter. $$

L'Ecusson (Place Malmédy, 4 blocks southwest of the train station, by Rue Madeleine) Superb cuisine at friendly prices. ☎ 03-8024-0382. X: Wed. eve., Sun. $$

Central (2 Rue Victor-Millot, a block east of the Hôtel-Dieu) A small hotel restaurant with excellent food. ☎ 03-8024-7724. X: Wed. and Thurs. lunch in winter and spring. $$

Auberge Bourguignonne (4 Place Madeleine, 4 blocks east of the Hôtel-Dieu, just outside the walls) Traditional cooking at a small inn. ☎ 03-8022-2353. X: Mon. $ and $$

La Gourmandin (8 Place Carnot, a block east of the Hôtel-Dieu) Traditional Burgundian specialties. ☎ 03-8024-0788. X: Sun. eve., Tues. $

Maxime (3 Place Madeleine, 4 blocks east of the Hôtel-Dieu) Great value in Burgundian cuisine, ☎ 03-8022-1782. X: Mon., Feb. $

SUGGESTED TOUR:

Numbers in parentheses correspond to numbers on the map.

Leave the **train station** (1) and follow the map through some colorful old streets to the **Tourist Information Office** (2). Here you can get an up-to-date list of the wine *caves* in town that offer tours or tastings *(dégustation)*. Many of these are located in ancient cellars dating from as far back as the 13th century and make intriguing places to visit. Some are free while others—often with better vintages—charge a nominal admission. Since the old part of Beaune is quite small you will be able to visit the cellars at your leisure anytime along the walking route. The locations of some of the better-known caves are shown on the map with circled numbers. They are:

Marché aux Vins, near the Hôtel-Dieu (8).

Caves des Cordeliers, near the Hôtel-Dieu (9).

La Halle aux Vins, facing Square des Lions on Blvd. Foch (10).

Maison Patriarche Père et Fils, on Rue de Collège (11).

Now for Beaune's major attraction, the:

*HÔTEL-DIEU *(also known as the Hospices de Beaune)* (3), ☎ 03-8024-4500. *Open a week before Easter to mid-Nov., daily 9–6:30; rest of year daily, 9–11:30 and 2–5:30. Adults 32FF, students and children 10–14 25FF.*

This exquisite structure—a major architectural achievement of the 15th century—was founded in 1443 by the chancellor of Burgundy, Nicolas Rolin, as a charity hospital to alleviate the misery of much of the town's population. This was perhaps only too fitting since it was Rolin—acting as

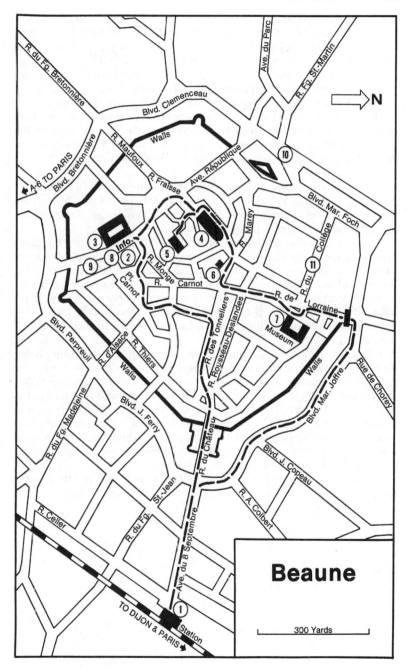

N

R. du Fg. Bretonnière

Ave. du Parc

R. Fg. St-Martin

Blvd. Clemenceau

Walls

R. Mauloux

R. Fraisse

Ave. République

Blvd. Bretonnière

A-6 TO PARIS

Blvd. Mar. Foch

R. Marey

10

3

Info.

4

8   2

5

R. Monge

11

9

R. du Collège

R. Carnot

6

Pl. Carnot

R. Carnot

R. de Lorraine

1

Museum

R. des Tonneliers

Blvd. Perpreuil

R. d'Alsace

R. Thiers

Walls

R. Rousseau-Deslandes

Walls

Blvd. Mar. Joffre

Rue de Chorey

Blvd. J. Ferry

R. du Fg. Madeleine

R. du Château

Blvd. J. Copeau

R. A. Colbert

R. Celler

St.-Jean

R. du Fg.

Ave. du 8 Septembre

Beaune

1

TO DIJON & PARIS

Station

300 Yards

tax collector for the dukes—who reduced them to poverty to begin with. Its use as a hospital continued until 1971, with much of it still functioning as an old-age home. Pick up a brochure in English at the entrance and wander through the restored rooms. At the end is a small art gallery featuring one of the most fabulous paintings from the Middle Ages, Roger van der Weyden's great polyptych of the *Last Judgement.

The Hôtel-Dieu is supported primarily by revenues from the 32 Côte de Beaune vineyards it owns, whose wines are sold at its famous auction, held on the third Sunday of each November. These tend to establish the prices for all Burgundy wines of the same vintage. The Hospices de Beaune label is highly regarded among lovers of fine wines.

Continue on to the **Collegiate Church of Notre-Dame** (4), begun during the 12th-century in the Cluniac tradition. Some of its works of art are truly astonishing—particularly the 15th-century tapestries depicting the life of the Virgin, displayed behind the altar.

Oenophiles—as well as normal folk—will appreciate the **Burgundy Wine Museum** (Musée du Vin de Bourgogne) (5), located in the medieval Mansion of the Dukes of Burgundy. Its many interesting displays cover the history and lore of local wine making from ancient times to the early 20th century. Don't miss the adjacent 14th-century press house (cuverie). ☎ 03-8022-0819. Open daily 9:30–6, closed Tues. from Dec.–March. Joint ticket with the Fine Arts Museum, below: Adults 25FF, seniors, students, and children over 12 15FF.

The walk now winds around past the picturesque 15th-century **Belfry** (6) of the former town hall to the **Museum of Fine Arts** (Musée des Beaux-Arts) (7). The rather miscellaneous collections, including some Gallo-Roman archaeological finds, are enlivened by a splendid group of paintings by the 19th-century romantic landscapist, Félix Ziem, a native son of Beaune. Another local lad, Étienne-Jules Marey, a 19th-century scientist who pioneered the principles of motion picture photography, has a separate gallery devoted to his work. ☎ 03-8024-5698. Open April–Oct., daily 2–6. Joint ticket with Wine Museum, above.

From here you can return to the station by walking along the ancient ramparts or, better still, return to town for another glass of wine.

Lyon

n the past, a daytrip to Lyon would have been nearly unthinkable as the second city of France lies some 288 miles southeast of Paris. All that changed with the introduction of high-speed TGV trains, which cover the distance in an astonishing two hours flat. This is a good excursion for railpass holders—you really get your money's worth—and an excellent reason to purchase one of these bargains.

Strangely, Lyon has never been much of a tourist attraction. Visitors yes—about seven million a year, nearly all on business—but travelers in search of pleasure have largely avoided it. Lyon deserves better than that. Its older sections are surprisingly beautiful, and endowed with enough first-rate attractions to make just about any other city in France besides Paris pale by comparison.

And then there is the food. Lyon is usually regarded as the gastronomic capital of all France, which in practical terms means that it probably has the best cooking in the world. You could make a trip there just to eat, especially if your object was to indulge in one of the legendary temples of *haute cuisine* the area is famous for.

Over two thousand years old, Lyon was founded in 43 BC as the Roman colony of *Lugdunum*. Even before then, the site at the confluence of two rivers had long been occupied by Celts and other people. Under the emperor Augustus it became the capital of Gaul and later, in AD 478, the capital of the Burgundians. The city's strategic situation at the crossroads of trade routes favored its development as a mercantile center, a position it still holds. Textile manufacturing took root in the early 16th century, establishing a strong economic base along with banking and printing. Although Lyon—sometimes spelled Lyons in English—is now a very modern city, the walking tour suggested below is limited to the handsome and very well-preserved older parts of town.

GETTING THERE:

TGV trains (reservations required) depart Gare de Lyon station in Paris frequently for the two-hour run to Lyon. Most of these stop at both of Lyon's two main stations, Part-Dieu and Perrache. If your train does this, do not get off at Part-Dieu but stay on to Perrache. If your train does not, you will have to get off at Part-Dieu and take another train to Perrache Station, where the walking tour begins. Return service operates until early evening.

By car, the distance from Paris is too great for a daytrip. You may, however, want to make a stopover en route to or from the Riviera. Lyon is 288 miles southeast of Paris via the A-6 Autoroute.

PRACTICALITIES:

Some of the major attractions are closed on Mondays, some on Tuesdays, and others on both days. The **Tourist Information Office**, ☎ 04-7277-6969, is located in Place Bellecour (2), with a branch at Perrache Station, another by the funicular station, and a third (seasonal) atop the Fourvière hill. Lyon has a city population of about 416,000, with well over a million in its greater urban area, and is in the Rhône-Alpes region.

FOOD AND DRINK:

Lyon abounds in superb restaurants and friendly cafés, with the selections listed below limited to a few along or near the suggested walking route. For choices in other parts of town you should consult an up-to-date restaurant guide.

Léon de Lyon (1 Rue Pleney, a block south of the Fine Arts Museum) Inspired Lyonnais cuisine in the grand tradition. Proper dress expected. For reservations ☎ 04-7210-1112. X: Sun., Mon., Aug. $$$

La Voûte—Chez Lea (11 Place Antonin-Gourju, a block northwest of Place Bellecour, near the river) Traditional Lyonnais cooking in an old establishment. ☎ 04-7842-0133. X: Sun. $$

Café des Federations (8 Rue Major-Martin, a block west of the Fine Arts Museum) An old-fashioned place with simple local cuisine. Reserve, ☎ 04-7828-2600. X: Sat., Sun., Aug. $$

Brasserie Georges (30 Cours de Verdun, near Perrache Station) This huge brasserie hasn't changed since the 1930s. Hearty food until midnight, every day. ☎ 04-7256-5454. $ and $$

Le Garet (7 Rue du Garet, 2 blocks east of the Fine Arts Museum) A friendly, neighborhood place. Reserve, ☎ 04-7828-1694. X: weekends, Aug. $ and $$

Au Petit Bouchon—Chez Georges (8 Rue du Garet, 2 blocks east of the Fine Arts Museum) An unpretentious place for traditional cuisine. ☎ 04-7828-3046. X: weekends, early Aug. $

SUGGESTED TOUR:

Numbers in parentheses correspond to numbers on the map.

Leave the **Perrache Train Station** (1), a huge modern complex that includes a bus terminal, and descend the escalators to Place Carnot. From here the pedestrians-only Rue Victor Hugo leads through a lively shopping district to **Place Bellecour** (2), a vast open space with a flower market, the main tourist office, and an equestrian statue of Louis XIV. Turn left and cross the Pont Bonaparte, a bridge spanning the Saône. Continue straight ahead to the funicular station, buy a ticket from the vending machine, and board the car on the right-hand side marked for Fourvière. This will take you to the top of a very steep hill, from which there is a wonderful panoramic view of Lyon. The outlandish **Basilique Notre-Dame-de-Fourvière** (3), at the top of the funicular and overlooking the city, has to be seen to be believed. This marvelously extravagant basilica, a curious mélange of architectural styles, was begun in 1870 as thanks to the Virgin for saving Lyon from the Germans during the Franco-Prussian War. Step inside for a look at the elaborate stained-glass windows, mosaics, and the crypt. A tower on the left affords an even better view of the city.

The Fourvière hill was the site of the original Roman settlement and is rich in archaeological finds. Follow the map to the:

*MUSÉE DE LA CIVILISATION GALLO-ROMAINE (4), ☎ 04-7238-8190. *Open Wed.–Sun., 9:30–noon and 2–6. Adults 20FF, students 10FF.*

This superb modern structure, mostly underground, spirals its way down part of the hillside. As you descend its ramps you will pass many fascinating artifacts from Lyon's ancient past. A descriptive booklet in English is available at the entrance.

Leave the museum from its lowest level and stroll over to the two **Théâtres Romains** (5), unearthed in the 1930s. The larger of these Roman theaters is the oldest in France and was built by the emperor Augustus in 15 BC. It is now used for occasional festival performances, but you can usually climb all over it.

Continue down the hill via Montée du Chemin Neuf to the **Cathedral of St.-Jean** (6). Begun in the 12th century, it displays a mixture of styles ranging from Romanesque to Flamboyant Gothic. The interior is noted for its 13th-century stained-glass in the choir, apse, and rose windows of the transepts. In the north transept there is an interesting 14th-century **astronomical clock** that puts on a show at noon, 2, 3, and 4 p.m. Don't miss the **Chapel of the Bourbons** on the north side of the nave. The **Treasury**, to the right of the entrance, exhibits rare pieces of religious art. *Cathedral open 7:30–noon and 2–7:30 p.m., closing at 5 on weekends and holidays.*

Adjacent to the cathedral, on its north side, is an outdoor archaeological garden with excavations of earlier churches. Stroll down Rue St.-Jean and turn left to the:

HÔTEL DE GADAGNE (7), ☎ 04-7842-0361. *Open Wed.–Mon., 10:45–6, remaining open until 8:30 on Fri. Adults 25FF, students 15FF.*

This magnificent l6th-century Renaissance mansion now houses both the **Musée Historique de Lyon** and the intriguing ***Musée de la Marionnette.** Puppets have been a tradition of the city since the late 18th century when one Laurent Mourguet, an unemployed silk worker who lost his job after the Revolution made silk undemocratic, created a satirical marionette character named Guignol. The plays, larded with broad humor in the local dialect, are still very popular. Ask at the tourist office for details of perfor-

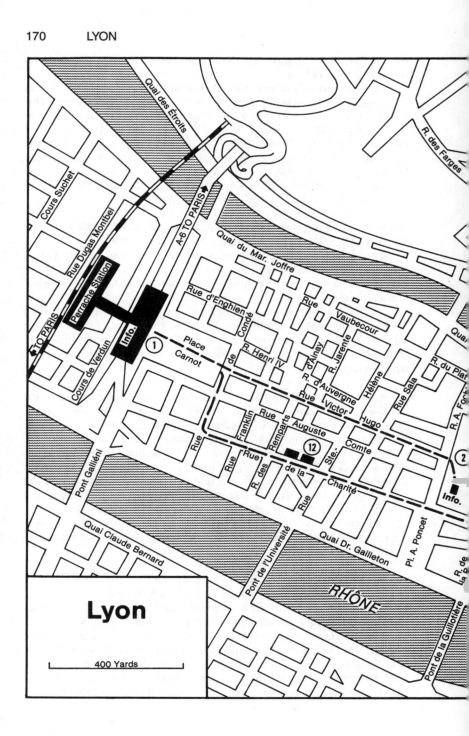

Lyon

400 Yards

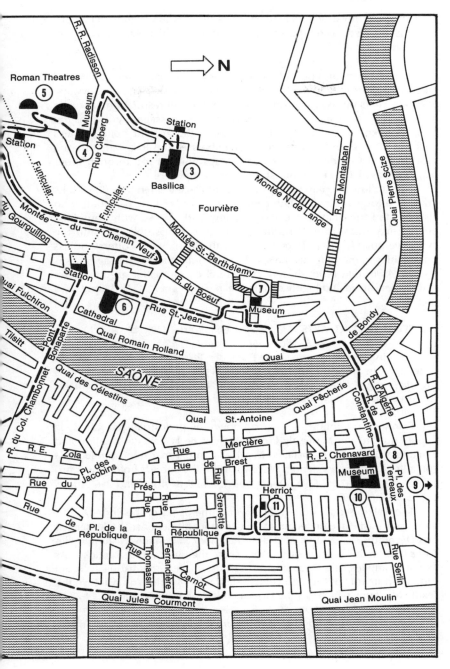

Roman Theatres

⑤

Station

Station

R.R. Radisson

Museum

Rue Cléberg

④

③

Basilica

Montée N. de Lange

R. de Montauban

Quai Pierre Scize

Fourvière

Montée du Gourguillon

Funicular

Montée du Chemin Neuf

Funicular

Montée St-Barthélemy

Station

ual Fulchiron

Cathedral

⑥

R. du Boeuf

Rue St. Jean

①

Museum

de Bondy

Quai Romain Rolland

Tilsitt

Pont Bonaparte

R. du Col. Chambonnet

Quai des Célestins

SAÔNE

Quai

Quai Pêcherie

R. d'Algérie

R. de Constantine

Quai St.-Antoine

R. E.

Zola

Pl. des Jacobins

Rue du

Prés.

Rue

Rue

de Brest

Mercière

Rue

R. P. Chenavard

⑧

Pl. des Terreaux

Rue

de

Pl. de la République

la République

Rue Thomassin

Ferrandière

Carnot

Grenette

Herriot

⑪

Museum

⑩

⑨

Rue Serlin

Quai Jules Courmont

Quai Jean Moulin

mances given in various theaters. Besides the classic Guignol characters, the museum also has puppets from all over the world, notably those from Cambodia.

While still in this colorful old area, known as **Vieux Lyon**, you should take the opportunity to explore its numerous tiny streets and alleyways. For many years this was a notorious slum, but recent restoration has made it fashionable once again. Some of its narrowest passages, known as *traboules*, make interior connections between the ancient buildings and adjacent streets, and were used by members of the Resistance during World War II to hide from the Nazis. Maps guiding you through these mazes are available at the tourist office and elsewhere.

Now follow the map across the river to **Place des Terreaux** (8) with its grandiose fountain by the 19th-century sculptor Frédéric Bartholdi, who also created the Statue of Liberty in New York. Those with boundless energy may want to head north up the Croix-Rousse hill and into the evocative quarter of **Les Traboules** (9, off the map), which offers endless possibilities to *trabouler,* as the sport of exploring the tiny passageways is known. As in Old Lyon, these architectural eccentricities are best seen with a specialized and highly detailed map. Don't get lost. And don't miss the:

*MUSEUM OF FINE ARTS *(Musée des Beaux-Arts)* (10), ☎ 04-7210-1740. *Open Wed.–Sun., 10:30–6. Adults 25FF, students 15FF.*

The Fine Arts Museum, facing Place des Terreaux, has one of the best collections in France. Originally a Benedictine nunnery, the building is slightly seedy, although not without charm. Its many rooms contain major works covering just about the entire scope of Western art.

Continue on, following the map down the pedestrianized Rue de la République, to the **Musée de l'Imprimerie et de la Banque** (Printing and Banking Museum) (11), installed in a 15th-century mansion on Rue de la Poulaillerie. This is a splendid place to visit if the subject holds any interest to you. ☎ 04-7837-6598. *Open Wed.–Sun., 9:30–noon and 2–6. Adults 25FF, students 15FF.*

The walking route now swings over to the banks of the Rhône, then leads past Place Bellecour (2) to two more attractions. The **Musée des Arts-Décoratifs** (12) and its next-door neighbor, the **Musée Historique des Tissus** (Historical Museum of Textiles), share the same admission ticket. As its name implies, the Decorative Arts Museum features exquisite room settings, primarily of the 18th century. If you like fabrics you will love the Textile Museum, which has the largest collection in the world. ☎ 04-7837-1505. *Both open Tues.–Sun., 10–5:30, closed holidays. The Decorative Arts Museum closes from noon to 2. Combined admission: Adults 28FF, students 15FF.*

From here it is only a short walk back to Perrache Station.

Section VI

DAYTRIPS FROM PARIS
THE LOIRE VALLEY

F ew regions of France are as quietly seductive as the Loire Valley. This huge area, whose prime attractions begin about one hundred miles southwest of Paris and extend westward for another hundred, is among the most satisfying of tourist destinations in the country. Drained by a broad, lazy river, the "Garden of France" offers a fine climate, bucolic scenery, unusual wines, a deep sense of history and, best of all, many of the very finest châteaux in the land. Some of these are massive fortifications dating from the Middle Ages, when the Loire Valley was a frequent battleground in the struggles between the French and the English. Others were built in more peaceful times and reflect the unparalleled luxury to which the Renaissance nobility had become accustomed.

Distance and the relative seclusion of many of its attractions do combine to make daytrips from Paris to this enchanting region somewhat of a problem. Fortunately, there are some notable exceptions: Angers, Tours, Amboise, and Blois not only sit squarely on major rail lines and highways, but they also rate high among the most fascinating destinations in the area.

Also included in this section is that quintessential French provincial town, Bourges. Although it lies a bit outside the region itself, it shares many of its characteristics and is served by the same rail line.

Trip 25

Angers

Situated on the Maine River, just north of the Loire, the ancient capital of Anjou attracts visitors with its mighty fortress—one of the most impressive feudal structures in France—and its fine cathedral. Angers is a fairly large and quite animated city that has managed to preserve much of its illustrious past despite heavy wartime damage.

Known to the Romans as *Juliomagus* and later conquered by the Normans, Angers had its true time of glory in the Middle Ages. Between the 10th and 12th centuries its counts had acquired power exceeding that of even the kings of France. One of these Angevin rulers, Henri Plantagenet, became Henry II of England in 1154 and fathered both Richard the Lionhearted and bad King John—a story of intrigue that makes for fascinating reading. Henry's wife, Eleanor of Aquitaine, had previously been married to Louis VII of France, thus making her queen of both countries at different times. Another local ruler, born in Angers early in the 15th century, was Good King René, duke of Anjou, count of Provence and king of Sicily. This remarkable man, among the most brilliant thinkers of his age, was largely responsible for the artistic tradition of Angers that continues to this day.

GETTING THERE:

Trains leave Montparnasse Station in Paris several times in the morning for Angers' St.-Laud Station. TGV Trains (reservations needed) make the run in about 80 minutes; regular trains (possible change at Le Mans) take 3 hours. Return service runs until mid-evening. This is a good excursion for railpass holders.

By car, Angers is 180 miles southwest of Paris. Take the A-10 and A-17 Autoroutes all the way.

PRACTICALITIES:

The castle is open every day except for a few major holidays, but the museums are closed on Mondays and some holidays. The local **Tourist Information Office**, ☎ 02-4123-5111, Internet: www.ville-angers.fr, is on Promenade du Bout du Monde opposite the castle.

FOOD AND DRINK:

Angers has an excellent selection of restaurants and cafés. Some good choices along or near the suggested walking route are:

Le Toussaint (Place Kennedy, near the tourist office and château) Local cuisine, especially seafood, in a refined atmosphere. Dress well and reserve, ☎ 02-4187-4620. X: Sun. eve., Mon. $$ and $$$

Lucullus (5 Rue Hoche, between the train station and château) Good value at lunch. ☎ 02-4187-0044. X: Sun. in summer, Mon. $$

Plantagenêts (in the Hôtel France, 8 Place de la Gare, opposite the train station) Good food in a convenient location. ☎ 02-4188-4942. X: Sat. lunch, Sun. eve. $ and $$

La Treille (12 Rue Montault, a block northeast of the cathedral) An unpretentious place for traditional dishes. ☎ 02- 4188-4551. X: Sun. $

La Soufflerie (8 Place du Pilori, 2 blocks northeast of the Hôtel-Pincé) All manner of soufflés. ☎ 02-4187-4532. X: Sun., Mon. $

SUGGESTED TOUR:

Numbers in parentheses correspond to numbers on the map. Leave the **Angers St.-Laud Train Station** (I) and head straight for the:

*CASTLE OF ANGERS *(Le Château d'Angers)* (2), ☎ 02-4187-4347. *Open June to mid-Sept., daily 9:30–7; rest of year daily 10 to 5 or 6. Closed major holidays. Adults 35FF, students 23FF.*

The forbidding bastion facing you was built in the 13th century by Louis IX, known to history as Saint Louis for his famous sense of moral authority. Previous fortresses have existed on the same site since 851; a 12th-century structure having been used by the Plantagenets. The thick curtain wall, over a half-mile in circumference, links 17 massive towers along a deep dry moat in which deer now roam.

With a design based on the Crusaders' castles in the Holy Land, this citadel was among the most powerful in the kingdom, and was never successfully taken by assault. It came close to being destroyed in the 16th-century Wars of Religion, however, not by attack but by an order from Henri III to dismantle the fortress before it could fall into enemy hands. Fortunately, the demolition went very slowly and before much damage was done peace had returned and the king was dead.

Cross the drawbridge and enter the castle grounds. The most famous sight here, well worth the journey in itself, is the monumental ***Apocalypse Tapestry**, housed in a specially built structure. This incomparable 14th-century series of wall hangings present a shattering representation of the text of Saint John in the Book of Revelations. Be sure to allow enough time to carefully study the 70 pieces that survived out of the original 90. An explanation in English will be loaned to you at the door, or you can purchase an illustrated booklet.

More outstanding medieval tapestries are displayed in the **Logis Royal** which, together with the superb **Chapel**, can be seen on guided tours included in the castle admission. The Logis du Gouverneur, beyond the gardens, also exhibits some of this art. A climb to the top of the highest

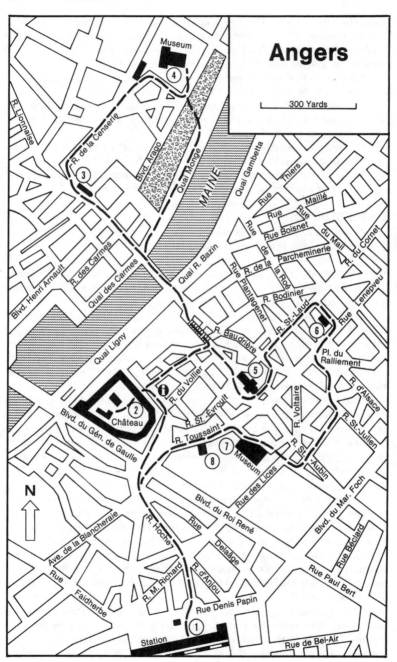

Angers

300 Yards

tower, facing the river, reveals a magnificent panorama of the city. From here it is easy to understand why the fortress was so impregnable. A walk around the ramparts and through the gardens will complete your visit.

Now follow the map across the river and into the colorful old quarter called La Doutre, noted for its ancient half-timbered houses. Turn right at the 12th-century **Church of La Trinité** (3) and continue on to the former **Hospital of St.-Jean** (4). Take a look at the elaborate 12th-century granary, whose cellars have some old wine presses, then enter the ancient hospital. Founded in 1175 by Henry II of England as part of his penance for the murder of Thomas à Becket, it cared for the sick until 1865. The very lovely interior now houses the **Jean Lurçat Museum**, displaying a huge modern ten-piece tapestry completed by Lurçat in 1966. You can also see the old dispensary, a medieval chapel, and the delightful 12th-century cloister. ☎ *02-4124-1845. Open mid-June to mid-Sept., daily 9–6:30; rest of year, Tues.–Sun. 10–noon and 2–6. Adults 20FF, under 16 free.*

The route now leads back across the river to the **Cathedral of St.-Maurice** (5). Dating from the 12th and 13th centuries, its unusual design is embellished with a peculiar central tower. Biblical figures decorate the splendid doorway, which opens into a very wide nave illuminated by stained-glass windows from the 12th century to modern times. The treasury, to the left as you enter, has some interesting artifacts including a Roman bathtub used as a baptismal font.

Continue on to the **Hôtel-Pincé** (6), a Renaissance mansion now used as a museum. The collections inside are rather eclectic, but focus mainly on the Ancient World as well as the Orient, especially on Japanese Ukiyo-é. *Open Tues.–Sun., 10–noon and 2–6, with slightly longer hours from June through Aug. Admission charged.*

One other major attraction remains before returning to the train station. This is the **Fine Arts Museum** *(Musée des Beaux-Arts)* in the **Logis Barrault** (7), an impressive 15th-century palace. Medieval and Renaissance items are displayed along with a fine collection of paintings by such artists as Boucher, Tiepolo, Fragonard, Davis, Géricault, Ingres, and Millet. Just around the corner is the outstanding **David d'Angers Gallery** (8), where heroic works by the locally-born 19th-century sculptor are exhibited in a 13th-century church. ☎ *02-4187-2103. Both attractions open mid-June to mid-Sept., daily 9–6:30; rest of year Tues.–Sun., 10–noon and 2–6. Adults 10FF, under 16 free.*

Tours

Tours, the major city of the Loire region, appears at first glance to be nothing but an endless sprawl of modern industries; certainly prosperous but hardly attractive to tourists. In its ancient heart, however, lurk enough medieval and Renaissance treasures to make this a highly worthwhile daytrip from Paris. A visit here is further enhanced by the presence of a large student population, breathing life into the picturesque alleyways of the Old Town district. All of this activity makes Tours one of the better spots in France to just relax at outdoor cafés and enjoy the passing parade.

GETTING THERE:

TGV trains (reservations required) depart Montparnasse Station in Paris frequently for the 70-minute ride to Tours. Regular trains take about 2.5 hours for the trip, and leave from Austerlitz Station in Paris. In either case it may be necessary to change trains at St.-Pierre-des-Corps on the outskirts of Tours. Return service runs until late evening.

By car, Tours is 145 miles southwest of Paris via the A-10 Autoroute, going by way of Orléans.

PRACTICALITIES:

Avoid coming to Tours on a Tuesday or major holiday, when many of its attractions are closed. The local **Tourist Information Office,** ☎ 02-4770-3737, Internet: www.tourism-touraine.com, is across from the train station on Rue Bernard Palissy.

FOOD AND DRINK:

Some good choices in the area covered by the walking tour are:

Barrier (101 Av. de la Tranchée, just across the Pont Wilson bridge) Classic French and Touraine cuisine from a renowned chef. Proper dress expected, for reservations ☎ 02-4754-2039. X: Sun. eve. $$$

Les Tuffeaux (19 Rue Lavoisier, across from the Château) A restful place for contemporary cuisine. ☎ 02-4747-1989. X: Sun., Mon. lunch. $$

L'Atelier Gourmand (37 Rue Étienne-Marcel, 2 blocks west of the Musée du Gemmail) A good value, indoors or out. ☎ 02-4738- 5987. $

Flunch (14 Pl. Jean-Jaurès, 3 blocks west of the station) A comfortable chain cafeteria with decent food. ☎ 02-4764-5670. $

Be sure to try the local Loire wines, especially the Vouvray!

SUGGESTED TOUR:

Numbers in parentheses correspond to numbers on the map. Leave the **train station** *(Gare)* (1) and follow the map past the tourist office and the Préfecture, housed in an 18th-century convent, to the:

*MUSÉE DES BEAUX-ARTS (Fine Arts Museum) (2), ☎ 02-4705-6873. *Open Wed.–Mon., 9–12:45 and 2–6. Closed major holidays. Adults 30FF, seniors and students 15FF.*

Tours' excellent art museum occupies the former Archbishop's Palace, which dates from the 17th and 18th centuries and incorporates vestiges of the Gallo-Roman town wall. The collections displayed in its elegant rooms were begun around 1800 with pieces seized during the French Revolution. Today they range all the way from the Italian Primitives to the most contemporary Moderns, including such masterpieces as Mantegna's *Christ in the Garden of Olives* and *The Resurrection*, Ruben's *Madonna and Child*, and Rembrandt's *Flight into Egypt*. The museum's courtyard and gardens are quite nice, shaded by a gigantic cedar tree planted in 1804.

Next to the museum stands the **Cathedral of St.-Gatien** (3), built between 1220 and 1547 in a variety of styles tracing the entire evolution of the French Gothic form. Its **flying buttresses** are particularly dramatic, especially when seen from the rear. Inside, the cathedral is most noted for its glorious 13th-century **stained-glass windows** in the chancel; and for the tomb of Charles VIII's infant children, guarded by small angels, just off the south transept. Try to see the adjoining **cloisters**, known as the Psalette, which has an elegant Renaissance staircase and offers close-up views of the buttresses. *The cathedral is usually closed between noon and 2 p.m. Cloister tours 15FF.*

One block to the north, facing the Loire River, are the scanty remains of the great **Château** (4) built in 1160 by Henry II of England. Part of the original structure, the **Tour de Guise,** has been restored and now houses an interesting wax museum called the **Historial de Touraine,** in which some 165 figures in 31 settings act out the history of the region from the 4th century until modern times. ☎ *02-4761-0295. Open daily 9–7. Adults 35FF, students 24FF.* There is also a **tropical aquarium** with a separate admission.

Follow the map down Rue Colbert, ambling through the **Beaune-Semblançay Garden** (5) with its nicely sculpted 16th-century fountain and the remains of a Renaissance mansion.

The nearby **Église St.-Julien** dates from the 13th century and has a belfry porch from the 11th, part of an abbey founded in the early 6th century by Clovis, king of the Franks. The ancient cellars of the complex now house the **Musée des Vins de Touraine** (6), a museum devoted to the local wines and their enjoyment. ☎ *02-4761-0793. Open Wed.–Mon., 9–noon and 2–6. Adults 15FF, seniors and students 10FF.*

Almost adjacent to it is the **Musée du Compagnonnage** (Craft Guilds

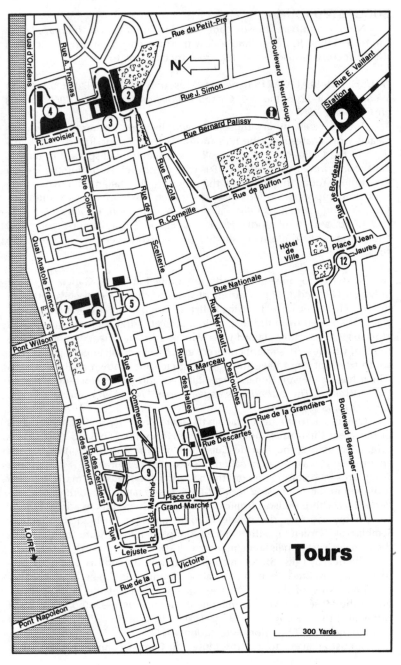

Tours

300 Yards

Museum) (7), located upstairs in a former monks' dormitory above a chapter house. The fascinating museum displays the masterpieces submitted by candidates for membership in craft guilds, many of which are bizarre in concept but of extraordinary quality. ☎ *02-4761-0793. Open daily in summer, 9–6:30; rest of year Wed.–Mon., 9–noon and 2–5 or 6. Adults 25FF, seniors and students 15FF.* From here you might want to stroll out on the Pont Wilson bridge for a good view of the Loire River, then return.

Continue down Rue du Commerce to the 16th-century **Hôtel Gouin** (8), a Renaissance mansion of exceptional beauty. Today it is home to an archaeological museum with collections of artifacts from the Gallo-Roman, medieval, and Renaissance periods. ☎ *02-4766-2232. Open July and Aug., daily 11–12:30 and 1:30–7; rest of year daily, 10–12:30 and 2–6:30, closing at 5:30 in winter and closed on Wed. in Oct. and Nov. Adults 20FF, seniors 15FF, students and children 12FF.*

You are now entering ***Vieux Tours** (Old Tours), a highly restored and very picturesque neighborhood of gabled façades and half-timbered houses connected by narrow pedestrian alleyways. Its most delightful square is **Place Plumereau** (9), lined with 15th-century houses and a multitude of outdoor cafés; the perfect spot for a break in your walk. When you feel like moving on, head north through a vaulted passageway to **Place St.-Pierre-le-Puellier** with its open Gallo-Roman excavations.

Wander over to the **Musée du Gemmail** (10) on Rue des Moûrier. Installed in a 19th-century mansion, this museum is devoted to the highly unusual (and very French) art of making three-dimensional backlit creations from broken fragments of colored glass. ☎ *02-4761-0119. Open April to mid-Nov., Tues.–Sun., 10–noon and 2–6:30; rest of year on weekends 10–noon and 2–6:30. Adults 30FF, students 20FF, children 10FF.*

Continue on the very attractive Rue Briçonnet and follow the map around, passing many old houses, artists' studios, and craft workshops, until you wind up at **Place de Châteauneuf** (11). This was the site of the once-great **Basilique St.-Martin**, built in the 11th century over the tomb of the 4th-century saint. For centuries this was a stop on the pilgrims' route to Spain, but it was sacked by the Huguenots in 1562 and fell to ruin during the Revolution. All that remains today is the **Tour de l'Horloge** on the Rues des Halles and the **Tour Charlemagne** on Rue de Châteauneuf.

Head south on Rue Descartes and Rue de la Grandière, then turn left on Boulevard Béranger to **Place Jean Juarès** (12). Facing the splendid **Hôtel de Ville** (Town Hall) of 1905, this shady square is lined with inviting sidewalk cafés, where you can once again just sit down and enjoy the fine old town. The best way to return to the train station is via Rue de Bordeaux.

Amboise

Rising majestically above the banks of the Loire, the magnificent château of Amboise totally dominates its attractive little town. A castle has stood on this rocky spur, guarding the strategic bridgehead since Gallo-Roman times, when it was known as *Ambacia*. The present structure, however, is a product of the 15th century and incorporates some of the earliest examples of Renaissance architecture in France. Charles VIII, who was born and raised at Amboise, had invaded Italy in 1494. While there, he became captivated by the new Italian style and brought some of its craftsmen back with him to finish off his favorite château.

The real effect of the Renaissance came with the succession to the throne of François I in 1515. This outstanding king also spent his childhood at Amboise and continued residence there during the first years of his reign. It was he who invited Leonardo da Vinci to France, installing him in a luxurious home just blocks from the château, where the great artist and inventor spent the last years of his life.

One of the most notorious carnages in French history occurred at Amboise in 1560 when Protestant militants plotted to capture the young king, François II, to demand their religious freedom. The coup was defeated and all involved were hideously executed, with corpses decorating the château and town for weeks afterward. After that, Amboise was rarely used except as a prison until the 19th century, when Louis-Philippe, the "Citizen King," lived there on occasion.

Amboise makes a good alternative base for visits to the famous châteaux of the Loire that lie beyond daytrip range of Paris. Ask at the tourist office about bus trips to these.

GETTING THERE:

Trains leave Austerlitz Station in Paris in the morning for Amboise, a trip of under 2.5 hours. Be careful to get on the correct car as some trains split en route. Return service operates until early evening. A change at Orléans or Blois might be necessary.

By car, take the A-1O Autoroute to Blois, then the D-751 or N-152 into Amboise, which is 137 miles southwest of Paris.

PRACTICALITIES:

Amboise may be visited at any time. The Postal Museum is closed on

Mondays and some holidays. The local **Tourist Information Office**, ☎ 02-4757-0928, Internet: www.amboise-valdeloire.com, is on the Quai du Général-de-Gaulle, near the bridge. Amboise has a population of about 11,000 and is in the Loire region.

FOOD AND DRINK:

Being a popular tourist center, the town has quite a few restaurants and cafés. Some of the better choices are:

La Manoir Saint-Thomas (Place Richelieu, 3 blocks south of the château) Superb local specialties in a Renaissance mansion with a garden. Proper dress expected, reserve by ☎ 02-4757-2252. X: Sun. eve., Mon. in off-season, Mon. and Tues. lunch in season, mid-Jan. to mid-March. $$$

Restaurant de la Poste (5 Rue d'Orange, a block north of the Postal Museum) Traditional cuisine at fair prices. ☎ 02-4723- 1616. X: Tues. in off-season. $ and $$

La Brèche (26 Rue Jules Ferry, 2 blocks south of the train station) A small inn with good meals, garden dining in season. ☎ 02-4757-0079. X: Sun. eve. and Mon. in off-season. $

SUGGESTED TOUR:

Numbers in parentheses correspond to numbers on the map. Leave the **train station** (1) and follow the map across the Loire to the:

*CHÂTEAU D'AMBOISE (2), ☎ 02-4757-0098. *Open Jan.–March, daily 9–noon and 2–5; April–June, daily 9–6:30; July–Aug., daily 9–7:30; Sept.–Oct., daily 9–6; Nov.–Dec., daily 9–noon and 2–5. Closed Christmas and New Year's Day. Adults 37FF, students 30FF, children 7–14 18FF.*

Amboise's magnificent castle is perched dramatically above the river and town, reached by a long ramp. During its time of glory the château was considerably larger than it is today, much of it having been demolished in the early 19th century for lack of maintenance funds. Some of the best parts, however, remained intact and have been beautifully restored to the delight of today's visitors.

Begin with the exquisite ***Chapel of St.-Hubert**, dedicated to the patron saint of huntsmen. Begun in 1491, shortly before Charles VIII acquired his passion for the Renaissance, it is a triumph of the Flamboyant Gothic style. What are thought to be the bones of Leonardo da Vinci are buried here, under a slab in the north transept.

Following this, enter the **Logis du Roi** (King's Apartments), consisting of two wings, one Gothic and the other Renaissance. These are the only major buildings of any size left at the castle. Their interiors are splendidly decorated in a variety of period styles, ranging from the 15th through the 19th centuries. From the fascinating **Minimes Tower** with its spiral equestrian ramp there is a stunning view up and down the Loire Valley. Don't miss taking a stroll through the ***gardens** behind the château before exiting.

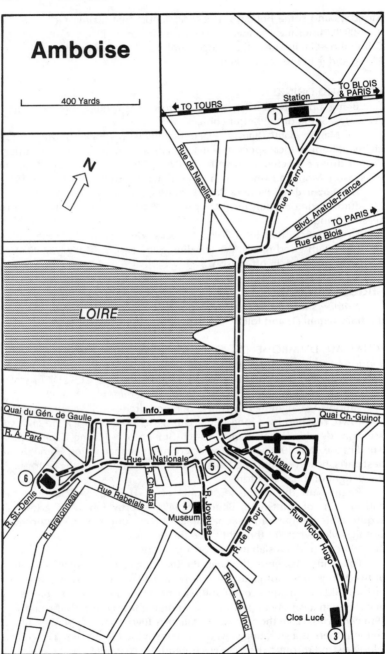

Amboise

400 Yards

N

TO TOURS   Station   TO BLOIS & PARIS

①

Rue de Nazelles

Rue J. Ferry

Blvd. Anatole-France

TO PARIS

Rue de Blois

LOIRE

Quai du Gén. de Gaulle   Info.   Quai Ch.-Guinot

R. A. Paré

Rue   Nationale

Château   ②

R. Chaptal

⑤

R. St-Denis

⑥

R. Bretonneau

Rue Rabelais

④
Museum

R. Joveuse

R. de la Tour

Rue Victor Hugo

Rue L. de Vinci

Clos Lucé

③

A ten-minute walk along Rue Victor-Hugo leads to **Clos Lucé** (3). This was the home of Leonardo da Vinci, that visionary genius of the Renaissance, from 1516 until his death three years later. Prior to that it was the residence of Anne of Brittany, the wife of King Charles VIII. The manor house has marvelous period furnishings, worth a visit in themselves, but the main interest lies in the many ***models of Leonardo's inventions**, built by IBM from his original plans. ☎ *02-4757-6288. Open daily; Jan., 10–5; Feb.–March, 9–6; April–June 9–7; July–Aug., 9–8; Sept.–mid-Nov., 9–7; mid-Nov.–Dec. 9–6. Adults 38FF, students 28FF, children 6–15 18FF.*

Return along Rue Victor-Hugo and follow the map to the **Postal Museum** (4). Located in an elegant 16th-century mansion, the museum features an intriguing exhibition of the history of transportation from horse-drawn coaches to modern airlines. There are also, of course, many rare stamps to be seen, along with old manuscripts and engravings. ☎ *02-4723-1980. Open daily except Mondays and some holidays: Jan.–March, 10–noon and 2–5:30; April–Sept., 9:30–noon and 2–6:30; Oct.–Dec., 10–noon and 2–5:30. Adults 20FF, students and children 10FF.*

Continue on to the 15th-century **Beffroi** (Clock Tower) (5), a picturesque structure built by Charles VIII on earlier foundations. Now follow the pedestrians-only Rue Nationale to the **Église St.-Denis** (6). This 12th-century example of the Romanesque style was built on the site of a Roman temple. Step inside for a look at some exceptional works of art, including a fine Pietà and an astonishingly realistic sculpture of a drowned woman.

Returning via Quai du Général-de-Gaulle you will pass an outstanding modern fountain designed by Max Ernst, the tourist office, the 15th-century Église St.-Florentin, and the 16th-century **Hôtel de Ville** (Town Hall). The latter has a small museum of local history. ☎ *02-4723-4723. Open July and Aug., 2–6.*

Trip 28

*Blois

While certainly not the loveliest château of the Loire, Blois may well prove to be the most interesting. Often called the "Versailles of the Renaissance" and for a crucial time virtually the capital of France—it exudes a deep sense of history exceeding even that of Angers or Amboise.

Although a castle had stood there since feudal times, it was not until the end of the 15th century that Blois became a royal residence. The first king to move in was Louis XII, in 1498, who promptly added a wing in the Late Gothic style. Another large section, in the new Renaissance style, was built by his successor François I. This flamboyant king later went on to greater architectural triumphs, notably the châteaux of Fontainebleau and Chambord, but he continued to use Blois as a waystop in an endless pursuit of courtly pleasure. Royalty remained in residence there until the Valois line died out in 1589 with the assassination of the miserable Henri III.

After that, the château was used by Louis XIII as a place to get rid of troublesome members of his family. The first to go was his mother, Marie de Medici, who was banished to Blois in 1617 but later managed to escape. He then gave it to his scheming brother, Gaston d'Orléans, to keep him out of political mischief. As did the previous owners, Gaston added a wing, thus completing the château you see today.

The town of Blois has several other nice attractions of its own, including a picturesque old quarter near the river. The name, incidentally, is pronounced "Blwah." It also makes a convenient overnight base for visits to those splendid châteaux that unfortunately lie beyond reasonable daytrip range of Paris, most notably Chambord and Chenonceau. You can ask at the tourist office about bus excursions to these, or rent a car and see them on your own.

GETTING THERE:

Trains for Blois depart Austerlitz Station in Paris several times in the morning. The run takes a bit over two hours, with return service until early evening. Be sure to get on the right car as some trains split en route.

By car, Blois is 112 miles southwest of Paris via the A-10 Autoroute.

PRACTICALITIES:

The Château is open every day, but is less crowded during the week.

Good weather will make this trip much more enjoyable. The local **tourist office**, ☎ 02-5490-4141, Internet: www.chambordcountry.com, is located at 3 Avenue Jean-Laigret, between the train station and the château.

FOOD AND DRINK:

There are quite a few restaurants and cafés along the walking route, of which some choices are:

L'Orangerie du Château (1 Ave. Jean-Laigret, near Pl. Victor-Hugo) Contemporary classic cuisine, elegant setting, terrace in summer. ☎ 02-5478-0536. X: Sun. eve., Wed. except holidays. $$ and $$$

Rendez-vous des Pêcheurs (27 Rue du Foix, 2 blocks southwest of Church of St.-Nicolas) Renowned for its seafood. Reserve, ☎ 02-5474-6748. X: Sun., Mon. lunch, Aug. $$ and $$$

Bouchon Lyonnais (25 Rue Violettes, behind Place Louis XII) Traditional French and Lyonnais cuisine at fair prices. ☎ 02- 5474-1287. X: Sun., Mon. $$

Le Maïdi (42 Rue St.-Lubin, a block southeast of the château) Moroccan cuisine, vegetarian or with meat. ☎ 02-5474- 3858. X: Thurs. off-season. $

SUGGESTED TOUR:

Numbers in parentheses correspond to numbers on the map.

Leave the **train station** (1) and follow Avenue Jean-Laigret past the tourist office to **Place Victor Hugo** (2). Before climbing the ramp to the château it would be a good idea to check your watch and decide whether you have enough time—well over an hour—to enjoy it properly before lunch, or whether to see some other sights and eat first. The walking route is quite short so you can always return to the château later.

*CHÂTEAU DE BLOIS (3), ☎ 02-5474-1606. *Open mid-March to mid-Oct., daily 9–6:30, closing at 8 in July and Aug.; rest of year, daily 9–noon and 2–5. Adults 35FF, students 25FF.*

The Château of Blois, overlooking the town and the Loire River, is a dramatic study in the evolution of French architecture from the Middle Ages to the Neo-Classical period. After the Valois line of kings died out in the late 16th century it ceased to be a royal residence and was used during Napoleon's time as an army barracks. What you see today is the result of a highly romanticized mid-19th-century restoration, perhaps more theatrical than accurate, but certainly fun to visit.

Pass through the doorway under the equestrian statue of Louis XII and enter the château. You are now in the **Louis XII wing**, built between 1498 and 1503. Purchase your ticket and decide whether to take a guided tour or just wander around on your own, which is entirely practical as there are printed explanations of everything in English.

Stepping into the inner courtyard you will see the famous open staircase of the ***François I wing**, dating from 1515–24. Climb this to the first

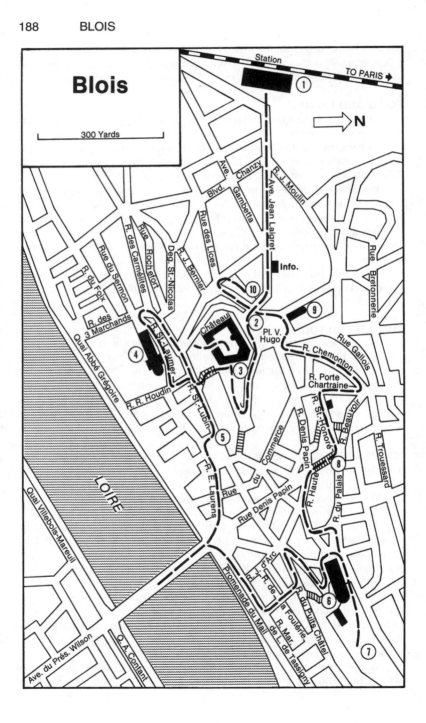

floor and go in. The route through this wing is well laid out, taking you eventually to the second floor, where a notorious assassination took place in 1588. Henri III, a weak and effeminate king, was able to remain in office only as long as it suited a powerful duke, Henri de Guise, Lieutenant-General of the kingdom and leader of the extremist Catholics. Guise threatened Henri's rule by forcing a meeting of the States-General at the château. While there, the king summoned him to a private meeting, on the way to which he was brutally murdered by 20 of the king's devoted minions. He died at the foot of the royal bed while the cowering Henri looked on through a peephole. The next day the king had the duke's brother, Cardinal de Lorraine, killed as well. But justice was to come. Within days, the king's scheming mother, Catherine de Medici, was dead and Henri III himself fell to an assassin's knife eight months later. He was the last of the Valois line.

The 13th-century **Salle des États**, the oldest surviving part of the château, joins the François I and Louis XII wings together. Take a look inside, then visit the adjacent archaeological museum and the **Fine Arts Museum** in the Louis XII wing.

At the far end of the courtyard stands the 17th-century **Gaston d'Orléans wing**, a Neo-Classical structure designed by François Mansart. Other interesting buildings are the **Charles d'Orléans Gallery** and the **Chapel of St.-Calais**, both dating from the late 15th century. Amble over to the 13th-century **Tour de Foix**, part of the old feudal walls, which offers a splendid panorama of the town.

Leave the château and follow the map down to the lovely **Church of St.-Nicolas** (4), whose interior merits a visit. Built in the 12th century as part of an abbey that was destroyed during the 16th-century Wars of Religion, it is noted for its harmonious blend of Romanesque and Gothic elements.

Continue on to **Place Louis XII** (5), with its Flamboyant Gothic fountain, passing some picturesque old houses on Rue St.-Lubin along the way. Now cut down to the river and stroll out on the elegant 18th-century bridge for a gorgeous view of the town and its château.

Return to the quay and follow the map through a delightful part of old Blois. Rue du Puits-Châtel has two particularly attractive houses at numbers 7 and 5, both dating from the time of Louis XII. When you come to Place Ave-Maria look to your left down Rue Fontaine des Élus, where the noteworthy Hôtel de Jassaud stands at number 5. Now turn hard right and climb Rue des Papegaults. Passing another 16th-century house, the Hôtel de Belot at number 10, this charming street leads to the Petits-Degrés-St.-Louis, which takes you uphill to Place St.-Louis.

The **Cathedral of St.-Louis** (6), facing you, was largely rebuilt in the 17th century. Although the church itself is not particularly outstanding, its 10th-century **Crypt of St.-Solenne** certainly is. Entry to this is from the side of the altar.

Continue around to the rear of the Town Hall, reached via a gate next to the cathedral. The **park** (7) beyond this commands an excellent vantage point for views of the Loire Valley.

Now thread your way through a maze of narrow streets lined with medieval and Renaissance houses, many of which are half-timbered. Follow the map up the Denis Papin stairs to the **Statue of Denis Papin** (8), a local lad of the 17th century who discovered many of the mysteries of steam power. He is shown holding his greatest invention, an early pressure cooker.

Turn left on Rue St.-Honoré past the Hôtel d'Alluye, a splendid Renaissance mansion whose double-galleried courtyard can be seen during office hours. Continue on Rue Porte-Chartraine and return on Rue Chemonton, noting the fine Hôtel de Guise at number 8. This returns you to Place Victor Hugo (2).

If you have a bit more time you may be interested in visiting the 17th-century **Church of St.-Vincent-de-Paul** (9) and, especially, the beautiful **Jardin du Roi** (10), all that remains of the château gardens that once extended all the way to the train station. From here you will get a magnificent close-up view of the château and a last glimpse of Blois before returning to Paris.

Bourges

Located in the very heartland of France, Bourges is an ancient and colorful town whose winding, cobbled streets contain some of the very best medieval architecture anywhere. Although relatively unknown to foreign tourists, it makes an excellent daytrip destination for seasoned travelers looking for a delightful new experience.

Originally populated by Gauls, Bourges fell to Caesar's legions in 52 BC and became the Roman town of *Avaricum*. Since AD 250 it was ruled by archbishops. Later, as the capital of Aquitaine, it passed into the hands of a succession of counts who in 1101 sold it to King Philip I of France. During the 14th century, Jean, duke of Berry and son of King John the Good, made Bourges the seat of his duchy. For a while the town became a flourishing center of the arts, a role enhanced by the immensely wealthy Jacques Coeur, whose palace there is probably the best example of a medieval town mansion to be found in France.

During the Hundred Years War, Charles VII, cynically referred to by the English as the "King of Bourges," sat in that beleaguered city and slowly gathered the strength, aided by Joan of Arc, which enabled him to drive the English out. His son, Louis XI, born in Bourges, was a brilliant schemer who overcame the feudal system and began development of the modern state. He also founded a university there that became a hotbed of the Reformation, thus plunging Bourges into the Wars of Religion, a catastrophe from which it never recovered.

In the ensuing centuries, Bourges fell into obscurity, far too poor to rebuild its narrow streets and ancient façades. Not until modern times did its economy revive, with industry locating outside the town proper. This newly found prosperity in the setting of a basically unchanged medieval town makes Bourges a fascinating place to visit.

GETTING THERE:

Trains leave Austerlitz Station in Paris several times in the morning for Bourges. Some of these may require a change at Vierzon. Be careful to board the correct car as some trains split en route. The fastest direct run takes a bit under two hours. Return service operates until early evening.

By car, take the A-10 Autoroute to Orléans, then the A-71 to Bourges, which lies 147 miles south of Paris.

PRACTICALITIES:

Avoid going to Bourges on a Tuesday or major holiday, when several of its best attractions are closed. The trip can be made in any season as the old part of town is quite small and most of your time will be spent indoors. The local **tourist office,** ☎ 02-4823-0260, Internet: www.ville-bourges.fr, is located on Rue Victor-Hugo, near the cathedral.

FOOD AND DRINK:

The cooking in this farmland region tends to be simple and whole-some. Some good restaurant choices are:

Abbaye St.Ambroix (in the Hôtel Bourbon, Blvd. de la République, opposite the Près-Fichaux Gardens) Gourmet dining amidst bits of a 16th-century abbey. ☎ 02-4870-8000. $$ and $$$

Jacques Coeur (3 Place Jacques-Coeur, across from the Jacques Coeur Palace) Traditional classic cuisine in the grand manner. ☎ 02-4870-1272. X: Sat., Sun. eve., Aug. $$ and $$$

D'Antan Sancerrois (50 Rue Bourbonnoux, 2 blocks north of the cathedral) Local cuisine of Berry. ☎ 02-4865-9626. X: Mon., Tues. lunch. $ and $$

SUGGESTED TOUR:

Numbers in parentheses correspond to numbers on the map.

Leave the **train station** (1) and follow the map to the **Church of Notre-Dame** (2), whose brooding atmosphere encompasses a wide variety of styles. Built in the early 15th century, it was badly damaged during the great fire of 1487 that consumed much of Bourges. Reconstruction began in 1520, with considerable later additions having been made.

Take a look down Rue Pelvoysin, which has some fine old houses, many of them half-timbered. The most noted of these is the **Maison de Pelvoysin** at number 17, built of stone in the 15th century. Continue on Rue Mirabeau and take the passageway through to Rue Branly, leading to the **Hôtel des Échevins** (3). This 15th-century guildhall features a marvelous octagonal stair tower of unusual design. It now houses the **Musée Estève**, featuring opulent modern works by the noted local 20th-century artist, Maurice Estève. ☎ *02-4824-2948. Open Wed.–Sat. and Mon., 10–noon and 2–6, Sun. 2–6. Free.*

The **Hôtel Lallemant** (4), just a few steps away on Rue Bourbonnoux, is an outstanding 15th-century mansion built for a wealthy cloth merchant. Heavily altered during the 17th century in the Renaissance style, it is now a museum of decorative art. Step inside to admire the richly decorated rooms, antique furniture and various objets d'art. ☎ *02-4857-8117. Open Wed.–Sat. and Mon., 10–noon and 2–6, Sun. 2–6. Free.*

Now follow the map past the Grange aux Dimes, a 13th-century tithe barn on Rue Molière, to the:

*CATHEDRAL OF ST.-ÉTIENNE (5). *Open 8 a.m.–9 p.m., closing at 6:30 or 7:30 in the off-season.*

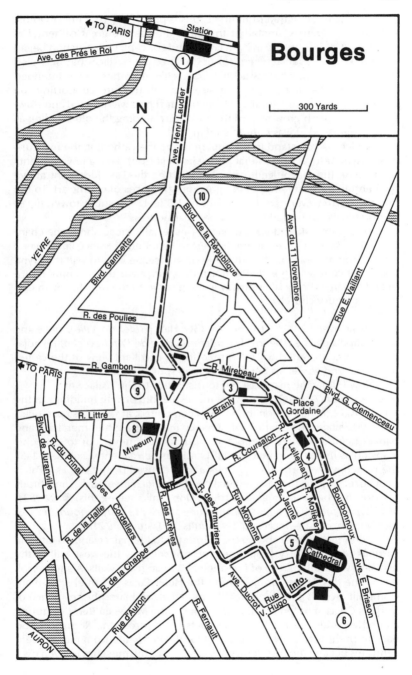

The major attraction of Bourges, this is one of the very finest Gothic structures in France. Erected at the same time as the great cathedral at Chartres, it differs greatly in both layout and concept. Construction began around 1192 as a replacement for a Romanesque basilica that occupied the site. The crypt, which was built first, is like no other. Never intended to house tombs or relics, it is basically a substructure supporting the cathedral over uneven ground. Above this the choir was erected and slowly the new church grew toward the west, surrounding the old building as work progressed. It was consecrated in 1324.

Notice, as you stand in the square facing the cathedral, the five curiously asymmetrical portals that pierce its west front. Take a few moments to examine the magnificent **carvings** depicting the Last Judgment above the central doorway—one of the great masterpieces of Gothic art. To the left, the north tower rises to a height of 213 feet. The south tower, never completed, is supported by a very peculiar buttress.

Inside, the ***stained-glass windows**—especially those above the chancel at the east end—are among the best to be found in France and cover a period from the early Gothic to the Renaissance. Be sure to visit the **crypt**, the entrance to which is by the north doorway. Near the reclining figure of Duke Jean of Berry is a stairway leading down to the remains of an earlier 9th-century church.

Stroll over to the 17th-century **City Hall** (Hôtel de Ville), once the archbishop's palace. The lovely **gardens** (Jardins de l'Archevêché) (6) adjacent to this, attributed to Le Nôtre, offer an excellent view of the cathedral's east end as well as being a welcome spot to relax.

Now follow the map past the tourist office to the ***Palace of Jacques Coeur** (7), surely one of the most splendid private buildings of the Middle Ages. It was begun in 1443 and completed, at fabulous cost, nearly ten years later for Charles VII's finance minister, a gifted merchant and banker named Jacques Coeur. Alas, poor Jacques never got to enjoy his mansion as he fell from grace in 1451 and was permanently exiled. In 1457 the palace was returned to his heirs and later used by the city as a Palais de Justice. Now restored to original condition, its marvelously sumptuous interior may be seen on guided tours. Don't miss seeing this. ☎ 02-4824-0687. Open July–Aug., daily 9–6; Apr.–June and Sept., daily 9–noon and 2–5; Oct.–March, daily 9–noon and 2–4. Adults 32FF, students 21FF.

Continue on, descending the steps next to the palace and go into the gardens of Place Berry. From here you can see how the west wall of the mansion was built on top of the original Roman town walls. A short stroll down Rue des Arènes brings you to the **Hôtel Cujas** (8), an elegant mansion built around 1515 for a wealthy merchant and later the residence of Jacques Cujas, a noted jurist. It now houses the **Musée du Berry**, featuring an archaeological exhibition of artifacts dating from the Roman period back to prehistoric times. Displays of local country life from more recent centuries occupy the first floor, while the rest of the museum is given over to the fine arts. ☎ *02-4857-8115. Open Wed.–Sat. and Mon., 10–noon and 2–6, Sun. 2–6. Free.*

Cross Place Planchat and turn left onto Rue Cambon. At number 19 stands the ornate **Maison de la Reine Blanche** (9), a 16th-century wooden house decorated with religious motifs. Farther on, at number 32, there is the Hôtel Dieu with its elaborate Renaissance doorway. Return to Place de Mirepied and continue down Avenue Jean-Jaurès past the beautiful **Prés-Fichaux Gardens** (10), where you can spend some delightful moments before returning to the station.

Section VII

DAYTRIPS IN
PROVENCE

Going to Provence is like stepping into a different world, one far removed from Paris and the north. This is a Mediterranean region with a distinctly Latin culture reflecting its ancient Roman heritage. It is also a sun-drenched land whose dazzling clarity was made famous by such painters as Van Gogh and Cézanne. Few areas of Europe—or of the world—can begin to match its broad variety of intriguing sights and delicious experiences.

The five destinations in this section are linked by frequent rail service and excellent highways. Any of them could be used as a base for exploring the others without having to change hotels. In terms of convenience, Marseille is the best situated for this purpose since it lies at the hub of major transportation routes. Those who prefer to avoid large cities will find that Arles or Avignon also make excellent bases, with Aix-en-Provence and Nîmes less handy, especially for rail travelers.

One-day bus excursions to other attractions in Provence, including the hauntingly beautiful Camargue, mysterious Les Baux, the Roman relics of Orange and the Pont du Gard, or the strange walled town of Aigues-Mortes are available from these base towns. Ask at the local tourist office for current information and schedules. Those with cars can easily visit several of these in one day. Descriptions are not included in this book since these places are a bit difficult to reach by regular public transportation and, being quite small, do not really lend themselves to structured walking tours.

Marseille
(Marseilles)

No one ever accused Marseille of being charming or quaint, or even lovely, but it certainly is unique—and more than a little intriguing. This brash, noisy, teeming metropolis throbs with such a vitality that to ignore it would be to miss out on a very colorful aspect of Mediterranean life.

Founded around 600 BC by Greek colonists from Phocea in Asia Minor, Marseille is the oldest city in France. Depending on how you count heads, it could also be the second largest. Then known as *Massalia*, it developed a network of satellite towns in Nice, Antibes, Arles and other places. Threatened by native tribes, the port later turned to Rome for defense and prospered for centuries afterwards. A major setback came in 49 BC when it backed Pompey in his dispute with Julius Caesar. The victorious Caesar got his revenge by shifting trade to Arles, but eventually the 11th-century Crusades brought about an economic resurgence.

Although it became a part of France in 1481, Marseille has always been more a Mediterranean than a French city, caring little for Paris and its kings. It enthusiastically joined the Revolution in 1789, and in 1792 its volunteers sang a new patriotic song with such lusty fervor that the tune became known as *La Marseillaise*, the French national anthem. Commercial development during the 19th century, especially the opening of the Suez Canal in 1869, greatly expanded the city into the metropolis it is today.

With all that history, it is amazing how little of the past remains. The *Marseillais* have never been much interested in antiquity, preferring to focus their energies on trade and the future. For this reason Marseille is more a city to relish for its spicy flavor than for the few bona-fide sights it offers.

Is Marseille really as wicked as its reputation suggests? No, despite the open prostitution that thrives between the Old Port and the Opéra, the drunken sailors and sleazy dives off La Canebière, it is no longer the drug capital of the world—if it ever was. There are, however, a few obvious areas that are best avoided at night.

With its superb transportation facilities and many hotels, Marseille is the most convenient base for daytrips throughout Provence. And it has a few other drawing cards as well, such as some of the best seafood restaurants in Europe and a truly spectacular setting on steep hills spilling down to the Old Port and the Mediterranean.

GETTING THERE:

Trains connect Marseille's St.-Charles Station with other towns in Provence at fairly frequent intervals. Average running times are: Aix-en-Provence—32 minutes, Arles—45 minutes, Avignon—I hour *(TGV service also available)*, and Nîmes—75 minutes. For more details consult the chapters for those specific towns. There are also convenient schedules to both the Riviera and Paris, the latter being served by speedy TGVs *(under 5 hours)* as well as conventional trains.

By car, Marseille is 19 miles from Aix-en-Provence, 57 miles from Arles, 62 miles from Avignon, and 75 miles from Nîmes. Recommended routes are given in the chapters dealing with those towns.

GETTING AROUND:

You may want to make use of the magnificent **Métro** (subway) or bus service during your exploration of Marseille. Both use the same tickets, sold singly or in a discounted *carnet* package of six. A ticket is valid for one continuous journey, which may combine both the Métro and bus, for a period of 70 minutes after cancellation on first boarding the bus or entering the subway station. A bargain one-day pass is available at the tourist office, which can supply you with a free map of the system. Rail travelers making Marseille their base will be happy to know that both Métro lines (and several bus routes) stop at St.-Charles Station.

PRACTICALITIES:

Marseille may be visited at any time, although good weather will make the suggested tour much more enjoyable. The museums are generally closed on Mondays.

The local **tourist office**, ☎ 04-9113-8900, Internet: www.marseilles. com, is located at the foot of La Canebière, near the Old Port, with a branch in the train station. They can arrange for hotel reservations and tours, as well as provide you with maps and transit information.

FOOD AND DRINK:

Bouillabaisse, a fish and seafood stew flavored with saffron, garlic, cayenne and other tasty ingredients, is the classic dish of Marseille—a treat not to be missed by seafood fanciers. As befits one of the world's greatest ports, the city has a wide selection of inexpensive foreign restaurants, particularly North African, Indian, and Vietnamese. Some of the better traditional restaurants are:

Michel (6 Rue des Catalans, near the Jardin du Pharo, facing the sea) Famous for its *bouillabaisse* and other seafoods. ☎ 04- 9152-3063. $$$

Les Trois Forts (36 Blvd. Charles-Livon, in the Sofitel Vieux-Port Hotel) Inspired contemporary regional cuisine with a view. ☎ 04-9115-5956. $$$

Chez Brun—Aux Mets de Provence (18 Quai Rive-Neuve, well hidden, near the Old Port) A traditional dining experience sampling seafood. Reservations, ☎ 04-9133-3538. X: Sun., Mon. lunch. $$$

Miramar (12 Quai du Port, at the northeast corner of the Old Port) Inventive seafood cuisine along with other dishes. ☎ 04- 9191-1040. X: Sun., Aug. $$$

L'Oursinade (in the Hôtel Mercure, 1 Rue Neuve St.-Martin, overlooking the archaeological gardens) Exceptionally good Provençal cuisine. ☎ 04-9139-2000. X: Sat., Sun., holidays, Aug. $$ and $$$

Chez Soi (5 Rue Papère, just south of the upper end of La Canebière) A bistro with good-value meals. ☎ 04-9154-2541. X: Mon. eve. $ and $$

La Kahena (2 Rue de la République, a block north of the Old Port) North African specialties. ☎ 04-9190-6193. $

Country Life (14 Rue Venture, a block north of the Cantini Museum) Healthy vegetarian meals. ☎ 04-9154-1644. X: weekends. $

SUGGESTED TOUR:

Numbers in parentheses correspond to numbers on the map.

Rail travelers using another base in Provence will begin their tour at **St.-Charles Station** (1), oddly located at the top of a hill. This marvelous old structure has been completely restored, with modern underground levels, while the exterior retains all of its considerable 19th-century charm. Walk outside for a panoramic view across the harbor, then descend the steps to Boulevard d'Athènes and walk downhill to **La Canebière**. Long known to foreign sailors as "The Can o' Beer," this once-glamorous main street of Marseille has faded somewhat in recent years, but its vitality remains as alive as ever.

Turn right and continue downhill past the tourist office to the Quai des Belges and the **Old Port** *(Vieux Port)* (2), the real start of this tour. Those in a hurry could also get here from the train station by Métro, although doing so misses a lot of the city's character. Until 1844 this was the only harbor at Marseille, but large ships now dock beyond the breakwater and the Old Port is used for fishing and pleasure vessels. If you arrive fairly early in the morning you will be treated to the sight of fishermen hawking their fresh catch right off the boats. Excursions by boat to the outlying islands are available here, but it is perhaps better to wait until you return to this spot for that exciting experience.

Follow the map along the Quai du Port past the elegant 17th-century **Town Hall** *(Hôtel de Ville)*, easily singled out among the hideous modern apartment blocks lining that side of the port. This was once a fascinating warren of narrow alleyways and fetid slums, but all that ended in 1943 when the occupying Germans blew the area up in an attempt to deny the Resistance a base of operations. They only got two blocks inland, however, and the rest of the colorful old quarter still survives intact.

Continue on to the 17th-century bastion of **Fort St.Jean** (3), which guards the narrow entrance to the harbor, and take the pedestrian promenade around it. In a few blocks you will come to a huge, remarkably

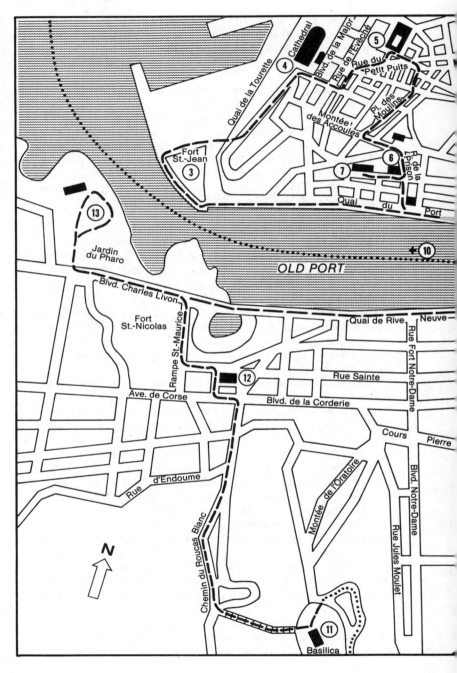

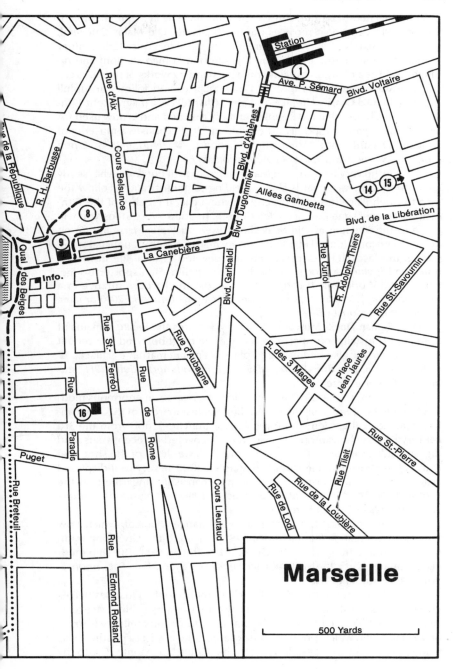

Marseille

500 Yards

ostentatious neo-Byzantine church, the **Cathédrale de la Major** (4). Built in the late 19th century, it replaces the much smaller **Old Major Cathedral**, which fortunately still stands directly to its side. This 12th-century Romanesque structure, erected on the site of a Roman stadium and no longer used as a church, contains some outstanding works of religious art.

The walk now enters the old Panier quarter and follows an uphill route to the **Old Charity Hospice** *(La Vieille Charité)* (5), a magnificent 17th-century almshouse that has been beautifully restored and is now used for archaeological and temporary art exhibitions. It also houses a museum of African, Oceanic, and American Indian art. ☎ *04-9156-2838. Open Mon.–Fri., 9–noon and 1:30–4:45. Admission 30FF.*

This is the very heart of Old Marseille, a colorful but somewhat seedy area of tiny alleyways that is slowly yielding to gentrification. Follow the map through Place des Moulins and downhill past the belfry of the 12th-century Notre-Dame des Accoules Church. In a few more steps you will come to the **Museum of Old Marsellle** *(Musée du Vieux Marseille)* (6) on Rue de la Prison. Housed in a 16th-century mansion with an unusual stone façade, the fascinating displays here are devoted to local life in former times and include a model of the highly intriguing Transporter Bridge, which until World War II carried traffic across the harbor entrance in a most unorthodox manner. *Closed for renovations until mid-2000 or later. Inquire at the tourist office.*

The **Roman Docks Museum** (7), nearby, features the *in situ* remains of Roman port installations discovered when the neighborhood was rebuilt in 1947. There are also interesting displays of ancient maritime artifacts. ☎ *04-9191-2462. Open Tues.–Sun., 10–5 (11–6 in summer) Adults 12FF, students 6FF, seniors free.*

Now return to the Old Port and follow the map to an enormous modern indoor shopping mall, the Centre Bourse. Just in front of this is a lovely archaeological garden where remains of the Greek port from the 3rd century BC may be explored. These were discovered in recent years, and digs are still going on. Adjoining this, on the lower level of the shopping mall, is the **Museum of the History of Marseille** (8). The very well-displayed artifacts include a 3rd-century Roman merchant ship unearthed on the spot in 1974. ☎ *04-9190-4222. Open Wed.–Sat. and Mon., noon–7. Adults 12FF, students 6FF, seniors free.*

Continue on past the former stock exchange *(Bourse)*, which now houses an interesting **Marine Museum** (9) devoted to the city's long tradition of maritime trade, from the Greek era to the present. The ship models alone are worth the visit. ☎ *04-9190- 4222. Open Mon.–Sat., noon–7. Adults 10FF, students 5FF.*

Turn the corner onto La Canebière and return to the Quai des Belges (2). Several establishments along the quay offer very enjoyable boat excursions to the ***Château d'If** (10, off the map), a 16th-century military fortress on a small island well beyond the breakwater. Long used as a prison, it was made famous by its description in The Count of Monte Cristo by

Alexandre Dumas. Many of these boats also call at the nearby Frioul Islands, where a pleasant resort village offers numerous outdoor cafés. Allow at least 90 minutes for the round trip and be prepared for a rough ride. Anyone foolish enough to sit on the outdoor deck will probably get wet. *Château* ☎ *04-9159-0230. Open April–Sept., daily 9–7; rest of year, Tues.–Sun., 9:15–5:15. Adults 26FF, students 17FF. Boats about 50–80FF round trip.*

Back at the Quai des Belges you will find a wide selection of restaurants and cafés in all price ranges. Stroll over to the adjacent Cours d'Estienne-d'Orves and board bus number 60—running every 30 minutes—for the very steep climb to Marseille's most spectacular landmark. The **Basilica of Notre-Dame de la Garde** (11), crowned with a huge golden statue of the Virgin, is yet another 19th-century neo-Byzantine monument. It is visible from virtually everywhere in the city, even at night, and after a while you may actually get to like it. Step inside to see the literally thousands of interesting sailors' ex-votos. The real reason to come up here, however, is for the fabulous *panorama it offers of the port, city, islands and seacoast.

Marseille does have at least one genuinely superb ancient church. Follow the map down a stepped path and along city streets to the **Abbey of St.-Victor** (12). The above-ground portion of this dates from the 11th to the 14th centuries and looks like a fortress, but the main interest lies in its spooky 5th-century crypt. Filled with a mysterious early-Christian atmosphere, the catacombs contain the relics of two 3rd-century martyrs. Don't miss exploring this strange, dark and wonderful place. ☎ *04-9611-2260. Open daily, 8:30–6:30, closed Sun. mornings. Admission 10FF.*

Continue on, following the map. When you come to a short tunnel be sure to use the sidewalk to the left; otherwise you will be caught in horrendous traffic. Just beyond this there is a Foreign Legion post, whose sidewalk recruiting office is open day and night—in case you feel so inclined. Those who would rather rest in a beautiful park with an unusually good view of the harbor will enjoy a visit to the nearby **Jardin du Pharo** (13). Luckily, it has an outdoor café overlooking the yacht basin, a perfect spot to unwind before walking or taking a bus back to the Quai des Belges. If you are heading for St.-Charles Station, you can take the Métro from there and avoid a long uphill climb.

ADDITIONAL SIGHTS:

Travelers staying in Marseille may want to see some of these attractions on another day:

The **Fine Arts Museum** *(Musée des Beaux Arts)* (14) has an extensive collection of works by major artists, especially those of native son Honoré Daumier. Located in the splendid 19th-century Longchamp Palace, it is a fairly long walk from the top of La Canebière, or can be reached by taking Métro line 1 to Cinq-Avenues Longchamp. ☎ *04-9114-5930. Open Tues.–Sun., 10–5 (11–6 in summer). Adults 12FF, students 6FF, seniors free.*

The same building also houses the Natural History Museum.

The **Grobet-Labadié Museum** (15) displays the private collections and furniture of a wealthy musician in his own 19th-century mansion. It is very close to the front of the Longchamp Palace, above, and has the same hours.

The **Cantini Museum** (16), close to downtown and just off Rue Paradis, features contemporary art along with traditional objects. It is open during the same times as the Fine Arts Museum, above. The closest Métro stop is Estrangin Préfecture on Line 1.

Aix-en-Provence

Only nineteen miles from Marseille, Aix-en-Provence is light years removed in character. Elegant, refined, gracious, dignified, sophisticated—all of these adjectives and more can be honestly used to describe the former capital of Provence, which many consider to be nothing less than the loveliest town in France. Whether you feel the same depends, of course, on your interests, but a few hours spent sitting at an outdoor café on the Cours Mirabeau does leave most visitors with a contended perspective on life.

First settled by the Romans in 122 BC after their victory over a local tribe, *Aquae Sextiae,* as it was then called, was already famous as a warm spring spa. By the 6th century AD, however, it was nearly abandoned, the ancient buildings being used as a convenient stone quarry. Good King René, that marvelous figure who keeps popping up in French history, made it his capital in the 15th century. René was the count of Provence, the duke of Anjou, and more or less the king of Sicily, albeit in exile. He was also a true Renaissance man—one of the most civilized, diversely educated and decent men of his age.

Though united to France in 1482, Provence retained much of its independence and maintained a parliament at Aix until the Revolution. After that the town declined in importance until the recent postwar era, which has seen a nearly explosive growth in population. Much of this is due to the development of modern light industries in the outlying areas, but some of the credit goes to both its university and to its world-famous summer music festival held annually during July and August.

Those with cars will find Aix to be a good base for exploring the rest of Provence, although it is somewhat inconvenient for rail travelers.

GETTING THERE:

Trains depart St.-Charles Station in Marseille nearly hourly for the 30-minute run to Aix-en-Provence, with returns until mid-evening. To get anywhere else in Provence or the Riviera by rail requires a change at Marseille. There is also fairly frequent bus service to other areas of Provence, leaving from near the tourist office.

By car, Aix is 19 miles north of Marseille via the A-7 and A-51 Autoroutes. Other distances are: Arles—47 miles, Avignon—50 miles, Nîmes—66 miles; all via the A-8 and A-7 Autoroutes followed by local roads.

PRACTICALITIES:
Good weather will make a stroll around Aix much more pleasant. Some of the major sights are closed on Tuesdays and holidays. Hotel rooms are scarce during July and August.

The local **tourist office,** ☎ 04-4216-1161, Internet: www.aix-en-provence.com, is conveniently located on Place du Général-de-Gaulle, near the foot of the Cours Mirabeau. Ask them about local bus service to Cézanne's studio, and about short regional tours. They can also find you a hotel room.

FOOD AND DRINK:
The many restaurants of Aix reflect a broad range of cuisines and prices. Some of the better choices are:

Clos de la Violette (10 Ave. Violette, 4 blocks north of the cathedral) Superb and imaginative regional cuisine in a garden setting. Dress properly and reserve, ☎ 04-4223-3071. X: Sun., Mon. lunch. $$$

Chez Jo (59 Rue Espariat, a block north of the lower end of Cours Mirabeau) Italian and Provençal cuisine, excellent pizza, very popular. ☎ 04-4226-1247. $$

Brasserie Royale (17 Cours Mirabeau) A traditional, old-fashioned brasserie with local specialties served in a spirited manner. ☎ 04-4226-0163. $ and $$

Chez Maxime (12 Place Ramus, 2 blocks west of the Granet Museum) Features the cuisine of Provence. ☎ 04-4226-2851. X: Sun., Mon. lunch. $ and $$

L'Hacienda (7 Rue Mérindol, 3 blocks west of the Town Hall) Home cooking in a family-style restaurant. ☎ 04-4227-0035. X: Sun. $

L'Arbre à Pain (12 Rue Constantin, 4 blocks east of the Museum of Old Aix) Vegetarian cuisine. ☎ 04-4296-9995. X: Sun. $

SUGGESTED TOUR:
Numbers in parentheses correspond to numbers on the map.

Leave the **train station** (1) and follow the map to Place du Général-de-Gaulle, also called La Rotonde, where the tourist office and gambling casino are located. In a few more steps you will be on the ***Cours Mirabeau** (2), one of the most utterly delightful avenues on Earth. It was named for the unscrupulous Count Mirabeau, a popular 18th-century demagogue who represented the common people of Aix in the States-General of 1789 that led to the French Revolution. Although only a quarter of a mile in length, it is very wide and completely shaded by four rows of ancient plane trees forming a cool green canopy. There are several fountains along its length, the most intriguing being the curious moss-covered Fontaine Chaude at the intersection of Rue Clemenceau, which runs with the warm thermal waters that made Aix famous. The south side is lined with strikingly elegant mansions while the north is the preserve of trendy shops and a great many outdoor cafés. One of the great pleasures of a trip to France is to sit

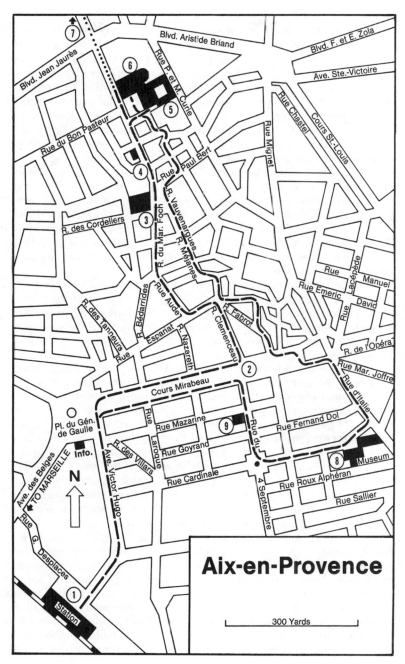

Aix-en-Provence

300 Yards

at one of these and just watch the world go by.

Stroll north on Rue Clemenceau and follow the map through a colorful old district of narrow streets to the **Town Hall** *(Hôtel de Ville)* (3), a 17th-century classical building with a lovely courtyard. Step into this, then climb the inside staircase to the first floor where there are some interesting displays in the Bibliothèque Méjanes. The handsome 16th-century **clock tower** in the adjacent square is topped with one of those ornate wrought-iron bell cages so typical to Provence. In a niche below this is a mechanical "calendar" that rotates wooden figures representing the seasons four times a year. A fountain graces the square, where an outdoor **flower market** is held on Tuesday, Thursday and Saturday mornings.

The **Museum of Old Aix** *(Musée du Vieil Aix)* (4), reached in a few minutes, has one of the best folklore collections in the south of France. Particularly noteworthy are the traditional *santons*—colored clay figures used in home Christmas displays—and larger puppets made to be drawn through the streets in the now-discontinued Corpus Christi processions. ☎ *04-4221-4355. Open April–Sept., Tues.–Sun., 10–noon and 2:30–6; Nov.–March, Tues.–Sun. 10–noon and 2–5. Closed Oct. and holidays. Adults 15FF, students 10FF.*

Continue on to the **Tapestry Museum** (5) in the former archbishop's palace. The inner courtyard of this building is the center of the annual music festival held in July and August. You may be interested in the outstanding collection of 17th- and 18th-century Beauvais tapestries, some of which depict the life of Don Quixote. ☎ *04-4223-0991. Open Wed.–Mon., 10–noon and 2–5:45. Adults 15F, students 9F.*

Next to this stands the **Cathedral of St.-Sauveur** (6), a curious architectural mélange incorporating elements from the 5th century onwards. Enter through an enchanting 12th-century Romanesque cloister, then step inside to enjoy the richly varied interior. The main attraction here is the famous ***Triptych of the Burning Bush***, painted about 1476 by Nicolas Froment for King René, who appears on the left panel, with his wife on the right panel. These are usually closed, but may be opened for you by the caretaker on request. Outside again, take a look at the west front. All of the sculptures except one are replacements, the originals having been destroyed in the Revolution. The sole survivor is that of the Virgin on the central pillar of the main portal, which escaped harm when some quick-witted person crowned her with a red cap of Liberty.

Art lovers might want to make a side trip at this point to the **Atelier Paul Cézanne** (7, off the map), the small studio where the renowned painter worked until his death in 1906. Although everything here is pretty much as he left it, the effect is curiously unmoving. Still, if you are an admirer of Cézanne—a native of Aix—this is a worthwhile stop. To get there on foot continue straight ahead and follow Avenue Pasteur a short distance, then make a right uphill on Avenue Paul Cézanne to the studio on the left. The distance is about three-quarters of a mile. It is also possible to take bus number 1 from the front of the tourist office to the

Cézanne stop, which follows an entirely different route. ☎ *04-4221-0653. Open April–Sept., daily 10–noon and 2:30–6; rest of year, daily 10–noon and 2–5. Closed holidays. Adults 25FF, seniors, students and children 12–16 10FF.*

Return to the cathedral and follow the map through a highly picturesque old part of town to the eastern end of the Cours Mirabeau. Continue on Rue d'Italie and turn right at the 13th-century **Church of St.-Jean-de-Malte**, the first Gothic structure in Provence—worth a visit for its stained-glass windows. Adjacent to this stands the **Granet Museum** (8), whose collections of fine art and pre-Roman archaeological artifacts are among the best in Provence. Some of the more outstanding paintings on display include a magnificent self-portrait by Rembrandt, several works by the locally-born early-19th-century artist François Granet, a portrait of Granet by Ingres, and a few works by Cézanne. ☎ *04-4238-1470. Open Wed.–Mon., 10–noon and 2–6. Closed holidays. Adults 18FF, children 12–16 10FF.*

You are now in the Mazarin Quarter, laid out in the 17th century by the archbishop of Aix, a brother of the great statesman. Stroll past the charming Fountain of the Four Dolphins, which has been merrily splashing away since 1667.

A right turn leads to the **Paul Arbaud Museum** (9), featuring interesting displays of local Provençal ceramics, art and culture. ☎ *04-4238-3895. Open Mon.–Sat., 2–5. Adults 15FF, students 10FF. From here it is only a few steps back to the Cours Mirabeau.*

*Arles

Few towns in France are as rich in ancient monuments as Arles, yet it remains a delightfully unpretentious country place, captivating in its honest simplicity. Virtually everyone who goes there enjoys the experience.

Founded by Greeks from Marseille in the 6th century BC, Arles became an important Roman colony in 49 BC after it sided with Julius Caesar in his victorious struggle against the rival general, Pompey. Having backed the wrong man, Marseille was humbled and its wealth transferred to Arles.

At that time the town was already a major port, linked to the Mediterranean by canal and set astride the main highway between Italy and Spain. The prosperity that followed brought about the construction of major public projects, several of which still stand today. Christianity came to Arles at an early date, along with political importance as the capital of Gaul. With the fall of the empire, however, the city fell to the barbarians from the north and was invaded by the Arab Saracens. Although later a kingdom in its own right, it never really recovered and soon drifted into the dreamy backwater that it is today.

Arles is probably best known for its association with the artist Vincent van Gogh, who created some 200 of his greatest works while living there in 1888 and 1889, just prior to his insanity and suicide.

As an alternative to Marseille, Arles is an excellent base for daytrips throughout Provence, particularly for those with cars. Ask at the tourist office for information about bus excursions to the Camargue region, Les Baux, Aigues-Mortes and other nearby attractions. They can also make hotel reservations for you.

GETTING THERE:

Trains depart St.-Charles Station in Marseille several times in the morning for the 45-minute run to Arles, with returns until late evening. There is also convenient service to and from Avignon and, less frequently, with Nîmes. Aix-en-Provence is reached via Marseille.

By car, Arles is connected via the N-113 road and the A-7 Autoroute to Marseille, 57 miles to the southeast. Other distances are: Aix-en-Provence—47 miles, Avignon—23 miles, and Nîmes—19 miles.

PRACTICALITIES:

Good weather, which fortunately is common in Provence, will

make this trip much more enjoyable. All of the major sights, except the Museon Arlaten and the Museum of Ancient Arles, are open every day except January 1st, May Day, and Christmas. An economical all-inclusive "global" ticket is available at the tourist office or sites. *Adults 60FF, students and children 40FF.*

The local **tourist office,** ☎ 04-9018-4120, is along the Boulevard des Lices, near the center of town. There is a branch at the train station. A useful Internet site is: www.arles.cci.fr.

FOOD AND DRINK:

Arles has a wide variety of restaurants and cafés, particularly near the Arena, on the Boulevard des Lices, and at Place du Forum. Some outstanding choices are:

Lou Marques (in the Jules César Hôtel on Blvd. des Lices, near the tourist office) Excellent classical and Provençal specialties as well as seafood. ☎ 04-9093-4320. X: Nov., Dec. $$$

Le Vaccarès (9 Rue Favorin, by Place du Forum) Traditional Provençal cuisine in a romantic upstairs setting. ☎ 04- 9096-0617. X: Sun. eve., Mon. $$ and $$$

Brasserie Nord-Pinus (Place du Forum) Superb Provençal cuisine in a stylish setting. ☎ 04-9093-0232. X: Feb., Tues. eve. and Wed. in winter. $$

Jardin de Manon (14 Ave. des Alyscamps, between the Theatre and Les Alyscamps) Good dining at fair prices, indoors or out. ☎ 04-9093-3818. X: Feb., Wed. $ and $$

Vitamine (16 Rue du Docteur-Fanton, between Pl. du Forum and the Baths of Constantine) Light meals for vegetarians. ☎ 04- 9093-7736. X: Weekends. $

SUGGESTED TOUR:

Numbers in parentheses correspond to numbers on the map.

Leave the **train station** (1) and stroll down to Place Lamartine, a good place to park if you came by car. Vincent van Gogh lived in a bistro here, sharing his place with the painter Gauguin for a while, and it was here that he cut off his ear. The house, alas, was destroyed by a bomb in 1944. Continue on through the town gates and follow the map to the:

*ARENA *(Les Arènes)* (2), ☎ 04-9096-0370. *Open daily; April–Sept. 9–7, rest of year 10–4:30. Closed during bullfights and other performances. Adults 15FF, students 9FF.*

Arles' arena is one of the largest, oldest and best-preserved Roman amphitheaters in existence. Probably built around AD 80 to seat some 25,000 spectators, it is now used for bullfights. During the Middle Ages the amphitheater was converted into a fortress, with the top rows of arches being demolished to furnish stones for the defensive towers. An entire town with a church and some 200 houses was built within it, and this provided some measure of safety from the marauding bands and incessant

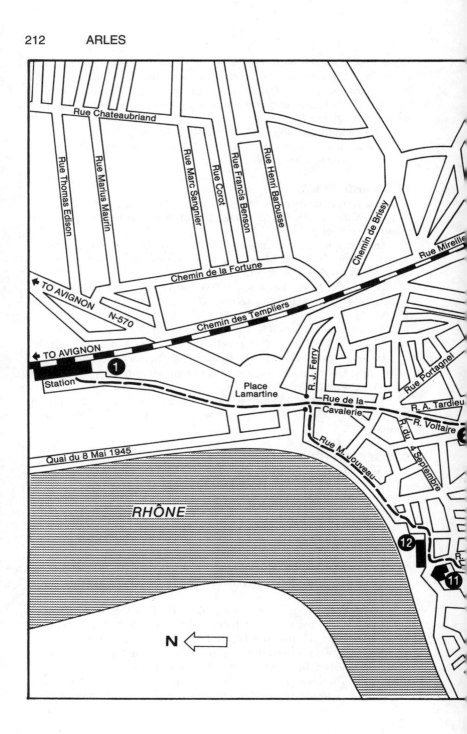

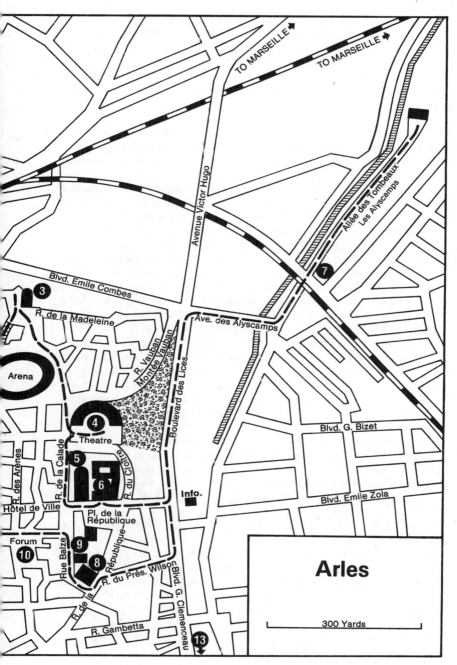

TO MARSEILLE

TO MARSEILLE

Avenue Victor Hugo

Allée des Tombeaux

Les Alyscamps

Blvd. Emile Combes

3

R. de la Madeleine

Ave. des Alyscamps

R. Vauban

Montée Vauban

Arena

Boulevard des Lices

7

4

Theatre

R. de la Calade

R. du Cloître

5

6

R. des Arènes

Blvd. G. Bizet

Info.

Hôtel de Ville

Pl. de la
République

R. de la République

Blvd. Emile Zola

Forum

10

Rue Balze

9

8

R. du Prés. Wilson

R. de la

Blvd. G. Clemenceau

Arles

R. Gambetta

13

300 Yards

wars of those troubled times. The arena was restored to its present condition only during the 19th century. Step inside and make a circular tour through the various passageways, exploring the inner chambers, then climb to the top of the medieval tower for a splendid view.

Both Spanish-style *(Corrida)* and Camargue-style *(Cocarde)* bullfights are held here; in the *corrida* the bull is killed, but in the *cocarde* he leaves unhurt to fight another day.

Walk up the stepped Rue Renan to the Romanesque **Notre-Dame-de-la-Major Church** (3), now closed. Directly aside of this there is a good lookout spot above the ancient ramparts that offers a spectacular panorama of the region.

Return via the arena and amble over to the nearby ***Roman Theater** *(Théâtre Antique)* (4). It was built during the reign of the emperor Augustus, toward the end of the 1st century BC, and was used for elaborate theatrical productions, which often tended to be obscene. The Christians put an end to all that and tore the place down, using most of the stones to build churches and convents. Miraculously, two Corinthian columns survived in situ and are still there. Excavations in the 18th century revealed the long-forgotten structure that, only partially restored, is now used for festival productions. You can wander inside for a close look at the stage and seating arrangements. ☎ *04-9096-9330. Open daily; April–Sept.9–7, rest of year 10–4:30. Adults 15FF, students 9FF.*

Continue on to Place de la République and the Romanesque former **Cathedral of St.-Trophîme** (5), now used as a parish church. Although parts of it may date from the Carolingian era, it is basically an 11th-century structure, much altered in later years. The marvelous **west front** is richly carved with a *Last Judgement* above the portal, a procession of the redeemed on the left frieze and, on the right, figures of the damned being marched naked into hell.

Next door to the cathedral is the entrance to the incomparable ***St.-Trophîme Cloister** *(Cloître)* (6), considered to be the best in Provence. Be sure to go upstairs to see the many small exhibits, and to carefully examine the marvelously sculpted details of Biblical stories and local legends on the pillars. ☎ *04-9049-3636. Open daily; April–Sept. 9–7, rest of year 10–4:30. Adults 20FF, students 14FF.*

Follow the map past the tourist office to **Les Alyscamps** (7), the strangely evocative remnant of what was once a great necropolis. Begun in pagan times and later taken over by Christians, it formerly covered an immense area nearly a mile in length, with many thousands of tombs. Desecrated during the 16th century, it fell to ruin, and what few sarcophagi survived were lined up along the sole remaining alley. Dante described the place in his *Divine Comedy,* while both Van Gogh and Gauguin painted its melancholy beauty. At the end of the lane stands the fittingly ruined remains of an ancient church. ☎ *04-9049-3636. Open daily; April–Sept. 9–7, rest of year 10–4:30. Adults 15FF, students 9FF.*

Return to the animated Boulevard des Lices and take Rue du Président-Wilson to the extraordinarily fascinating ***Museon Arlaten** (8), whose name is appropriately in the Provençal language. Allow yourself at least an hour to get lost in this vast storage attic of a museum, filled to the brim with just about everything imaginable that might relate to Provençal folklore. It was founded by the noted writer Frédéric Mistral using funds he received for winning the Nobel Prize in 1904, and many of the faded display cards are still in his hand. The total disregard for conventional museum values is what makes this place so intriguing, like a perverse visit to a huge junkshop. Don't miss seeing this. ☎ *04-9096-0823. Open 9–noon and 2–5, closing at 6 in April, May, and Sept., 6:30 in June, and 7 in July and Aug. Closed Mon. from Oct. to June. Adults 20FF, students 15FF.*

Turn the corner to the **Cryptoportiques** (subterranean galleries) (9), a very spooky underground place built by the Romans in the 1st century BC as a storage center for grain. The passageways were probably the substructure of the original Roman forum, near today's Place du Forum. *Open daily April–Sept. 9–7, rest of year 10–4:30. Adults 12FF, students 7FF.*

Continue on through the **Place du Forum** (10), a charming square with several inviting outdoor cafés, a statue of Frédéric Mistral, and a few relics of the Roman forum. **The Baths of Constantine** *(Palais des Thermes)* (11), nearby, are all that remain of a great 4th-century bathing establishment built by the emperor Constantine. The water came via an aqueduct some 40 miles long that crossed the wide Rhône River. *Open daily; April–Sept., 9–noon and 2–7; rest of year 10–noon and 2–4:30. Adults 15FF, students 9FF.*

The last sight to visit on this walk is right next door, the **Museum of Fine Arts** (Musée Réattu) (12). Located in the 15th-century former priory of the Knights of Malta, it is best known for its collection of late Picasso drawings, donated by the artist just prior to his death in 1973. There is also a fine collection of other modern works by French artists as well as local art, 17th-century tapestries, and a famous section devoted to photography. ☎ *04-9049-3758. Open daily; April–Sept. 9–noon and 2–7; rest of year 10–noon and 2–4:30. Adults 20FF, students 14FF.*

From here you can walk along the banks of the Rhône to the town gates, or return through the town.

ADDITIONAL SIGHT:

*MUSEUM OF ANCIENT ARLES *(Musée de l'Arles Antique)* (13), Presqu'île du Cirque Romain, ☎ 04-9018-8888. A 10-minute walk west on Blvd. G. Clemenceau, bearing left and following signs. *Open Apr.–Sept., Wed.–Mon., 9–7; rest of year Wed.–Mon. 10–6. Adults 35FF, students 25FF, children 5FF.*

Erected on a Roman archaeology site, this modern structure houses a vast collection of Roman artifacts along with detailed models of ancient achievements.

Trip 33

*Avignon

Lively, cosmopolitan Avignon is far more sophisticated than its size would suggest. Ever since the 14th century, when it was the capital of Christendom, it has retained a worldly atmosphere that today makes it a popular tourist and convention center as well as the setting for one of Europe's major theatrical festivals.

Although the town has existed since Gallo-Roman times, and its famous bridge has stood since the 12th century, Avignon did not really gain significance until 1309. Pope Clement V, a Frenchman, was driven from Rome by the endless wars between the Guelfs and the Ghibellines. Desiring to be closer to the French king, he moved the Papacy to a territory it owned on the banks of the Rhône, on the edge of France. Avignon, although a part of Provence, bordered on this, and was the town best suited as their new capital. The "Second Babylonian Captivity" had begun, lasting through seven French Popes, until Gregory XI moved back to Rome in 1377. This did not sit well with a faction of Cardinals who preferred to remain in Avignon. They resisted by electing their own Pope, thus creating the "Great Schism" in which the Pope in Rome and the Antipope in Avignon hurled anathemas at one another until 1403.

After that, Avignon became a peaceful but still worldly place. Having been purchased from Provence in 1348, it remained the property of the Papacy right up until the French Revolution, when it was annexed to France.

With its superb tourist facilities, Avignon makes a fine base for daytrips throughout Provence. Those staying there may want to explore the city in greater depth, or make short excursions to nearby Villeneuve-les-Avignon, Orange, Pont du Gard, Tarascon or Les Baux. Avignon plays host to its famous drama festival from early July until early August.

GETTING THERE:

Trains, including speedy TGVs, connect St.-Charles Station in Marseille with Avignon at fairly frequent intervals, with return service until late evening. Regular trains take about one hour, TGVs at bit less. There is also direct service to and from Arles (under 20 minutes) and with Nîmes (about 30 minutes, with faster TGV service available). To get to Aix-en-Provence requires a change at Marseille.

Avignon is connected with Paris by direct TGV service, taking a bit under four hours.

By car, Avignon is 62 miles northwest of Marseille via the A-7 Autoroute and the N-7 road. Other distances are: Aix-en-Provence—50 miles, Arles—23 miles, and Nîmes—27 miles.

PRACTICALITIES:
The Palace of the Popes is open daily except for a few major holidays. Most of the museums close on Tuesdays and holidays. Good weather will make this trip more rewarding. The town is crowded during the international drama festival held from early July until early August. Find out more about this on the Internet at: www.festival-avignon.com.

The helpful **tourist office**, ☎ 04-9082-6511, Internet: www.ot-avignon.fr, is located at 41 Cours Jean-Jaurès, not far from the train station. They can make hotel reservations for you.

FOOD AND DRINK:
Sophisticated Avignon is endowed with an exceptional selection of restaurants and cafés in all price ranges. Some excellent choices are:

Hiély-Lucullus (5 Rue de la République, at Place de l'Horloge) Traditional gastronomy in an upstairs dining room. For reservations ☎ 04-9086-1707. X: Mon., Tues. lunch. $$$

Brunel (46 Rue de la Balance, a block northwest of the Palace of the Popes) Refined regional cuisine in a pleasant atmosphere. ☎ 04-9085-2483. X: Sun., Mon. $$$

Le Vernet (58 Rue Joseph-Vernet, opposite the Calvet Museum) Modern cuisine in a luxurious old house or garden. ☎ 04-9086-6453. X: Sun., Mon. lunch except in summer, Feb. $$ and $$$

L'Isle Sonnante (7 Rue Racine, a block west of Place de l'Horloge) Excellent Provençal cuisine and wines. Reserve. ☎ 04-9082-5601. X: Sun., Mon., Aug. $$ and $$$

La Fourchette (17 Rue Racine, a block west of Place de l'Horloge) Good food at moderate prices brings in crowds. ☎ 04-9085-2093. X: Sat., Sun. $$

Crêperie du Cloître (9 Place du Cloître St.-Pierre, 3 blocks east of Place de l'Horloge) Crêpes, salads, and the like. ☎ 04-9085-3463. X: Sun., Mon. lunch. $

Song Long (1 Place Carnot, 2 blocks southeast of the Palace of the Popes) Vietnamese specialties, including vegetarian dishes. ☎ 04-9086-3500. $

Simple Simon (26 Rue de la Petite-Fusterie, 2 blocks west of Place de l'Horloge) Light English meals and teas, indoors or out. ☎ 04-9086-6270. X: Sun., Aug. $

The local wines are those from the Côtes du Rhône, especially Châteauneuf-du-Pape.

SUGGESTED TOUR:
Numbers in parentheses correspond to numbers on the map.

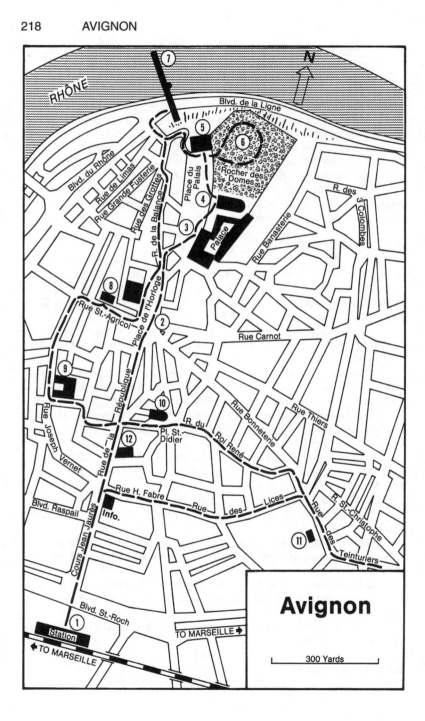

Leave the **train station** (1) and follow the map through the 14th-century ramparts, which completely encircle the old part of town. They were restored in the 19th century by Viollet-le-Duc, the architect who did so much to preserve medieval France. Continue past the tourist office to **Place de l'Horloge** (2), a delightfully animated spot on the site of the ancient Roman forum, with many outdoor cafés, a 14th-century clock tower, and the Town Hall. Just beyond this is Avignon's stellar attraction, the:

*PALACE OF THE POPES *(Palais des Papes)* (3), ☎ 04-9027-5074, Internet: www.palais-des-papes.com. *Open daily April–Oct., 9–7; Nov.–March, 9:30–5:45; remaining open until 9 p.m. in July and 8 p.m. in Aug. and Sept. Last entry one hour before closing. Closed on New Year's Day and Christmas. Admission 45FF each for the palace and the summer art exhibition; both for 55FF.*

Looking more like a mighty fortress than the residence of a religious leader, this is really two very different structures joined together. The austere **Old Palace**, to the left, was built by Benedict XII between 1335 and 1342. His successor, Clement VI, was a more flamboyant Pope, as the **New Palace** (1342–52) on the right suggests. Both buildings were badly damaged and looted during the Revolution, then used as a prison and, later, as an army barracks until 1906. An enormous amount of restoration has been done since then, but most of the rooms are still pretty much devoid of furnishings. Still, they are extremely interesting and well worth the visit. One-hour guided tours are offered in French, English, or German; but you can just walk through on your own if you wish, using a printed guide or the audiotour device. Art exhibitions (separate admission) are held here from May to September.

The **Cathedral of Notre-Dame-des-Doms** (4) stands next to the palace. Dating from the 12th century, it was greatly altered in later years. The gilded statue of the Virgin atop the steeple, added in 1859, is visible from all over town. Step inside to see the 12th-century white marble archbishop's throne and the fine canopied tomb of Pope John XXII.

Stroll down to the nearby ***Petit Palais** (5), built in 1317 as a palace for the Archbishop of Avignon and greatly altered in later centuries. It now houses the splendid **Museum of Medieval Painting and Sculpture** *(Musée du Petit Palais)*. Aside from the quality of the art, which is quite high, this is a beautiful example of museum organization at its very best—a situation all too rare in provincial France. Don't miss ambling through the lovely rooms. ☎ *04-9086-4458. Open Wed.–Mon., 9:30–noon and 2–6. Closed major holidays. Adults 30FF, seniors and students 15FF. Entry free on Sun. from Oct.–Feb.*

Climb up to the **Rocher des Doms** (6), a beautiful park on the site of Avignon's prehistoric origins. The highest point in town, it overlooks a bend in the river and the famous **Pont St.-Bénézet** (7), a 12th-century bridge known to generations of French children as the *Pont d'Avignon* of the familiar nursery rhyme. Storms and floods over the centuries have reduced the original 22 arches that were once the only stone span across the Rhône south of Lyon to a mere four, but these certainly make a spectacular sight. According to legend, the bridge was begun after a young shepherd lad named Bénézet experienced a Divine vision, then by performing a miracle convinced the authorities to construct the span. It turned out to be a good investment, bringing prosperity to Avignon for centuries to come. If you wish to walk out on it you can follow the map—steeply downhill—to its foot, where the entrance is combined with an annex of the tourist office. ☎ *04-9085-6016. Open Tues.–Sun., 9–1 and 2–5, later in summer. Adults 17FF, seniors and students 9FF. A temporary span will replace the missing arches during 2000 but will be torn down later.*

Return to Place de l'Horloge (2), using the route on the map if you went down to the bridge. A right on Rue St.-Agricol leads to the interesting **Church of St.-Agricol** (8), up a flight of stairs, rebuilt in the 14th century and much altered since. It contains several excellent works of art including a superb altarpiece.

Continue on Rue Joseph-Vernet to the **Calvet Museum** (9), housed in a magnificent 18th-century mansion. The collections of art, displayed in an old-fashioned manner, are certainly an eclectic lot, with several great masterpieces by such talents as Breughel, David, Géricault, Manet, Corot, Toulouse-Lautrec, Dufy, and Utrillo scattered among a mass of decidedly lesser works. There is also a fascinating collection of medieval wrought-iron objects. The museum has a certain charm about it that is difficult to describe but worth experiencing. ☎ *04-9086-3384. Open Wed.–Mon., 10–1 and 2–6. Adults 30FF, seniors and students 15FF.*

Follow the map to the 14th-century **Church of St.-Didier** (10). In the first chapel on the right you will see a noted altarpiece of 1478, called *"Our Lady of the Spasm"* for its realistic depiction of the Virgin in anguish. There are also some outstanding 14th-century frescoes in the first chapel on the left.

The route now wanders through a picturesque old part of town to the **Rue des Teinturiers**, an ancient cobbled street running along a stream lined with old water wheels once used in the production of dyed fabrics. Stop in at the **Chapel of the Grey Penitents** *(Pénitents Gris)* (11) to admire its splendid 17th-century golden glory. Continue on to the ramparts, then return to the tourist office, following the map. You may be interested in visiting the nearby **Lapidary Museum** (12) on Rue de la République, which features Gallo-Roman and prehistoric archaeological finds from the region, housed in a former Jesuit chapel of the 17th century. ☎ *04-9086-3384. Open Wed.–Mon., 10–1 and 2–6. Entrance 10FF.* From here it is only a short stroll back to the station.

Nîmes

Some of the most remarkable Roman structures outside Italy are to be found in Nîmes, a handsome city on the fringe of Provence that bills itself as *"La Rome Française."* A visit here will be made even more enjoyable by the magnificent gardens, the fine museums, and by a stroll through the colorful medieval quarter.

Centered around a sacred spring, Nîmes was already a large tribal settlement when the Romans came in 121 BC. Then known as *Nemausus,* it flourished as a colony of veterans set at the junction of several trade routes. During this time it became a showplace of the Roman Empire, with many fine buildings, some of which are still in excellent condition.

Occupation by the Visigoths in the 5th century AD prevented the spread of Christianity, which did not arrive until the 8th century. After that, the town was annexed to the Counts of Toulouse. During the 16th century Nîmes became a Protestant stronghold, with religious strife continuing until the Revolution. Since then it has prospered with the development of various light industries.

The city is noted for the manufacture of textiles, particularly of a rough twill fabric long marketed abroad as being *"de Nîmes,"* from which we get the word denim.

Nîmes can be used as a base for daytrips in Provence, although it is not as convenient for this purpose as Marseille, Arles or Avignon. Other short excursion possibilities are to the ancient walled town of Aigues-Mortes or the famous Roman aqueduct at Pont du Gard, both served by regional buses. Ask at the tourist office for current schedules.

GETTING THERE:

Trains depart St.-Charles Station in Marseille in the morning for Nîmes, a trip of about 75 minutes. Return service operates until early evening. Most of these also stop at Arles en route. There are direct trains between Nîmes and Avignon, including TGVs, taking about 30 minutes. To get to Aix-en-Provence requires a change at Marseille.

Nimes is connected to Paris with direct TGV service, the run taking about 4.5 hours.

By car, Nîmes is easy to reach following local maps. Distances are: 75 miles northwest of Marseille, from Aix-en-Provence—66 miles, Arles—19 miles, and Avignon—27 miles.

PRACTICALITIES:

The Roman monuments of Nîmes are open daily except on a few major holidays, although the Arena cannot be visited on bullfight days. The museums are closed on Mondays and public holidays. The local **tourist office**, ☎ 04-6667-2911, Internet: www.nimes.mnet.fr or www.ot-nimes.fr, is located at 6 Rue Auguste, close to the Maison Carrée. They can find hotel rooms for you and provide bus schedules for nearby excursions. There is also a branch office in the train station.

FOOD AND DRINK:

Nîmes offers a fairly good selection of restaurants, several of which are in hotels. Among the best choices are:

Le Magister (5 Rue Nationale, 2 blocks west of the Augustus Gate) An elegant restaurant with good-value lunches. ☎ 04-6676-1100. X: Sat. lunch, Sun. eve. $$ and $$$

L'Enclos de la Fontaine (in the Hôtel Impérator on Quai de la Fontaine, a block southeast of the Fountain Gardens) Imaginative cuisine in lovely surroundings. ☎ 04-6667-7025. $$ and $$$

Le Lisita (2 Blvd. des Arènes, just north of the Arena) A popular favorite. ☎ 04-6667-2915. X: Sat. $$

Aux Plaisirs des Halles (4 Rue Littre, 2 blocks north of the cathedral) Good food at decent prices, near the heart of Old Nîmes. ☎ 04-6636-0102. $ and $$

Crêperie Les 4 Saisons (3 Rue des Greffes, 2 blocks southwest of the Archaeology Museum) A wide variety of crêpes in the Old Nîmes district. ☎ 04-6667-2170. X: Sun. $

There are quite a few inviting sidewalk cafés behind the arena and along Boulevard Victor-Hugo.

SUGGESTED TOUR:

Numbers in parentheses correspond to numbers on the map. Leave the **train station** (1) and follow the map to the:

*ROMAN ARENA *(Arènes)* (2), ☎ 04-6676-7277. *Open to tourists when not in use for concerts, shows, or bullfights; daily in summer, 9–7; daily in winter 9–noon and 2–5:30. Closed Christmas, New Year's, and May Day. Adults 28FF, students and children 20FF.*

Built in the late 1st century AD, Nîmes' Arena is a bit smaller than its counterpart in Arles, but is actually in better condition. Following the fall of the empire it became a fortress, and during the Middle Ages a slum with some 150 houses erected within its walls. As a result of a complete renovation carried out in the 19th century, the amphitheater is now used for occasional bullfights, concerts and other events. If you happen to come on a bullfight day, don't despair—the running of the bulls down Boulevard Victor-Hugo is an exciting event in itself.

Continue along Boulevard Victor-Hugo to the *Maison Carrée (3) which, despite its name, is rectangular in shape. This splendid Greek-style temple was built around 5 AD and is probably the best-preserved Roman temple anywhere. Unlike most structures from antiquity, it has been in continuous use for a variety of functions for over two thousand years, which no doubt accounts for the fine shape it is in today. In the late 18th century it even provided inspiration for Thomas Jefferson in his design of the Virginia State Capitol. ☎ 04-6636-2676. Open daily in summer, 9–noon and 2:30–7; daily in winter 9–noon and 2–6. Free.

To the right of it stands the Carrée d'Art, a distinguished museum of contemporary art and a striking piece of modern architecture in its own right. ☎ 04-6676-3570. Open Tues.–Sun., 10–6. Closed Mon. and public holidays. Adults 28FF, students 20FF.

Now follow the map past the tourist office to the very impressive Fountain Gardens (Jardins de la Fontaine) (4), laid out in the 18th century around the sacred spring of Nemausus. Stroll over to the exquisite Temple of Diana (5), a highly romantic 2nd-century ruin that was part of a long-vanished Roman sanctuary dedicated to an emperor-worshiping cult.

The route now climbs through a park to the Tour Magne (6), a massive Roman defensive tower that was once part of the town walls. At the time of its construction, about 16 BC, it was some 30 feet taller than it is today, but it is still a fairly stiff climb to the top. The magnificent panoramic view from up there, extending as far as the Pyrenees on a clear day, makes it all worth the effort. ☎ 04-6667-6556. Open daily 9–7, closing at 5:30 in winter. Closed Christmas, New Year's, and May Day. Adults 15FF, students and children 10FF.

Return to the Fountain Gardens (4) and follow Quai de la Fontaine to Boulevard Gambetta. Those interested in early Roman plumbing may want to make a short side trip up Rue du Fort and Rue de la Lampèze to the Castellum (7), an ancient distribution center for water flowing in via the Pont du Gard aqueduct.

Continue along to the Augustus Gate (Porte Auguste) (8), a well-preserved part of the Roman ramparts from the 1st century BC. A few blocks beyond this lies a 17th-century Jesuit monastery that now houses the intriguing Museum of Archaeology (9), displaying many artifacts from prehistoric as well as Roman times. The Natural History Museum, in the same building, is also worth a visit. ☎ 04-6667-2557. Open Tues.–Sun., 11–6. Closed Mon. and certain holidays. Adults 28FF, students 20FF.

You are now on the edge of Old Nîmes (Vieux Nîmes), the medieval core from which the modern city emerged. Follow the map to the Cathedral of St.-Castor (10), a small and much-altered structure with its roots in the 11th century. The partly Romanesque frieze on its west front depicts scenes from the Old Testament.

Step over to the former Bishop's Palace, a 17th-century mansion that now houses the Museum of Old Nîmes (11), whose collections include furniture in beautiful surroundings along with displays devoted to textiles

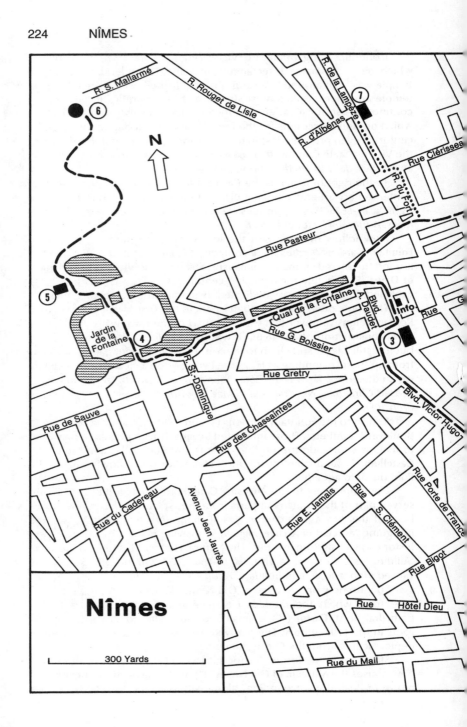

R. S. Mallarmé
R. Rouget de Lisle
R. de la Lampèze
6
7
R. d'Albénas
Rue Clérissea
N
R. du Fort
Rue Pasteur
5
Quai de la Fontaine
Blvd. A Daudet
Info
Rue
G
Jardin de la Fontaine
4
Rue G. Boissier
3
Rue Gretry
R. St. Dominique
Rue de Sauve
Blvd. Victor Hugo
Rue des Chassaintes
Rue E. Jamais
Rue
S. Clément
Rue Porte de France
Rue du Cadereau
Avenue Jean Jaurès
Rue Bigot
Rue
Hôtel Dieu
Nîmes
Rue du Mail
300 Yards

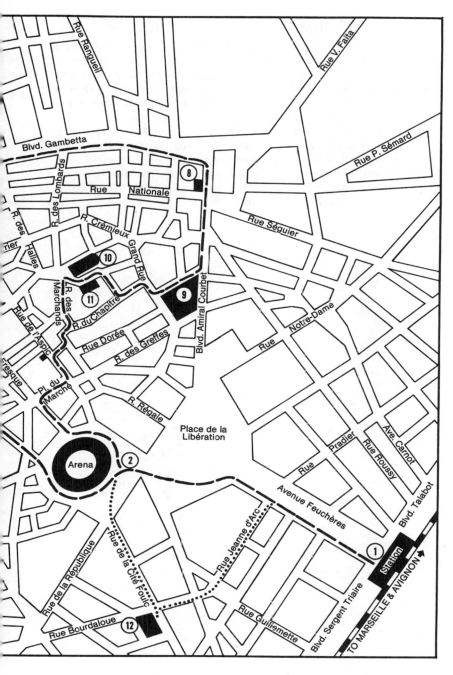

and bullfighting. ☎ *04-6636-0064. Open Tues.–Sun., 11–6, closed holidays. Adults 28FF, students 20FF.*

The route now leads through some highly picturesque streets lined with nicely restored houses of mixed ages, several of which are medieval. Take a look into the courtyard at number 14 Rue de l'Aspic, noted for its magnificent double staircase. There are many other pleasant surprises in this charming neighborhood, best seen by just wandering around and poking your head into doorways.

Return to the station via the Arena. You may be interested in making a slight detour to the **Fine Arts Museum** *(Musée des Beaux-Arts)* (12). The most remarkable item there is a major Roman mosaic on the ground floor. There are also a number of paintings representing various European schools from the 16th through the 19th centuries. ☎ *04-6667-3821. Open Tues.–Sun., 11–6, closed holidays. Adults 28FF, students 20FF.*

Section VIII

DAYTRIPS ON
THE RIVIERA

There is something for everyone on the French Riviera. Whether your tastes run to hedonistic resorts, half-hidden hill towns, vibrant art colonies, medieval strongholds, golden beaches, mountains and forests, sophisticated urban centers or gambling casinos, you're sure to find some little corner of this enchanted, sun-drenched land that will call you back again and again. And that, precisely, is the reason why daytrips throughout the region are such a good idea. They allow you to sample many different facets of the Riviera in a relatively short time and at reasonable cost, so when you return—and you probably will return—you'll know just where to head.

There is no exact definition of what constitutes the Riviera or, as it is often called, the Côte d'Azur. For the purposes of the book, however, it includes the Mediterranean seacoast from St. Tropez to the Italian border, and extends north to the beginnings of the Alps.

Although almost any of the coastal towns can be used as a base for your daytrips, there is no denying that Nice is the most convenient for those traveling by rail or bus since it is the transportation hub of the entire region, with frequent services to the other attractions. A large and very attractive city with a Mediterranean flair all its own, Nice has a broad range of hotels and restaurants in every conceivable price bracket. Other towns that make particularly good bases are Cannes, Antibes, Monaco and Menton.

Trip 35

Old Nice

Nice is, well, nice. That is probably the best possible word to describe this appealing city—the fifth-largest in France—beautifully situated on the edge of the Mediterranean and practically in the shadow of the Alps. Not extravagantly spectacular in any one aspect, its harmonious blend of qualities makes it quite endearing to the many visitors who return year after year. A great commercial center in its own right, Nice does not have to depend on tourists for a living and is all the more attractive for that.

Since there is an excellent chance that Nice will be the base for your Riviera daytrips, two walking tours are included that cover the most interesting parts of town. Either of these can be done in just a few hours, leaving the rest of the day free for a possible half-day excursion to a nearby uncomplicated destination such as Cagnes-sur-Mer or Menton. Or for taking the other tour, or for just relaxing.

The first walking tour explores the picturesque narrow alleyways, outdoor markets, hilltop fortress and bustling port of Old Nice, a delightful district that retains much of its ancient charm. The second tour—described in the next chapter—turns inland to the relics of Roman Nice on the Cimiez hill.

Founded as a trading post by the Phocean Greeks of Marseille around 350 BC, the settlement was first called *Nikêa* in honor of Nike, the goddess of victory, following a defeat of the local Ligurian tribes. Two centuries later, the Romans established a town—*Cemenelum*—on the Cimiez hill, but this was later destroyed by the Barbarians and the Saracens. In the 10th century AD Nice came to life again and prospered, first as a part of Provence and later under the Italian House of Savoy. Although it changed hands several times, the city remained essentially a Savoyan one until 1860, when it was ceded to France after a popular plebiscite. Much of its ancient heritage still lingers in the twisting lanes of Old Nice, and especially on the menus of many of its best restaurants.

GETTING THERE:
   Trains connect Nice with virtually all coastal towns along the Riviera, from St. Raphaël to the Italian border, at frequent intervals, with service operating until late evening. Expresses stop at major towns including St. Raphaël, Cannes, Antibes, Monaco and Menton; while locals *(omnibus)* make halts virtually everywhere. Typical running times to Nice are: from

Cannes—under 30 minutes; from Antibes—15 minutes; from Monaco—20 minutes; and from Menton—under 30 minutes.

There is direct train service to and from Paris, with the TGV types making the run in 7 hours.

The main station in Nice *(Gare Nice-Ville)* is about a 10- to 15-minute stroll from the starting point of this walking tour, Place Masséna. There is also frequent bus service, as well as taxis. You can get a free city map at the tourist office adjacent to the train station.

By car, Nice is 11 miles from Monaco, 17 miles from Menton, 8 miles from Cagnes-sur-Mer, 15 miles from Antibes and 21 miles from Cannes. Recommended routes are given in the chapters dealing with those and other towns.

By air, the Nice-Côte d'Azur Airport is only four miles southwest of the city center and has frequent flights to Paris and to all over Europe, North Africa, the Middle East, and North America.

PRACTICALITIES:

Old Nice may be explored at any time, but note the schedules of the museums if these are of interest to you.

Nice has several **tourist offices**. One of these is located next to the main train station, ☎ 04-9387-0707. Another convenient branch, ☎ 04-9214-4800, is at 5 Promenade des Anglais, just west of the Jardin Albert I near the Old Town and Place Masséna. There is also an office on the road leading in from the airport. Be sure to ask for a city map—essential for finding your way around the parts of town not covered by these walking tours. A useful Internet site is: www.ville-nice.fr.

FOOD AND DRINK:

Nice is blessed with an exceptionally wide range of restaurants at every possible price level. Many of these feature seafood, Niçoise or Italian cuisine. The choices listed below are located in or near the old part of town covered by this walking tour. For restaurants in other parts of Nice you should consult a reliable guide such as the red-cover *Michelin France*.

Don Camillo (5 Rue des Ponchettes, near the base of the elevator to Le Château) Italian and Niçoise specialties in a relaxed setting. ☎ 04-9385-6795. X: Sun., Mon. lunch. $$$

Ane Rouge (7 Quai des Deux-Emmanuel, a block beyond the east side of Port Lympia) Exquisite seafood. ☎ 04-9389-4963. X: Wed. $$ and $$$

Chez Rolando (3 Rue Desboutins, 2 blocks southwest of Place Masséna) Italian cuisine. ☎ 04-9385-7679. X: Sun., holidays, July. $$ and $$$

Les Dents de la Mer (2 Rue St.-François-de-Paule, just east of the Opéra) Contemporary classical seafood dishes in a very nautical environment. ☎ 04-9380-9916. $$ and $$$

La Merenda (4 Rue de la Terrace, 2 blocks northwest of the flower market) A tiny and very popular restaurant with authentic Niçoise cuisine. No phone, stop by and reserve. X: Sat., Sun., early April, late July to mid-Aug.

$$

L'Olivier (2 Place Garibaldi) A small place for home cooking, Provençal style. Reserve, ☎ 04-9326-8909. X: Sun., Wed. lunch, Aug. $$

La Nissarda (17 Rue Gubernatis, 6 blocks north of the Opéra) Niçoise, French and Italian dishes in a traditional neighborhood restaurant. ☎ 04-9385-2629. X: Sun., holidays, Aug. $

Nissa Socca (5 Rue Sainte-Réparate, by the cathedral) Niçoise home cooking at bargain prices—very popular, so wait in line. ☎ 04-9380-1835. X: Sun. $

SUGGESTED TOUR:

Numbers in parentheses correspond to numbers on the map.

Begin your walk at the very heart of Nice, the elegant **Place Masséna** (1), located near the beach and many of the city's best hotels and shopping areas. It can be easily reached from other parts of town by bus or on foot. For those lucky enough to be in Nice during the annual Carnival, held during the last two weeks of February, this is the best possible place for viewing the festivities.

Continue around the **Jardin Albert I**, a lovely garden filled with exotic plants and palm trees. The Quai des États-Unis is an extension of the world-renowned **Promenade des Anglais**, a seaside avenue laid out by the resident English colony in the early 1800s and soon taken over by the town. The beach along here is certainly pretty to look at but not very comfortable for sunbathing since it is all pebbles.

A left turn at the handsome, late-19th-century **Opéra** leads to the Cours Saleya and the outdoor **Flower Market** (2), a colorful spot that comes to life with the vending of flowers and produce from early morning until mid-afternoon, every day except Mondays and Sunday afternoons.

Follow the map to the base of a steep, rocky plateau overlooking the city, port and seacoast. An **elevator** *(ascenseur)* (3), reached through a short tunnel, will quickly lift you some 300 feet for a marvelous view from the top. *Operates daily, 9–5:50, until 7:50 in summer. Fare up: 5FF.* It is also possible to walk up. Still known as ***Le Château** (4), its summit is crowned with the ruins of a 16th-century fortress, destroyed in 1706 on orders from Louis XIV. Close by are the foundations of an 11th-century cathedral and some early Greek structures. A stroll through the lush gardens leads to a viewing platform, several outdoor cafés, and an utterly delightful artificial waterfall *(cascade).*

On the way back be sure to stop at the **Bellanda Tower**, a 16th-century circular bastion near the elevator, now housing the **Naval Museum**. Step inside to admire the splendid ship models and nautical artifacts. ☎ 04-9380-4761. *Open Wed.–Sun., 10–noon and 2–7, closing at 6 from Oct.–May. Closed Mon., Tues., and holidays. Adults 15FF, students 9FF.* Interestingly, the tower was once occupied by Hector Berlioz, who composed the music to *King Lear* in these rooms. From here you can easily walk down or rejoin the elevator—it makes a stop at the museum, part way down the hill.

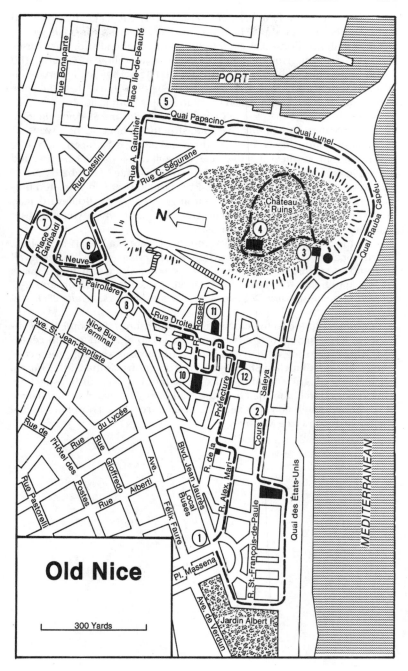

Old Nice

300 Yards

Continue around the base of the hill to **Port Lympia** (5), the lively old harbor of Nice. Begun in 1750, it provides a safe haven for boats which, prior to that, just docked along the foot of the castle hill. Regular cruises are offered to other points along the Riviera, as well as to Corsica. The north end of the harbor, known as Place de l'Ile-de-Beauté, is very reminiscent of Italy, and it was in fact near the Customs House that Giuseppe Garibaldi, the hero of the Italian Revolution, was born in 1807.

Now follow the map to the **Church of St.-Martin and St.-Augustin** (6), a richly-decorated 17th-century baroque structure that contains a wonderful *Pietà* by Louis Bréa. It was here that Garibaldi was baptized. Continue down the narrow alleyways to **Place Garibaldi** (7), a magnificent arcaded square in the 18th-century Savoyan style with a statue of Garibaldi.

Rue Pairolière leads to **Place St.-François** (8), where an animated outdoor fish market is held in the mornings. Nearby, on Boulevard Jean Jaurès, is the modern bus terminal *(Gare Routière)*, which you might be using for some of the other daytrips.

A stop at the **Lascaris Palace** (9) on Rue Droite is a "must" for visitors to Old Nice. This 17th-century mansion in the Genoese style has been well restored and furnished with period pieces along with fascinating displays of folk traditions. ☎ *04-9362-0554. Open Tues.–Sun., 10–noon and 2–6. Closed late Nov. to mid-Dec., Mon. and some holidays. Adults 25FF, students 15FF.*

Wander around to the **Cathedral of Ste.-Réparate** (10), a mid-17th-century classical building with a fine dome of glazed tiles and an 18th-century tower. Step inside to view the marvelous baroque carvings, then continue on to the **Church of St.-Jacques** (11), also known as the Gesù Church. Again, there is a truly magnificent baroque interior well worth inspecting. One other church you may be interested in is the **Chapel of St.-Giaume** (12), another splendid example of baroque decoration. From here follow the map back to Place Masséna.

*Nice-Cimiez

When the Romans came to Nice around 150 BC, they immediately moved inland to the heights of Cimiez, commanding a view of the surrounding countryside. Previously, this had been the site of a Ligurian fort. Known as *Cemenelum*, the Roman town rapidly grew to an estimated population of 20,000, and soon acquired the usual features including an arena, baths and so on. This gradually fell to ruin during the Barbarian invasions and was abandoned by the 6th century AD.

Cimiez is now an attractive residential area with many splendid homes. During the 19th century it was especially favored by the British. Queen Victoria was a frequent winter guest, staying at the old Hôtel Régina at the top of the main boulevard, from which her statue still surveys the scene.

Scattered among the elegant homes and gardens on the Cimiez hill are two outstanding art museums, some fascinating Roman ruins, and an interesting monastery. This trip can easily be done in half a day, leaving the remaining hours to explore Old Nice.

GETTING THERE:

City buses (Route #15) leave from Place Masséna in downtown Nice (see map on page 231) very frequently for the starting point of this tour, the Marc Chagall Museum (1). Get off at the "Chagall" stop. The same bus continues on to the Roman Arena (2), whose stop is marked "Arènes."

Those starting at the **main train station** in Nice can easily walk to the Chagall Museum, using the city map offered by the tourist office as a guide. This should take about ten minutes but does involve a short, steep climb. Taxis are also available.

By car, start at the wide promenade between Place Garibaldi and the Palais des Congrès, then follow Boulevard Carabacel and Boulevard de Cimiez to the Chagall Museum. Ample parking is available everywhere.

PRACTICALITIES:

The Chagall and Matisse museums are closed on Tuesdays, while the Archaeological Museum closes on Mondays, some holidays, Sunday mornings, and most of November. The Franciscan Museum is closed on Sundays and holidays. Good weather will make this trip much more enjoyable.

See page 229 for the location of **tourist offices** in Nice. A good Internet site to check for current exhibitions is: www.ville-nice.fr.

FOOD AND DRINK:

There are virtually no restaurants in the Cimiez area, so plan on eating in Nice proper (see page 229). Snacks and drinks are available outdoors at or near each of the attractions.

SUGGESTED TOUR:

Numbers in parentheses correspond to numbers on the map. Begin at the renowned:

*MARC CHAGALL MUSEUM (*Musée National Message Biblique Marc Chagall*) (1), ☎ 04-9353-8720. *Open Wed.–Mon., 10–6, closing at 5 from Oct.–June. Admission in July–Sept., adults 38FF, seniors and students 28FF; rest of year, adults 30FF, seniors and students 20FF.*

The Marc Chagall Museum was opened in 1973 as the only national museum dedicated to a then-living artist. It is devoted primarily to a series of large canvases created during the 1960s in which Chagall depicted his own unique version of stories from the Bible. These were donated to the State on the condition that the government would erect a suitable museum. Chagall's strange and colorful fantasies are enormously popular, attracting a great many visitors to this rather out-of-the-way spot. The museum itself is a delightful place—modern, well lit and beautifully arranged. In addition to the Biblical series, don't miss the sculptures, tapestries, stained-glass windows, graphic works and, especially, the outdoor mosaic of the prophet Elijah rising to Heaven. Chagall, who died nearby in 1985 at the age of 97, was himself a sometime visitor to the museum.

From here it is a pleasant but slightly uphill walk of a bit less than a mile to the **Roman Arena** (2), located in a public park. You can also get there by taking bus number 15 from the stop on the far side of Boulevard de Cimiez. One of the smallest amphitheaters in the Roman world, it probably dates from the 1st century AD and could seat some 5,000 spectators after its enlargement in the 3rd century. Although in poor condition, the arena is still used for occasional performances.

Stroll over to the charming 17th-century Villa des Arènes, home of the:

*MATISSE MUSEUM (3), ☎ 04-9381-0808. *Open Wed.–Mon., 10–6, closing at 5 from Oct.–March. Closed Christmas, New Year's, May Day. Adults 25FF, students 15FF, under 18 free.*

The collections here span the entire career of the famous artist Henri Matisse. Born in 1869, Matisse spent much of his life around Nice and died in Cimiez in 1954. It is absolutely fascinating to see such a broad scope of artistic talent, covering such a long period of time, displayed in these 18

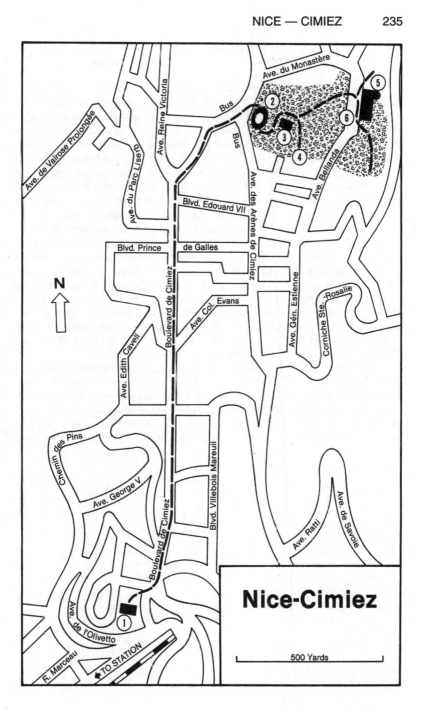

Nice-Cimiez

500 Yards

rooms. Don't miss his sketches and models for the Chapel of the Rosary in Vence (see page 281).

Nearby is the *Archaeological Museum (4) with its exhibits of local artifacts from the 7th century BC through the Roman era. Step outside to visit the adjacent Archaeological Site, where you can wander around a large area of Roman ruins. The 3rd-century AD baths, one of which is incorrectly called the "Temple of Apollo," are possibly the best to be found in Gaul. Just south of the villa are the remains of a 5th-century Palaeo-Christian basilica. A guide booklet in English is available to help you understand the digs. ☎ 04-9381-5957. Open April–Sept., Tues.–Sun., 10–noon and 2–6; rest of year, Tues.–Sun., 10–1 and 2–5. Closed Mon., Sun. mornings, some holidays, and from mid-Nov. to early Dec. Adults 25FF, students 15FF.

A short stroll through the park leads to the Cimiez Monastery (5), heavily rebuilt in the 19th century. This originally dates from the 16th century, when it replaced a 9th-century Benedictine monastery erected on the site of a temple of Diana. The church interior contains some remarkable *works of art including both a 15th-century Pietà and a Crucifixion by Louis Bréa. The Franciscan Museum (6), next to this, tells the story of the order's life and works in several intriguing displays, with a re-created 17th-century monk's cell and an 18th-century chapel as highlights. A descriptive brochure in English is available. ☎ 04-9381-0004. Open Mon.–Sat., 10–noon and 3–6. Closed Sun. and some holidays. Free.

Be sure to stroll out into the magnificent terraced gardens that overlook the city and the Mediterranean. The view from here is just fabulous. Before leaving, you may want to stop at the little cemetery just north of the church. Both Matisse and his fellow artist Raoul Dufy are buried here. Return to the arena to take bus number 15 back to Nice proper. You can also take bus number I7 from the opposite corner, whichever comes first.

Villefranche, Cap-Ferrat, and Beaulieu

D espite rampant commercialization, isolated pockets of the romantic old Riviera do still exist, largely unchanged since the Roaring Twenties. This classic daytrip from Nice takes you just a few miles in distance, but decades in time, to some very unusual sights in a setting of spectacular natural beauty.

The picturesque old port of Villefranche is a largely unspoiled 18th-century town whose ancient streets sometimes tunnel under the jumble of colorful houses. Among its attractions is a bizarre art museum in the dungeons of a 16th-century fortress, and a highly unusual chapel decorated by Jean Cocteau. From there you can walk (or take a bus) along the coast and out onto the Cap Ferrat peninsula, whose lush Mediterranean vegetation shelters homes of the rich and famous. One of the most magnificent of these, a villa built for the Baroness Ephrussi de Rothschild, is open to the public, as are the lovely gardens.

Passing through the port village of St.-Jean-Cap-Ferrat, the route follows a coastal promenade to the old resort of Beaulieu-sur-Mer, snuggled between mountains and the sea, which is noted for its exceptionally mild climate. Its sole tourist attraction, the strange Villa Kérylos, is alone worth a trip.

GETTING THERE:

Trains depart Nice frequently for the 7-minute ride to Villefranche-sur-Mer. Be sure to take a local *(Omnibus)*. Return service from Beaulieu-sur-Mer operates until late evening. The same line serves practically all spots on the Riviera coast.

By car, take the N-98 Basse Corniche road, which begins in Nice as Boulevard Carnot. Exit to the center of Villefranche-sur-Mer, less than 4 miles to the east. By modifying the route, you can drive the entire suggested tour route and not have to walk.

PRACTICALITIES:

The Rothschild estate and the Villa Kérylos are open daily, while the Cocteau chapel is closed on Mondays, and the Citadel on Tuesdays.

The local **Tourist Information Offices** are: **Villefranche**, 1 Square Binon,

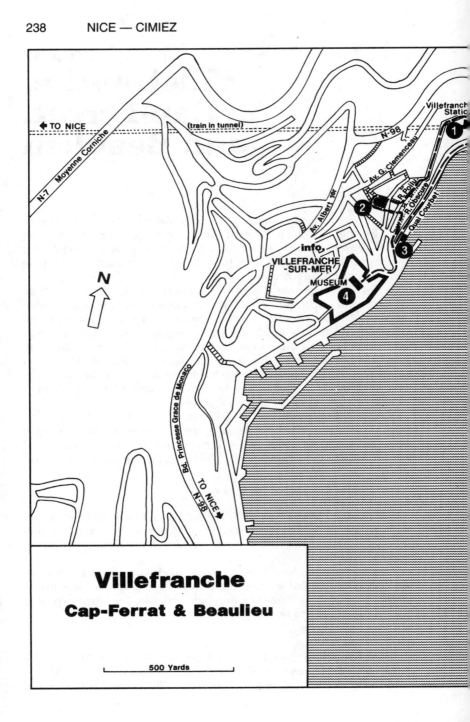

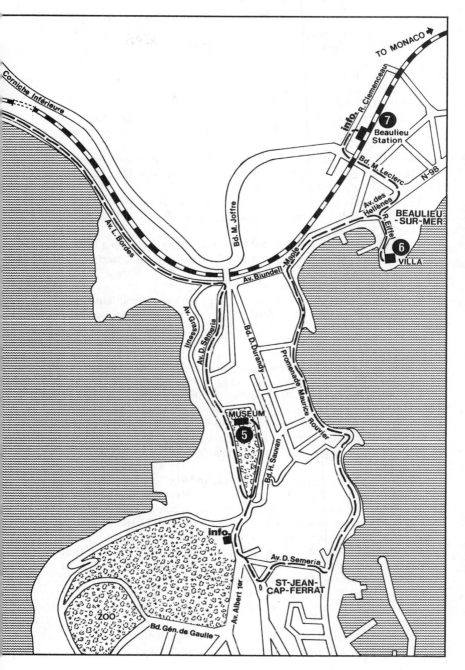

3 blocks west of the Citadel, ☎ 04-9301-7368; **St.-Jean-Cap-Ferrat**, 59 Avenue Denis-Semeria, 3 blocks south of the Rothschild estate, ☎ 04-9376-0890; and **Beaulieu**, by the train station, ☎ 04-9301-0221.

FOOD AND DRINK:

Some restaurant suggestions are:
IN VILLEFRANCHE-SUR-MER:
Le Saint-Pierre (1 Quai Courbet, near the Cocteau chapel) Classical cuisine overlooking the sea, with a glassed-in terrace. ☎ 04-9376-2727. $$ and $$$

Provençal (4 Av. Maréchal-Joffre, 2 blocks northwest of the Citadel) A small hotel with good-value meals. ☎ 04-9301-7142. X: Nov., Dec. $$

IN ST.-JEAN-CAP-FERRAT:
Le Provençal (2 Av. Denis-Semeria, 1 block west of the port) Specializes in fish, especially *bouillabaisse*. ☎ 04-9376-0539. X: Nov.–March. $$$

Le Sloop (at the north end of the port) Inventive cuisine on a terrace facing the yachts. ☎ 04-9301-4863. X: Wed. off season, Wed. and Thurs. lunch in season. $$

IN BEAULIEU-SUR-MER:
Les Araves (4 Ave. Mar.-Foch, by the train station in Beaulieu) Good food at reasonable prices. ☎ 04-9301-1312. X: Sun. eve and Mon. except in July–Aug. $$

SUGGESTED TOUR:

Numbers in parentheses correspond to numbers on the map.
Leave the **Villefranche Station** (1) and follow the map to Rue du Poilu, a main street of the **Old Town** *(Vieille Ville)*. Parallel to this, towards the sea, is the mysterious **Rue Obscure**, a dark passageway tunneling beneath the brightly-colored houses. One block to the west stands the **Église St.-Michel** (2), a 17th-century church in the Italian Baroque style, noted for its striking figure of Christ carved from a single piece of wood by a forgotten 17th-century convict.

Continue on Rue de l'Église and the vaulted Rue Obscure to the **Old Port**, founded in the 14th century as a duty-free area. It faces a sheltered bay of exceptional depth, a roadstead that easily accommodates large liners and warships. Next to the harbor is the **Chapelle St.-Pierre** (3), a 14th-century fishermen's chapel that was decorated in 1957 by the avant-garde writer and film maker Jean Cocteau. His staring-eye ceramics represent the flames of the Apocalypse, while the pastel frescoes depict the life of Saint Peter, gypsies, and the women of Villefranche. ☎ 04-9376- 9070. *Open Tues.–Sun., 10–noon and 4–8:30 in summer; 9:30–noon and 2–6 in fall; 9:30–noon and 2–5 in winter; 9:30–noon and 3–7 in spring. Entrance 12FF.*

The huge **Citadel** (4) overlooking the port was built in the 16th-century by the dukes of Savoy, who then ruled this region. Today it houses the

Volti Museum, where strange modern sculptures by a local artist are displayed in the courtyard and deep in the surrounding casemates. ☎ *04-9376-3327. Open Mon. and Wed.–Sat., 10–noon and 2–5, 3–8 in summer; Sun. 2–5, 3–8 in summer. Free.*

Now follow the map on foot (or take a bus) around the bay and out onto the **Cap Ferrat peninsula,** a hilly spit of land covered with exotic vegetation and dotted with the mansions of the super rich. Nearly all of these are exceedingly private, but you can visit one of the grandest of them all, the:

*VILLA EPHRUSSI DE ROTHSCHILD (5), ☎ 04-9301-3309. *Open mid-Feb. to Oct., daily 10–6 (7 in July and Aug.); rest of year, Mon.–Fri. 2–6, weekends 10–6. Adults 46FF, students 35FF, plus 15FF for the upper floor.*

Built in 1912, the villa was bequeathed in 1934 to the Académie des Beaux-Arts and is now the **Île-de-France Museum,** where the rather eclectic collections of the Baroness de Rothschild are displayed in a jewel of a setting. Among the many treasures are Renaissance furniture, Aubusson tapestries, Sèvres porcelains, period costumes, and paintings by Boucher and Fragonard. One gallery is devoted to the 19th-century Impressionists, with important works by Renoir, Sisley, and Monet. Surrounding the villa are some 17 acres of fabulous ***gardens** in various styles, some with dramatic views over the Mediterranean.

The route leads across the peninsula to the former fishing village of **St.Jean-Cap-Ferrat,** now a small resort. From its harbor follow the **Promenade Maurice Rouvier,** a coastal pedestrian path with fabulous views, to the old resort of **Beaulieu-sur-Mer.** The sole tourist attraction in this lovely town is the curious:

*VILLA KÉRYLOS (6), ☎ 04-9301-0144. *Open July–Aug., daily 10–7; Sept. daily 10–6; rest of year, daily 10:30–12:30 and 2–6; closed weekday mornings from mid-Dec. to mid-Feb., Christmas and New Year's. Adults 40FF, students 25FF.*

Built in 1900 by the archaeologist Théodore Reinach as an exact replica of a Greek villa from antiquity, Villa Kérylos is perched on a promontory overlooking the town and bay. Its library displays genuine art from that era, while the furniture is mostly reproductions copied from those depicted on ancient vases. Classified as a historic monument, the villa has belonged to the Institut de France since the owner's death in 1928. Entering it is like stepping back three millennia in time, at least visually, yet it retains a strangely decadent ambiance from the early 1900s. Don't miss this very unusual sight. From here it is a short walk to the **Beaulieu Train Station** (7).

Trip 38

Èze

L ooking down from a rocky perch high above the Mediterranean, the incredibly picturesque village of Èze draws a steady stream of visitors to its enchanted site. Add to the spectacular setting the fact that it's right on the main road linking Nice with Monaco and you have the makings of a classic tourist trap. Fortunately, Èze survives the onslaught with grace and offers many hidden charms to those who will seek them out.

Èze's history goes back to pre-Roman times, when it was an ancient Ligurian *oppidum*, most likely established by the Phoenicians. A Roman highway, the Haraklean Way, passed by here as the area entered into four centuries of peace under the Pax Romana. During the Dark Ages, Èze, weakened by famine and plague, was taken over by the Saracens, whose rule lasted into the 10th century. Following liberation under William, Count of Provence, the village prospered and in 1860 became a part of France.

There are no famous sights or great museums in Èze, just the delightfully medieval pedestrian lanes carved into the rocky mountainside, the ancient stone buildings and, above all, the fantastic views over the Mediterranean. This is the perfect place to unwind, perhaps sitting at a café and absorbing the atmosphere, or visiting the many tiny craftsmen's shops in search of an unusual souvenir.

GETTING THERE:

Buses depart the bus station *(Gare Routière)* on Boulevard Jean-Jaurès in Nice fairly frequently for Èze, a stop on the route to Monaco. Be sure to sit on the right-hand side of the bus to enjoy the spectacular views.

Trains connect Èze-sur-Mer, a sea-level village well below the hill town, with Nice and virtually all other places along the Riviera, at frequent intervals. From there you would have to climb up some 1,200 feet on a rocky path, or take a roundabout route by cab (there are also local buses in summer). You might want to return this way, however.

By car, Èze is about 7 miles northeast of Nice on the N-7 Moyenne Corniche road. Traffic is often congested along here, so allow enough time—and enjoy the fantastic views. There is a large parking lot at the entrance to the village, charging 5FF per hour.

PRACTICALITIES:

Good weather is essential for enjoyment of this trip, which can be

made on any day or in any season. The local **tourist office,** ☎ 04-9341-2600,
Internet: www.eze-riviera.com, is by the parking lot.

FOOD AND DRINK:

You won't go hungry—or thirsty—in Èze, given its numerous restaurants and cafés. Just a few of the better choices are:

Château de la Chèvre d'Or (Rue Barri, near the southeast corner of the
village) Renowned for its regional cuisine served in a pretty setting,
indoors or out. Reservations, ☎ 04-9210-6666. $$$+

Troubador (Rue du Brec, a block south of the church) Traditional
French cuisine in a typical 16th-century house. Reserve, ☎ 04-9341-1903. X:
early July, Dec., Feb., Sun., Mon. lunch. $$ and $$$

L'Olivier (Pl. Gén. de Gaulle, by the parking lot) Well regarded cuisine.
☎ 04-9341-0523. X: Nov. to mid-Dec., Mon., Tues. lunch. $$ and $$$

Bistrot Loumiri (Ave. Jardin Exotique, on the way into the village) A
good-value choice. Reservations suggested, ☎ 04-9341-1642. X: Feb., Mon.,
Wed. eve. $$

SUGGESTED TOUR:

Numbers in parentheses correspond to numbers on the map.

Whether you came by bus or by car, you'll be starting out at the parking lot at **Place Général de Gaulle** (1). From here it's an uphill stroll along
Avenue du Jardin Exotique and into **Èze-Village,** as the upper town is properly known. The sole entrance is by the ancient 14th-century **fortified gateway** *(Porte Fortifiée).* Continue on through the tiny, stepped stone streets,
turning right onto Rue du Brec, becoming Rue de l'Eglise. This leads to the
Parish Church (2), reconstructed in the Classical style in 1772. Within its
Baroque interior is a fine statue of the Assumption as well as a remarkable
baptismal font. A reliquary below the altar contains the remains of Saint
Germain, a martyr of the 4th century.

Return on Rue du Brec, passing the **Local History Museum** (3), a tiny
place that is open only on request. ☎ *04-9210-6060.* Now follow Rue
Principale to Place du Planet, where you'll find the historic **White Penitents'
Chapel** (4). Dating from the 14th century, it was the meeting place of the
White Penitents brotherhood, who for centuries took care of burying
Èze's dead, as well as taking care of its needy. The simple interior is deco-
rated with fine religious art, both medieval and contemporary.

Now follow the route through the narrow alleyways, heading uphill
to the famous ***Tropical Gardens** (Jardin Exotique)* (5). Suspended some
1,400 feet above the blue Mediterranean, the garden offers a breathtaking
***panorama** over the tiled rooftops, the sea, and much of the Riviera.
Established in 1949 around the ruins of a 14th-century castle that was
destroyed in 1706 on orders from Louis XIV, the gardens are filled with
many varieties of cacti and succulents, mostly from the Americas. ☎ *04-
9341-1030. Open daily, 9–6, 7, or 8, depending on season. Admission 12FF.*

Wander down through the village, picking your way through the tiny

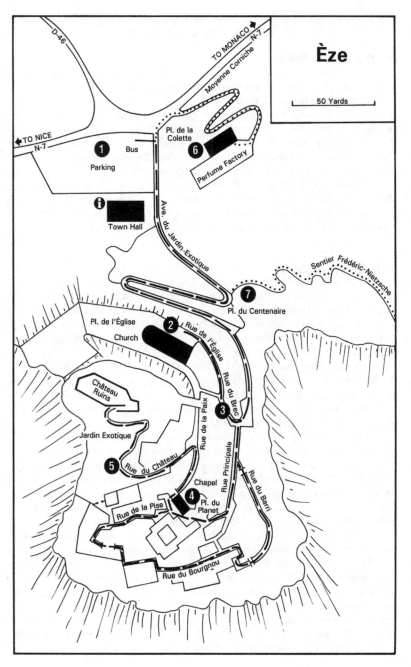

Èze

50 Yards

TO MONACO
Moyenne Corniche N-7

D-46

TO NICE
N-7

1 Bus
Parking

Pl. de la Colette

6 Perfume Factory

i Town Hall

Ave. du Jardin-Exotique

Sentier Frédéric-Nietzsche

7 Pl. du Centenaire

Pl. de l'Église
Church

2 Rue de l'Église

Rue du Brec

Château Ruins

Jardin Exotique

Rue de la Paix

3

5 Rue du Château

Rue Principale

Rue du Barri

Chapel

Rue de la Pise

4 Pl. du Planet

Rue du Bourgnou

passageways and passing several craftsmen's shops, art galleries, boutiques, and souvenir shops. You'll also pass some inviting restaurants and
cafés, many of which offer wonderful views from their outdoor terraces.

Before leaving Èze, you may wish to visit one of its perfume establishments. **Parfumerie Fragonard** (6), near the parking lot, has a perfume
factory as well as a shop, both open to the public. ☎ *04-9341-0505. Visits
daily, 8:30–6:30. Free.*

If you came by bus—and didn't buy a round-trip ticket—you may prefer to return by train instead. The **Sentier Frédéric-Nietzsche** (7) is a steep
woodland path leading sharply down to the station at **Èze-sur-Mer**, from
which trains run frequently to Nice and practically anywhere else on the
Riviera. The great German philosopher Frederic Nietzsche worked out his
masterpiece, *Thus Spake Zarathustra*, while hiking this trail; perhaps you'll
be similarly inspired. Parts of it are rocky, so be sure you have adequate
shoes, and allow a full hour for the 1,200-foot descent.

Monaco

Somewhat less than a square mile in size, the Principality of Monaco is an independent country that thrives on tourism. Its casino is world famous, and the palace adds a touch of theatricality that only a mini-state could muster. The panoramic view from its heights is simply stupendous. Not surprisingly, the two towns of Monaco-Ville and Monte-Carlo, separated by a small harbor, offer more than their share of attractions.

The Grimaldi family has more or less ruled Monaco since 1297, when they liberated it from the Genoese. They also once controlled other choice pieces of real estate along the coast, including Antibes and Cagnes. The last of their holdings, Menton, was sold to France in 1860 at the same time that Nice was ceded and the French-Italian border moved eastward. The family did, however, manage to hang on to Monaco, which was then practically bankrupt. Financial salvation came with the opening of the Principality's first successful casino in 1865 and the arrival of the railroad in 1868. Growth since then has been spectacular, with much of the land now covered by concrete high-rises. Gambling is no longer the major industry, having been replaced by tourism, conventions, and more traditional businesses.

Although it is not a part of France, French money is used in Monaco along with its own coinage. There are no customs to go through between the two countries; in fact the border is practically invisible. As you probably know, the lucky *Monégasques* pay no taxes.

GETTING THERE:

Trains connect Monaco/Monte-Carlo with virtually all coastal towns along the Riviera at frequent intervals. Service operates until late evening. From Nice the ride takes about 20 minutes.

By car, Monaco is best reached via the N-7 road, the famous Moyenne Corniche. It is 11 miles northeast of Nice. There are many underground parking lots—just follow the "P" signs.

GETTING AROUND:

Two-dimensional maps make Monaco seem like a walker's paradise. It isn't. Most of the Principality is extremely hilly, so much so that public elevators have been installed between some streets. You will probably wind up using buses for part of the walking tour. These run quite frequently, with route maps at the bus stops. Fares may be paid directly to the driver.

PRACTICALITIES:

Monaco is always open for business, but some of the sights may be closed in winter or on major holidays. Visits to the Prince's Palace can be made from June through October. The Monaco **tourist office,** ☎ 9216-6116, Internet: www.monaco.mc, is at 2a Boulevard des Moulins in Monte-Carlo, near the casino. They can make hotel reservations for you. Note that the **telephone system** uses 8-digit numbers for local calls. To call a Monaco number from France you must prefix the number with 00, then the country code for Monaco, 377. To call France from Monaco, you dial 00, then 33, then the 10-digit number in France.

FOOD AND DRINK:

Sumptuous dining in Monaco can be a very expensive proposition. Those with thinner wallets will find adequate meals in the many bistro-type places near the station, by the harbor, and in the alleyways behind the Prince's Palace. Some outstanding choices are:

IN THE OLD TOWN:

Castelroc (in front of the Prince's Palace) Monégasque specialties, with outdoor tables overlooking the palace. ☎ 9330-3668. X: Sat., Dec., Jan. $$

Le Pinocchio (30 Rue Comte-Félix-Gastaldi, just north of the cathedral) Italian cuisine, with outdoor tables available. ☎ 9350-9620. X: Wed. in winter, Dec., Jan. $$

U Cavagetu (14 Rue Comte-Félix-Gastaldi, a block north of the cathedral) Local specialties and grills, outdoor seating available. ☎ 9330-3580. X: Fri. $

Saint-Nicolas (6 Rue de l'Eglise, on the west side of the cathedral) Traditional Monégasque and Italian cooking at modest prices. ☎ 9330-3041. X: Wed. $

IN MONTE-CARLO:

Le Louis XV (in the Hôtel de Paris, across from the casino) The finest and most luxurious dining imaginable. Dress accordingly and reserve, ☎ 9216-3001. X: Tues., Wed. $$$+

Le Grill (in the Hôtel de Paris, across from the casino) On the rooftop of a sumptuous hotel, an experience to remember. For reservations ☎ 9216-2966. $$$+

Le Saint-Benoît (l0 ter, Av. de la Costa, 5 blocks southwest of the tourist office. Noted for its seafood and Italian specialties. ☎ 9325-0234. X: Mon. $$$

Café de Paris (Pavilion St.-James, facing the casino) A brasserie with good French food. ☎ 9216-2020. $$$

Polpetta (2 Rue Paradis, 5 blocks southwest of the tourist office) Fine Italian cuisine in a romantic atmosphere. ☎ 9350-6784. X: Tues., Sat. lunch. $$

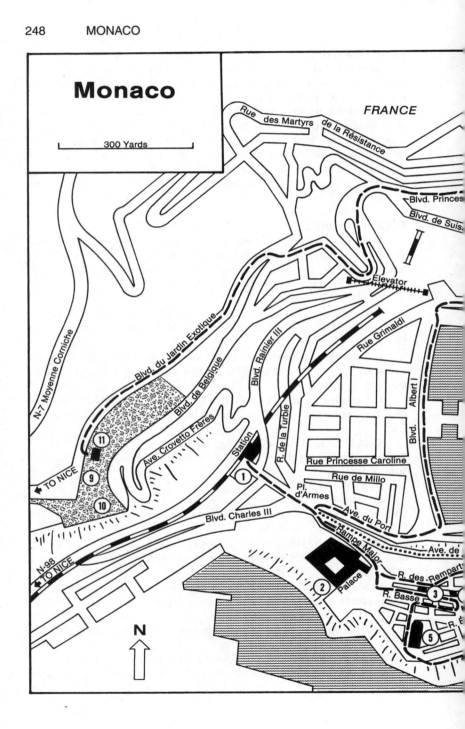

Monaco

300 Yards

FRANCE

Rue des Martyrs de la Résistance

Blvd. Princes

Blvd. de Suis.

Elevator

Blvd. du Jardin Exotique

Blvd. Rainier III

Rue Grimaldi

N-7 Moyenne Corniche

Blvd. de Belgique

Ave. Crovetto Frères

R. de la Turbie

Blvd. Albert I

Rue Princesse Caroline

Station

Rue de Millo

TO NICE

Pl. d'Armes

Ave. du Port

Blvd. Charles III

Hampe Major

Ave. de

N-98 TO NICE

R. des Rempart

R. Basse

Palace

R. É

N

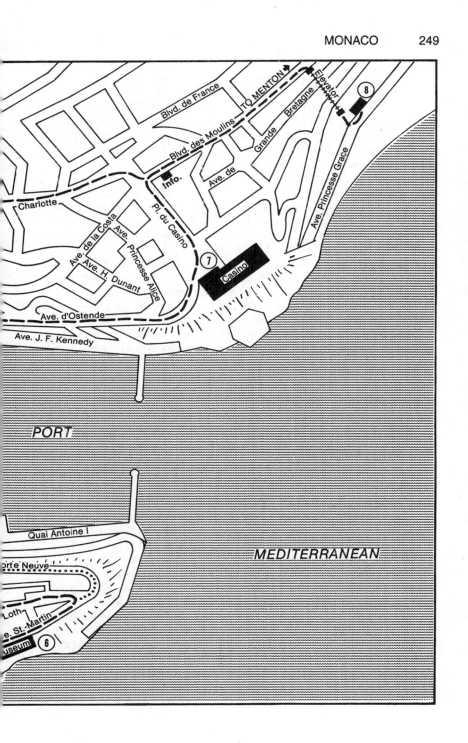

SUGGESTED TOUR:
Numbers in parentheses correspond to numbers on the map.

Leave the **train station** (1) and walk straight ahead to Place d'Armes. From here you can climb up the Rampe Major to the **Old Town** *(Monaco-Ville)*, perched high above the port on a promontory rock *(Le Rocher)*. Alternatively, you can take a bus that drops you off a few level blocks from the first attraction. However you get there, you will have the first of many spectacular views. Begin at the:

PRINCE'S PALACE *(Palais du Prince)* (2), ☎ 9325-1831. *Open from June through Oct., daily 9:30–6:20. Frequent half-hour guided tours in English. Napoleonic Museum open year round, Tues.–Sun., 9:30-6:30, closed Nov. Palace tours: Adults 30FF, children 15FF. Combination ticket with the adjacent Napoleonic Museum: Adults 40FF, children 20FF.*

Surveying the entire domain, the Prince's Palace is open to tourists when the reigning prince is not in residence. Even if you miss this, however, you can still enjoy the slightly ludicrous operetta-like changing-of-the-guard ceremony held daily at 11:55 a.m. in front of the palace. Several outdoor cafés are grouped around here so you can watch in comfort.

The palace itself was begun in 1215 and greatly altered during the ensuing centuries. Besides being home to Prince Rainier III, whose wife, Grace Kelly, was tragically killed in a car accident in 1982, it also houses the small but interesting **Napoleonic Museum** *(Musée des Souvenirs Napoléoniens)*. Step inside to see the many personal effects of the great French leader along with items relating to the history of Monaco.

Several of the narrow lanes in Monaco-Ville are now reserved for pedestrians. Stroll down Rue Basse to the **Historial des Princes de Monaco** (3), a beautifully arranged wax museum that depicts the history of the Grimaldi family in 24 life-size scenes. The costumes are authentic and were donated by the family. ☎ 9330-3905. *Open daily 9:30–6:30 or 7:30; shorter hours off season. Closed Dec. and Jan. Admission charged.*

Continuing down the street, you will pass the **Misericord Chapel** (4), a 17th-century structure whose interior features a fine high altar in polychrome marble and a splendid statue of Christ, which is carried through the Old Town on Good Fridays.

The **Cathedral of Monaco** (5), built at the end of the 19th century in a somewhat ostentatious Neo-Romanesque style, reflects the sudden prosperity brought about by the opening of the casino. It inherited several excellent works of art from the 13th-century church that stood on the same site, including a superb 16th-century altarpiece by Louis Bréa in the right transept. The tomb of Princess Grace (1929-82) is among those of the princes of Monaco.

A stroll through the lovely St.-Martin Gardens leads to the renowned ***Oceanographic Museum** (6), considered to be the best of its kind in the world. Once directed by the noted underwater explorer Jacques

Cousteau, it was founded in 1910 by Prince Albert I, who had a passion for the sea. The large aquarium in its basement is a fascinating treat for all visitors, while the upper floors are devoted to the many aspects of oceanography. ☎ 9315-3600. *Open daily 9–7, remaining open until 8 in July–Aug. Adults 60FF, students 30FF.*

Now follow the map back to Place d'Armes and continue on past the bustling harbor. This is a good place to stop for a rest as there are many outdoor cafés along the waterfront. From here the route leads uphill along Avenue d'Ostende to the town of **Monte Carlo**. You may prefer to take a bus and avoid the rather steep climb to the:

*CASINO OF MONTE-CARLO (7), ☎ 9216-2300. *Entry to first section free; passport and proof of age (at least 21) required. Entry to Salon Ordinaire, 50FF; to Salons Privés, 100FF. Proper dress required, meaning no shorts in salons, tie and jacket for men in Salons Privés.*

The Casino of Monte-Carlo is undoubtedly the most famous gambling establishment in the world. The older section of this highly elaborate structure was designed in 1878 by Charles Garnier, the architect of the Paris Opéra—which it somewhat resembles. To your left as you enter are the gambling rooms, whose extravagant décor is worth seeing even if you're not a gambler. Admission to the first section requires only a passport to prove that you are over 21 and not a local citizen. An entrance fee is charged for the more exclusive—and much more intriguing—salons beyond that. Don't miss the bar with its fantastic ceiling depicting naked ladies puffing on cigars. The casino also contains a magnificent opera house, which can only be seen by attending a performance.

A short walk through the gardens brings you to the tourist office on Boulevard des Moulins. From here you may want to make a little side trip to the **National Museum** (8), housed in a charming mansion also designed by Charles Garnier. Appropriately enough for a toy nation, the enchanting displays here feature hundreds of dolls and mechanical toys *(automata)* in exquisite settings. To reach the museum just follow the map and take the elevator down the hill. ☎ 9330-9126. *Open Easter to Sept., daily 10–6:30; rest of year, daily 10–12:15 and 2:30–6:30. Adults 26FF, students 15FF.*

From the corner near the tourist office you can take bus number 2 (or take a long, boring walk) to the next attraction, the:

*EXOTIC GARDENS *(Jardin Exotique)* (9), ☎ 9315-2980. *Open daily 9–7, closing at 6 or dusk from mid-Sept. to mid-May. Adults 37FF, students 18FF; admission includes the Museum of Anthropology and the caves.*

Clinging to the side of a cliff overlooking the entire Principality, the gardens contain literally thousands of varieties of weird and wonderful plants, especially a broad range of cacti from Africa and Latin America. Near the bottom of this are the **Observatory Caves** *(Grottes de l'Observatoire)* (10), where prehistoric man once lived. Guided tours are conducted through this magic world of stalactites and stalagmites at frequent intervals, a great treat for the energetic who don't mind all the hoofing involved.

Back at the entrance to the gardens is the **Museum of Prehistoric Anthropology** (11) with its collections of ancient relics.

The easiest way to get back to the station is by taking a bus to Place d'Armes. You could also walk part of the way, then take the escalator and elevator down to the port.

Menton

The last town before the Italian border, Menton is a pleasantly picturesque resort blessed with the mildest climate on the Riviera. Long favored by British vacationers, it has become somewhat of a cultural center in recent years. The old quarter, remarkably well preserved, exudes a quiet charm of times gone by. Menton is famous for its citrus fruit, particularly lemons. It makes a good half-day trip since all of the sights can be seen in a few hours; unless you would rather linger and enjoy yourself— not a bad idea.

GETTING THERE:

Trains link Menton with other coastal towns on the Riviera at frequent intervals, with returns until mid-evening. From Nice, the trip takes about 30 minutes.

By car, Menton lies 17 miles northeast of Nice via the A-8 Autoroute or the N-7 road.

PRACTICALITIES:

Sunny Menton may be savored at any time, but note that the museums are closed on Tuesdays and holidays. The local **tourist office,** ☎ 04-9357-5700, is at 8 Avenue Boyer, near the casino.

FOOD AND DRINK:

This old resort offers a good selection of restaurants and cafés, especially along the Promenade du Soleil and near the port. Some choices are:

Café Fiori (in the Hôtel Ambassadeurs, 3 Rue Partouneaux, a block north of the tourist office) The most elegant place in Menton for traditional French cuisine. ☎ 04-9328-7575. $$ and $$$

Chaudron (28 Rue St.-Michel, near the market place) Good French cuisine at fair prices. Reservations advised. ☎ 04-9335- 9025. Mon. eve. off-season, Tues. $$

Au Pistou (9 Quai Gordon Bennett, by the port) An excellent value, indoors or out. ☎ 04-9357-4589. X: Mon. $

SUGGESTED TOUR:

Numbers in parentheses correspond to numbers on the map.

Leave the **train station** (1) and follow the map through the lovely Biovès Garden along Avenue Boyer. Turn around for a splendid view of the nearby mountains framed by orange trees. Along the way you will pass the impressive **Palais de l'Europe** (2), a cultural center in the Belle Époque style

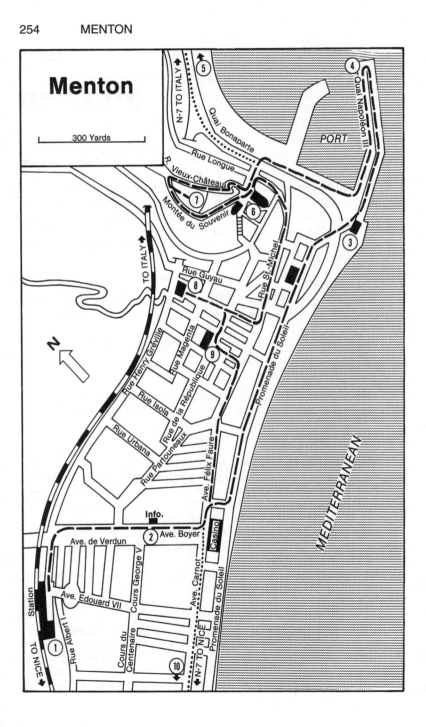

Menton

300 Yards

N-7 TO ITALY

Quai Bonaparte

Quai Napoléon III

PORT

Rue Longue

R. Vieux-Château

Montée du Souvenir

TO ITALY

Rue Guyau

Rue St-Michel

Rue Henry Gréville

Rue Magenta

Rue Isola

Rue de la République

Promenade du Soleil

Rue Urbana

Rue Partouneaux

Ave. Félix Faure

MEDITERRANEAN

Info.

Ave. Boyer

Ave. de Verdun

Cours George V

Casino

Ave. Carnot

Promenade du Soleil

Station

Ave. Edouard VII

Rue Albert I

Cours du Centenaire

N-7 TO NICE

TO NICE

that houses the tourist office.

Continue on past the casino to the *Promenade du Soleil, an elegant avenue running alongside the beach. Follow this to the Municipal Market brimming with morning activity in an old Victorian structure. The Jean Cocteau Museum (3) lies just beyond this, housed in a small fortification erected during the 17th century by the rulers of Monaco, which once owned Menton. Cocteau, who died in 1963, was primarily known as a talented poet, writer, film maker and general leader in French avant-garde circles. His reputation as a graphic artist is less secure, but the works displayed here are nonetheless fascinating. There is also an outstanding drawing of him by Picasso. ☎ 04-9357-7230. Open Wed.–Mon., 10–noon and 2–6. Closed holidays. Adults 20FF, students 15FF, children free.

Stroll out on the Quai Napoléon III Jetty (4), climbing the steps next to the museum for a marvelous view of the Old Town. When you get to the lighthouse at the end, descend to the lower level and return.

Continue along the port and climb the steps to Quai Bonaparte, a broad street supported by arches. From here you can make a short side trip to the Tropical Garden (Jardin Botanique) (5, off the map) in the suburb of Garavan. Turn left on Chemin St.-Jacques to enter the magnificent gardens, located one-half mile from the Italian border. Open Feb.–Sept., daily 9–noon and 3–8, closing at sunset when earlier.

Back at the port, climb the massive staircase to the Church of St.-Michel (6) in the Old Town. Facing a charming little Italianate square where outdoor concerts are given in August, the 17th-century baroque church has a richly decorated interior that should be seen. At the end of the square stands another interesting church, the Chapel of the Pénitents-Blancs.

Now follow Rue du Vieux Château to the Old Cemetery (7), built on the site of a former castle, which offers splendid *views from its grounds. Return via Montée du Souvenir and descend the steps as far as Rue Longue. A right leads through a picturesque neighborhood to the new town.

Stroll down Rue St.-Michel and turn right to the Museum for Regional Prehistory (8). The displays here are concerned with local history, folk art and archaeology. ☎ 04-9335-8464. Open Wed.–Mon., 10–noon and 2–6, closing earlier in winter. Closed holidays.

Continue on to the Town Hall (Hôtel de Ville) (9), which features a fantastic Marriage Room (Salle des Mariages) wildly decorated by Jean Cocteau in 1957. Step inside and ask to see it. ☎ 04-9210-5000. Open Mon.–Fri., 8:30–12:30 and 1:30–5. Closed holidays. Admission 10FF.

While in Menton you may be interested in visiting the Palais Carnolès Museum (10, off the map), a walk of nearly a mile from the casino. There is also bus service to it. Devoted to the fine arts, and located in a gorgeous old mansion once used by the princes of Monaco, it is noted for its exceptionally lovely gardens. ☎ 04-9335-4971. Open Wed.–Mon., 10–noon and 2–6. Closed holidays.

Trip 41

Cagnes-sur-Mer

Primarily a modern seaside resort, Cagnes-sur-Mer offers two magnificent attractions that make a daytrip there highly worthwhile. First, there is Haut-de-Cagnes, an ancient walled village perched high atop a hill overlooking the Riviera. The other lure is Les Collettes, the enchanting country villa of the famous Impressionist painter Pierre-Auguste Renoir. Both can be seen in the same day, making this an ideal little excursion. You may, however, want to linger and have dinner at one of the attractive restaurants in the upper town. This trip could be combined with one to Antibes or Cannes.

GETTING THERE:

Trains connect Cagnes-sur-Mer with other coastal Riviera towns at frequent intervals, with returns until late evening. Not all expresses stop at Cagnes.

By car, take the coastal road or the A-8. Cagnes is 8 miles west of Nice.

PRACTICALITIES:

Cagnes may be visited at most any time, but note the opening times of the castle and the Renoir villa. Avoid coming in November.

The local **tourist office, ☎** 04-9320-6164, Internet: www.cagnes.com, is at 6 Boulevard Maréchal Juin in the lower town.

FOOD AND DRINK:

The walled hilltop village of Haut-de-Cagnes offers a number of charming restaurants and outdoor cafés. Among the better choices are:

La Cagnard (Rue du Pontis-Long, 2 blocks southwest of the castle) A famous old inn with classic cuisine. ☎ 04-9320-7321. X: Thurs. lunch, Nov. $$$

Josy-Jo (2 Rue Planastel, near the Chapel of Notre-Dame) Excellent uncomplicated cuisine in pleasing surroundings. ☎ 04-9320-6876. X: Sat. lunch, Sun., early Aug., late Jan. $$$

Le Jimmy's (Place du Château, just north of the castle) Charming outdoor tables, a good place for snacks or drinks. ☎ 04-9213-0593. $

SUGGESTED TOUR:

Numbers in parentheses correspond to numbers on the map.

Stepping out of the **train station** (1) may leave you with that awful

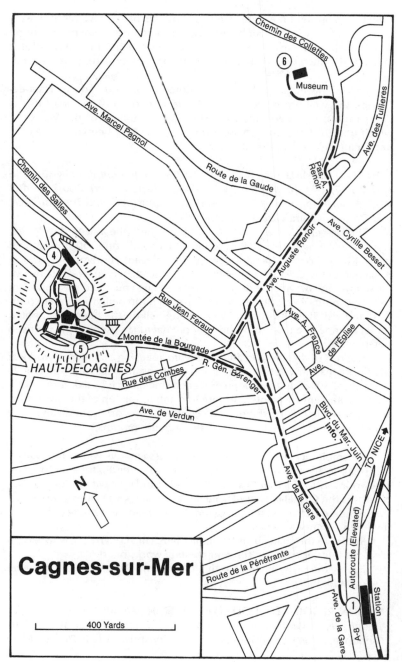

Cagnes-sur-Mer

400 Yards

"what-ever-brought-me-here" feeling. Don't despair. A few minute's walk past the highway intersection and tacky modern developments will bring you to the foot of one of the nicest hilltowns on the Riviera. You could also take a taxi, which would eliminate the interesting but somewhat strenuous climb.

Follow the map up the steep Montée de la Bourgade to **Haut-de-Cagnes**, the well-preserved medieval village whose history as a fortress dates from pre-Roman times. Overlooking the mouth of the Var River, which until 1860 was the Italian border, this has long been a strategically important stronghold, the site of the:

*CHÂTEAU GRIMALDI (2), ☎ 04-9320-8557. *Open July–Sept., daily 10–noon and 2:30–7; rest of summer, Wed.–Mon. 10–noon and 2:30–7; winter Wed.–Mon. 10–noon and 2–5. Closed Nov., Christmas, and Tues. on Oct., and Dec.–June. Adults 20FF, children 10FF.*

The present Castle *(Château)*, around which the village developed, was originally begun in 1309 by Rainier I Grimaldi, ruler of Monaco and other Riviera towns. Transformed into an elegant residence in 1620, it remained in the Grimaldi family until 1792. The château now contains two museums, one of which is devoted to everything you could possibly want to know about olive cultivation. Stroll through the delightful inner courtyard and visit the 17th-century banqueting hall on the main floor, noted for its trompe l'oeil fresco of the **Fall of Phaeton*, a triumph of contrived perspective.

The rest of the castle in an **art museum**, focusing on modern works of Mediterranean inspiration. One room contains an unusual display of 40 portraits of Susy Solidor, a popular French singer, each by a different well-known 20th-century painter. Be sure to climb to the top of the tower for a spectacular view. An exhibition of contemporary art from all over the world is held in the château during the summer months.

An amble up and down the stepped passageways within the walls— too small to be shown on the map—leads to serendipitous discoveries. Find your way to **Place du Château** (3), a delightful spot with outdoor cafés. Nearby is the **Chapel of Notre-Dame-de-Protection** (4), a 14th-century structure whose charming setting inspired Renoir. Step inside to see the primitive 16th-century frescoes.

Return to the château and visit the **Church of St.-Pierre** (5), whose double-nave interior contains some interesting works of art.

Follow the map downhill to the lower town. From here it's a relatively short walk to the:

*MAISON RENOIR—LES COLLETTES (6), ☎ 04-9320-6107. *Open late May through Sept., Wed.–Mon. 10–noon and 2–5; rest of year Wed.–Mon., 10–noon and 2–6. Closed Tues., Nov., and Christmas. Adults 20FF, children 6–12 10FF.*

The great painter Renoir spent the last ten years of his life in this love-ly country villa. Now housing the **Renoir Museum**, it has been faithfully restored to the condition it was in when he died there in 1919. Although Renoir was very ill during his last years, he continued to paint from a wheelchair with brushes tied to his fingers. This touching scene is loving-ly evoked in the studio, and throughout the property. Ten original paint-ings, along with sculptures created on the premises during his "Cagnes period," are featured. Don't miss seeing this

Antibes

Dating from the 4th century BC, the ancient Greek trading post of *Antipolis* grew up to become the delightfully unpretentious Antibes of today. The narrow streets of its picturesque Old Town are an open invitation for pleasant wanderings, particularly to the seaside promenade and its castle, which today houses the fabulous Picasso Museum. Ambitious walkers, or those with cars or rented bicycles, can also explore the lovely Cap d'Antibes, a place of great natural beauty.

GETTING THERE:

Trains depart Nice frequently for the 15-minute ride to Antibes, with returns until late evening. The same line serves practically all coastal towns on the Riviera.

By car, use the N-7 or N-98 road. Antibes is 15 miles southwest of Nice.

PRACTICALITIES:

The Picasso Museum is closed on Mondays and some major holidays. Good weather is essential for a pleasant side trip to Cap d'Antibes.

The local **Tourist Information Office**, ☎ 04-9290-5300, is at 11 Place du Général-de-Gaulle, 5 blocks south of the train station. The town's full name is Antibes-Juan-les-Pins. A useful Internet site is: www.guide-azur.com.

FOOD AND DRINK:

Antibes has a broad range of restaurants in all price brackets. Some excellent choices are:

Bacon (Blvd. de Bacon, near Pointe Bacon) Renowned for its fresh seafood. Dress properly and reserve, ☎ 04-9361-5002. X: Mon. except July–Aug. $$$+

L'Oursin (16 Rue de la République, 6 blocks west of the Picasso Museum) A popular place for seafood. ☎ 04-9334-1346. X: Sun. eve., Mon. in winter. $$

Le Marquis (4 Rue Sade, 2 blocks west of the Picasso Museum) A convenient location near the market place. ☎ 04-9334-2300. X: Mon., Tues. lunch. $$

Le Brûlot (3 Rue Isnard, 2 blocks west of the cathedral) A thriving bistro with hearty dishes. ☎ 04-9334-1776. X: Sun., late Aug., Mon. lunch. $

SUGGESTED TOUR:

Numbers in parentheses correspond to numbers on the map.
Leave the **train station** (1) and follow the town map, passing the tourist office on Place du Général-de-Gaulle. Rue de la République leads to Place Nationale. You are now entering the **Old Town** *(Vielle Ville)* with its picturesque maze of narrow streets. Thread your way through past the colorful market place on Cours Masséna to the:

*CHÂTEAU GRIMALDI—MUSÉE PICASSO (2), ☎ 04-9290-5428. *Open in summer, Tues.–Sun., 10–6; winter Tues.–Sun. 10–noon and 2–6. Closed Mon. and holidays. Adults 30FF, students 13FF, under 15 free.*

Built between the 13th and 16th centuries, this medieval stronghold overlooking the sea was for centuries home to a branch of the ruling Grimaldi family of Monaco. After seeing service as a governor's residence and later as an army barracks, the castle was bought by the town after World War I for use as a museum.

In 1946, Pablo Picasso was invited to use part of it as a studio. During the months that followed he produced some of his greatest works, many of which the artist later donated to the museum in memory of the happy times he had there. Although primarily devoted to Picasso, the museum also displays works by other contemporary artists along with some archaeological pieces. To wander through its well-arranged rooms and passageways is a sheer joy. Don't miss the sculpture-filled terrace overlooking the sea.

The **Church of the Immaculate Conception** (3), next door, is still referred to as a cathedral although it lost that status as far back as 1244. Much of the present structure is from the 17th century, but the 12th-century belfry is original. Step inside to see the noted altarpiece in the south transept, attributed to Louis Bréa.

Now meander through the oldest parts of Antibes and follow the 16th-century ramparts to the **Musée d'Archeologie** (4) in the 17th-century Bastion of St.-André. The archaeological collections in this museum, covering some 4,000 years of local history, include jewelry, coins, and pottery. ☎ *04-9290-5435. Open Tues.–Sun., 10–noon and 2–6. Closed Mon. and holidays. Adults 10FF, students 5FF, under 15 free.*

Ambitious walkers have a real treat ahead of them. Turn to the area map and follow the coastal road past the public beach to **Pointe Bacon** (5) on Cap d'Antibes, a distance of slightly over one mile. The views from here are spectacular, encompassing the Bay of Angels as far as Nice. Those with cars or rental bicycles can, of course, drive or pedal there and continue completely around the wooded peninsula, long a haunt of the very rich.

Retrace your steps and turn into a stepped path called Chemin du Calvaire. This leads uphill past some Stations of the Cross to the **La Garoupe Plateau**, which offers a sweeping ***panorama** of the seacoast,

PORT

TO NICE

Station

Ave. de la Libération

Ave. du 11 Novembre

Ave. de Verdun

Soleau

Pasteur

Ave.

Thiers

Robert

Ave.

Rue F. Mistral

Blvd. de l'Aiguillon

Rue Thuret

Info.

Rue Vauban

Pl. des Martyrs

Ave.

Pl. du Gén. De Gaulie

Rue de la République

Pl. Nationale

Rue James Close

Rue Sade

Rue Fersen

Masséna

Rue de Grasse

Cours

Prom. Amiral

N

Blvd. Albert I

MEDITERRANEAN

Blvd. du Mar. Foch

Antibes
Town

200 Yards

SEE NEXT MAP

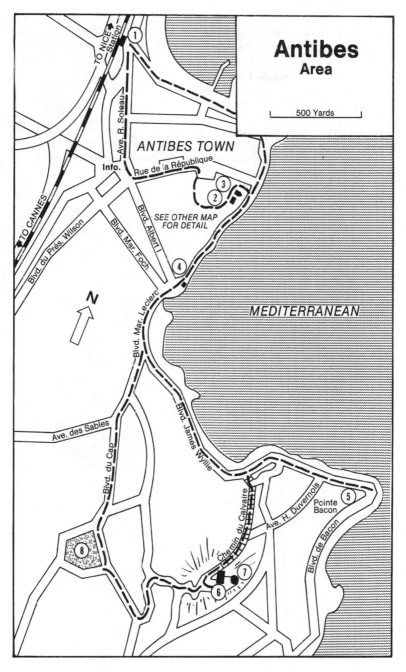

Antibes
Area

500 Yards

extending from Cannes to Nice, with part of the Alps in the background. The delightful **Chapel of Notre-Dame-de-la-Garoupe** (6), dating in part from the Middle Ages, has a strange and wonderful interior. Its walls are covered with touchingly naïve ex-votos offered by sailors and others in thanks for deliverance from some awful fate. You could literally spend hours examining the tales they so graphically depict. *Open daily, 10:30–12:30 and 2–5, with shorter hours in the winter.* Nearby is a **lighthouse** *(phare)* (7), which may also be visited.

The route shown on the map takes you past the interesting **Jardin Thuret** (8), a research garden for exotic trees and plants. ☎ *04-9367-8800. Open Mon.–Fri., 8:30–5:30. Closed some holidays.* Return to Antibes via Boulevard du Cap.

*Cannes

Cannes was just a sleepy fishing village until that fateful day in 1834 when Lord Brougham, an English ex-chancellor en route to Italy, was turned back at the then-nearby border on account of an outbreak of cholera. Determined to have his vacation in the sun anyway, he built a villa near Cannes and spent the next 34 winters there, encouraging other aristocrats to follow suit. By the time the railway arrived in 1863, the town's destiny was sealed and the rush to build hotels began.

What was once upper class has now become commercial chic, existing for sensual pleasure. Cannes' main thoroughfare—La Croisette—is lined with luxury hotels, its harbor a flotilla of sumptuous yachts. This is truly the playground of the rich and famous. Fortunately, there are other diversions as well—the nearby Lérins Islands, the Old Port and the tiny medieval quarter each offer their own special charms.

A daytrip to Cannes could be combined with one to Antibes or Cagnes-sur-Mer; or by really rushing, with one to Grasse.

GETTING THERE:

Trains connect Cannes with other Riviera coastal towns, with frequent service operating until late evening. The ride from Nice takes about 30 minutes. Cannes also has direct TGV service with Paris, a ride of 6.5 hours.

By car, Cannes is best reached via the A-8 Autoroute or the N-7 road. It is 21 miles southwest of Nice.

PRACTICALITIES:

You can enjoy yourself in Cannes at any time. It may be crowded during festivals, but that's part of the fun. Boat service to the Lérins Islands is excellent from June through September, but reduced the rest of the year.

The local **tourist office,** ☎ 04-9399-1977, is upstairs in the train station. There is another office, ☎ 04-9339-2453, in the Convention Center by the port. A useful Internet site is: www.cannes-on-line.com.

FOOD AND DRINK:

Cannes has an enormous selection of restaurants and cafés, not all of which are expensive. Some of the better choices are:

La Palme d'Or (in the Hôtel Martinez at 73 La Croisette, 10 blocks southeast of the Convention Center) Innovative modern cuisine in a 1930's setting. For reservations ☎ 04-9298-7414. X: Mon.,Tues. lunch, mid-

Nov. to mid-Dec. $$$+

La Poêle d'Or (23 Rue des États-Unis, 4 blocks east of the Convention Center) A good value in the luxury category. ☎ 04- 9339-7765. X: Mon., Tues. lunch. $$$

La Mère Besson (13 Rue des Frères Pradignac, 5 blocks southeast of the station) A favorite for Provençal cuisine. ☎ 04-9339-5924. X: Mon. lunch, Sat. lunch, Sun. $$ and $$$

Le Caveau 30 (45 Rue Félix-Faure, 3 blocks northwest of the boat terminal) An old-fashioned bistro with sidewalk tables and good food. ☎ 04-9339-0633. $$

Chez Astoux (43 Rue Félix-Faure, 3 blocks northwest of the boat terminal) A boisterous place for seafood. ☎ 04-9339-0622. $$

Au Mal Assis (15 Quai St.-Pierre, 3 blocks east of the Le Castre Museum) A colorful large bistro with superb seafood. ☎ 04-9339-1338. $$

Gaston Gastounette (7 Quai St.-Pierre, 3 blocks east of the Le Castre Museum) Featuring Provençal cuisine. ☎ 04-9339-4792. $$

Oscar (16 Rue des Frères Pradignac, 5 blocks southeast of the station) Traditional cuisine of Provence. ☎ 04-9339-9600. X: Sun., Mon. lunch. $ and $$

Au Bec Fin (12 Rue du 24-Août, 2 blocks southwest of the station) An unpretentious place for good home cooking. ☎ 04- 9338-3586. X: Sat. eve., Sun. $

Le Monaco (15 Rue du 24-Août, 2 blocks southwest of the station) A popular neighborhood restaurant with good food at modest prices. ☎ 04-9338-3776. X: Sun. $

SUGGESTED TOUR:
Numbers in parentheses correspond to numbers on the map.

The **train station** (1) has a tourist office upstairs, reached by an outdoor staircase. Stop there for a map that lists the schedule of boats to the Lérins Islands along with other useful information. Now follow Rue des Serbes to *La Croisette, an elegant seaside promenade of world renown.

From here you may want to take a delightful walk along the bay to the **Palm Beach** (2, off the map), a distance of less than a mile and a half. Along the way you will pass beaches, gardens, and several opulent marinas.

Returning along the sandy beach brings you to the **Convention Center** *(Palais des Festivals)* (3), home to the International Film Festival held each year in May, as well as many other events. The **Casino Croisette**, part of the same complex, offers roulette, blackjack, and slots all year round. Stroll through the lovely gardens behind it and over to the **Boat Terminal** *(Gare Maritime)* (4), where you can take an enjoyable cruise to the nearby *Lérins Islands (5). For many, this is the highlight of a visit to Cannes. ☎ 04-9338-6633. *Round trip to Sainte-Marguerite 45FF, both islands 70FF.*

There are two islands in the group, and it is quite possible to visit both. Most tourists, however, are content to explore just the first, **Sainte-Marguerite**, reached in 15 minutes. About two miles long by a half-mile in

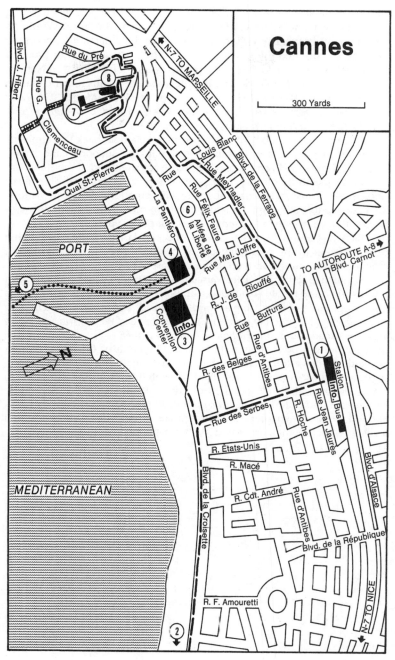

Cannes

300 Yards

width, it is mostly covered with a dense forest cut through with charming pathways. A massive 17th-century **fortress** lies near the dock. Within its forbidding walls you can visit the prison cell of the enigmatic "Man in the Iron Mask," confined there for 16 years by Louis XIV, along with those of several Protestants locked up after the revocation of the Edict of Nantes. There is also the **Musée de la Mer**, an interesting museum of marine archaeology. ☎ 04-9343-1817. *Open in summer, Wed.–Mon., 10:30–12:15 and 2:15–6:30; rest of year, Wed.–Mon., 10–12:15 and 2:15–4:30 or 5:30. Closed Tues. and holidays. Admission 10FF.*

Returning to the docks, you can either take a boat back to Cannes or continue on for another 15-minute cruise to the second island, **Saint-Honorat**. Considerably smaller but more enchanting, it contains an ancient 11th-century fortified monastery that may be explored. The newer Abbaye de Lérins, still in use, opens its church and museum to visitors. Boat service to both islands operates quite frequently from June through September, with reduced schedules the rest of the year.

Back in Cannes, step over to the **Allées de la Liberté** (6), alive with a flower market in the mornings and games of boules in the afternoons. From here it is a short climb up to the old part of town known as **Le Suquet**. Follow the map to the **La Castre Museum** (7), a former citadel containing an interesting—and highly eclectic—assemblage of art, antiquities, and items of ethnographic interest from around the world. ☎ 04-9338-5526. *Open in summer, Wed.–Mon., 10–noon and 3–7; rest of year, Wed.–Mon., 10–noon and 2–6. Closed Tues. and holidays. Admission 10FF.*

Continue around to the 16th- and 17th-century **Church of Notre-Dame-d'Espérance** (8), a late-Gothic structure featuring some fine polychrome statues. The route now leads downhill through the old town to the port. Quai St.-Pierre is a particularly colorful spot with its popular restaurants and outdoor cafés. Wander around the lively old market area and follow Rue Meynadier—the former Main Street when Cannes was still a village—back in the direction of the train station.

1000000000000000000000000

Grasse

The medieval hill town of Grasse is widely known as the undisputed world center of perfume essences. A visit to one of its scent factories is a must, of course, but don't miss exploring the town itself. A veritable maze of ancient alleyways and half-hidden passages wind their way along the hillside, opening here and there for magnificent views. With its interesting cathedral and four small but intriguing museums, Grasse offers enough attractions to entertain you for an entire day.

GETTING THERE:

Buses to Grasse depart fairly often from the east side of the train station in Cannes, easily reached from Nice in 30 minutes by frequent trains. The bus ride takes about 45 minutes, with return service until early evening. There is also some direct service between the bus terminal in Nice and Grasse.

By car, take the N-85 north from Cannes, a distance of 10 miles. Grasse is 26 miles west of Nice. Park by the bus station.

PRACTICALITIES:

Grasse may be visited at any time, but at least one museum is closed on Sundays, others on Mondays and Tuesdays in winter, and most in November and early December.

The local **Tourist Information Office**, ☎ 04-9336-0356, is on Cours Honoré Cresp, just north of the Villa-Musée Fragonard. From May through September a little tourist "train" operates from here, stopping at points of interest throughout the Old Town. There is also a branch tourist office at 3 Place de la Foux, near the bus station.

FOOD AND DRINK:

Grasse has an adequate number of restaurants, some good choices being:

Amphitryon (16 Blvd. Victor-Hugo, 2 blocks west of the Fragonard Villa Museum) Light classical cuisine from the southwest of France in a small traditional restaurant. ☎ 04-9336-5873. X: Sun., holidays, Aug. $$

Le Baltus (15 Rue Fontette, 2 blocks east of Pl. aux Aires) A tiny, romantic restaurant with traditional cuisine. ☎ 04-9336- 3290. X: Wed. eve., Sat. eve. $ and $$

La Voûte (24 Place aux Aires) Provençal cooking, grills, and pizza. ☎ 04-9336-1143. $

SUGGESTED TOUR:
Numbers in parentheses correspond to numbers on the map.

Leave the **bus station** *(Gare Routière)* (1) and follow the map to **Place aux Aires** (2). This thoroughly delightful open area has some fine arcaded 18th-century houses and several sidewalk cafés arranged around a bubbling fountain. A lively outdoor market is held there in the mornings.

Follow the map down Rue des 4 Coins and descend the steep Rue de Fontette to Place Jean-Jaurès. Continue on, trying not to get lost in the tiny alleyways, to the 12th-century **Cathedral of Notre-Dame-du-Puy** (3), heavily restored in the 17th century. Step inside to view the two paintings by Rubens in the south aisle, an altarpiece attributed to Louis Bréa and, above the sacristy door, one of Fragonard's rare religious works, the *Washing of the Feet.*

The square in front of the cathedral has an impressive square tower from the 12th century. Stroll around to **Place du 24 Août** (4), which offers a sweeping panorama of the countryside.

A series of steps leads to Rue Mirabeau and the ***Musée d'Art et d'Histoire de Provence** (5). Housed in an 18th-century mansion, the museum's splendid collections are mostly concerned with the folk arts and traditions of the region, although there are also some fine paintings and archaeological displays. ☎ *04-9336-0161. Open June–Sept., daily 10–7; Oct. and Dec.–May, Wed.–Sun., 10–noon and 2–5. Closed Mon. and Tues. in winter, all of Nov., and holidays. Adults 25FF, students 20FF.*

Grasse produces most of the world's supply of the essences used in perfume manufacturing. This industry had its origins in the 16th-century fashion for scented gloves, which were made locally. It grew with the nearby cultivation of roses, jasmin and other plants; with more exotic ingredients now being imported from all over the world. Several of the larger factories offer free guided tours explaining their operations. One of the most interesting of these is the **Parfumerie Fragonard** (6), conveniently located a few steps away, whose tours in English are given daily at frequent intervals.

Now wander past a lovely park to the **Villa-Musée Fragonard** (7). If that name seems common around here, it is because the famous painter Jean-Honoré Fragonard was born in Grasse in 1732. Although he lived most of his life in Paris, he returned to his hometown during the Revolution and spent a year in this villa. Most of the paintings on display are copies, albeit very good ones; the originals being in the Frick Museum in New York. Still, a visit to this charming small museum is very worthwhile. ☎ *04-9336-0161. Open June–Sept., daily 10–7; Oct. and Dec.–May, Wed.–Sun., 10–noon and 2–6. Closed Mon. and Tues. in winter, all of Nov., and holidays. Adults 25FF, students 20FF.*

The ***International Perfume Museum** (8) brings to life the history of perfume making from ancient times to the present. There's a hall filled with antique bottles, a greenhouse where exotic plants are grown, essences to smell, and a section devoted to the fascinating business of perfume marketing. ☎ *04-9396-8020. Open June–Sept., daily 10–7; Oct. and Dec.–May,*

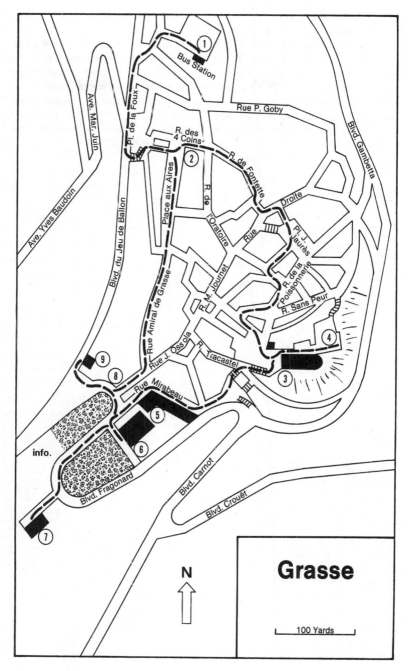

Grasse

100 Yards

Wed.–Sun., 10–noon and 2–7. Closed Mon. and Tues. in winter, all of Nov., and holidays. Adults 25FF, students 20FF.

American tourists will be particularly interested in the **Musée de la Marine** (9), devoted primarily to the life of Amiral de Grasse. Born in nearby Bar-sur-Loup, this 18th-century French naval hero is remembered for his role in the American War of Independence, when he blockaded the British at Yorktown, Virginia. Souvenirs of the battle are on display along with ship models and related items. *Inquire as to current opening times and admission.* From here follow the map back to Place aux Aires and the bus station.

St. Tropez

Fame and notoriety have not managed to spoil St. Tropez, which preserves all of its considerable charm. Isolated by geography from the main stream of the Riviera and far off the highways and rail line, this deliciously hedonistic place is well worth the effort of reaching. There are many faces to St. Tropez. It is at one and the same time an art colony, a haunt of the intelligentsia, a bohemian resort, a center of fashion, and—yes—even a sleepy old fishing port. These and other facets of its paradoxical existence may or may not appeal to you, but the easiest way to at least sample its heady lifestyle is to go there for a day and try the place on for size. Who knows? You may decide to return for a real vacation. If you do, you'll be happy to know that there are sandy beaches for every taste, all within a short distance of the town.

GETTING THERE:

Trains in the morning connect coastal towns along the Riviera with St. Raphaël, a one-hour ride from Nice. From the St. Raphaël station you can get a bus for the 80-minute ride to St. Tropez. Return service operates until early evening. During the summer there are also boats from the St. Raphaël port (not far from the station) to St. Tropez, a cruise of about 50 minutes and not much costlier than the bus.

By car, take the A-8 Autoroute to the Fréjus exit, then the N-98 to St. Tropez. It is 68 miles southwest of Nice.

PRACTICALITIES:

Good weather is essential for a visit to St. Tropez. The museums are closed on Tuesdays, major holidays, and November. Unlike the rest of the Riviera, St. Tropez faces north and experiences cold winters.

The local **tourist office,** ☎ 04-9497-4521, Internet: www.nova.fr/saint-tropez, is on the quay by the port.

FOOD AND DRINK:

As you might expect, St. Tropez abounds in restaurants and outdoor cafés. Some choices are:

Les Arcades (at the Byblos Hotel on Ave. P. Signac, south of the Citadel) Luxurious poolside dining at the poshest of inns. ☎ 04-9456-6800. X: winter. $$$

Bistrot des Lices (3 Place des Lices/Place Carnot) A trendy bistro with classic and modern dishes. ☎ 04-9497-8282. X: Tues. off-season, Jan. to Mar. $$$

Le Girelier (Quai Jean-Jaurès, near the tourist office) Seafood specialties in the Provençal style, also meat dishes. ☎ 04-9497-0387. X: Mon. lunch in July-Aug., winter. $$

Café des Arts (Place des Lices/Place Carnot) A long-time favorite for simple bistro food. ☎ 04-9497-0225. $$

Lou Regalé (12 Rue Colonel Guichard, by the Parish Church) Inexpensive dining right in the center of town. ☎ 04-9497-1618. $

SUGGESTED TOUR:
Numbers in parentheses correspond to numbers on the map.

Leave the **bus station** (1) and follow the map to the port. Filled with all kinds of boats, from humble fishing vessels to luxury yachts, this is the very heart of St. Tropez. Don't be surprised to see oceangoing sailboats with American registrations docked here. The quays are often the scene of uninhibited exhibitionism or joyous revelry, which can be best savored by sitting down at one of the seemingly endless sidewalk cafés, especially **Le Gorille** or **Sénéquier's**.

Be sure to stroll out to the end of the ***Môle Jean Réveille** (2), a massive breakwater that encloses the harbor. The panoramic vistas from its upper level are fantastic.

Return to the quay and turn left on Rue de la Mairie, passing the Suffren Castle and the **Town Hall** (3). You are now in the picturesque Old Town, where several narrow passageways lead to lovely views. Continue on Rue de la Ponche to its end, poke around the alleyways there, then follow the map uphill to a path that goes to the nearby Graniers beach. Stroll a short way down this to a **point** (4) where you will be treated to a magnificent perspective of the town and the sea.

Walk uphill to the **Citadel** (5), a 16th-century fortress that now houses the fascinating **Maritime Museum** *(Musée Naval)*. Step inside to see the marvelous reconstruction of a Greek galley, displays on the manufacture of torpedoes (a local industry), and a section devoted to the Allied landing of 1944—when this bastion was the last stronghold of German resistance. A climb to the roof reveals yet another fabulous panorama. ☎ *04-9497-5943. Open daily 10–5, 6 or 7. Closed Nov. and holidays. Adults 25FF, students 15FF.*

Returning to town, you may want to make a little side trip to witness a more traditional aspect of life in St. Tropez. Known to residents as **Place des Lices** (6) but called Place Carnot on some maps, the town's main square is a delightfully shady spot where men play *boules* all day and a market is held on Tuesday and Saturday mornings. Stop in for a drink at the Café des Arts, then stroll over to the 18th-century **Parish Church** (7) to see its remarkable bust of Saint Tropez himself.

No visit to St. Tropez is complete without a stop at the:

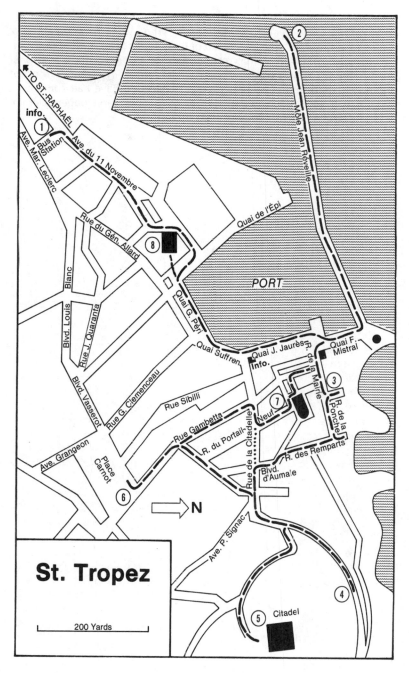

St. Tropez

200 Yards

TO ST.-RAPHAËL

info.
①

Bus Station

Ave. du 11 Novembre

Ave. Mar. Leclerc

Rue du Gén. Allard

Blanc

Blvd. Louis

Rue J. Quaranta

Blvd. Vasserot

Rue G. Clemenceau

Ave. Grangeon

Rue Sibilli

Rue Gambetta

Place Carnot

⑥

Quai G. Péri

Quai de l'Épi

Quai Suffren

Quai J. Jaurès

Info.

Quai F. Mistral

R. de la Ponche

R. de la Mairie

③

⑦

Neuf

R. du Portail-

Rue de la Citadelle

R. des Remparts

Blvd. d'Aumale

Ave. P. Signac

PORT

Môle Jean Réveille

②

⑧

N

Citadel
⑤

④

*ANNONCIADE MUSEUM (8), ☎ 04-9497-0401. *Open June–Sept.,
Wed.–Mon., 10–noon and 3–7; rest of year, Wed.–Mon., 10–noon and 2–6.
Closed Tues., some holidays, and all of Nov. Adults 30FF, students 15FF.*

Housed in a 16th-century chapel right by the port, this is—surprisingly—one of the best small museums of modern art in all France. Most of the artists represented in its permanent collection have had some connection with the town, and include Signac, Matisse, Van Dongen, Derain, Bonnard, Dufy, Vuillard, Roussel and others.

*St. Paul

Totally enclosed by its ancient ramparts, the tiny fortified hill town of St. Paul is today both an art colony and a magnet for discerning tourists. Often referred to as St.-Paul-de-Vence after its larger neighbor, this charming village is home to one of the world's greatest museums of contemporary art.

Once occupied by Ligurians, and then Romans, St. Paul was converted into a military stronghold in the 16th century by François I, who needed to defend his frontier against the dukes of Savoy. Its importance declined after the Revolution, only to be rediscovered by artists in the 1920s.

This classic daytrip is customarily combined with one to nearby Vence, described in the next chapter.

GETTING THERE:

Buses depart the bus station *(Gare Routière)* on Boulevard Jean Jaurès in Nice about every hour for the 45-minute ride to St. Paul. They then continue on to Vence. Return buses run until early evening. A special round-trip ticket allowing stops at both towns is available.

By car, take the A-8 Autoroute or other coastal roads to Cagnes-sur-Mer, then the D-6 and D-107 north to St. Paul. From there the D-102 continues on to Vence, three miles to the north. St. Paul is 12 miles northwest of Nice.

PRACTICALITIES:

This trip can be made at any time. Good weather will make it much more enjoyable. The local **tourist office**, ☎ 04-9332-8695, is at 2 Rue Grands, just inside the town gate. A useful Internet site is: www.stpaulweb.com.

FOOD AND DRINK:

The village of St. Paul has several restaurants, most of which are quite simple. A few of the better choices are:

La Colombe d'Or (at the entrance to the town) World-famous for its magnificent collection of modern art, given to the owner by the painters in payment for meals. The terrace restaurant of this inn is enchanting. For reservations ☎ 04-9332-8002. X: Nov. to mid-Dec. $$$

Le Saint-Paul (86 Rue Grande) An elegant small inn with an excellent restaurant. ☎ 04-9332-6525. $$

SUGGESTED TOUR:

Numbers in parentheses correspond to numbers on the map.

Leave the **bus stop** (1) and stroll past the famous Colombe d'Or inn to the North Gate of the village. Just inside this is the **tourist office** (2) and an exhibition of contemporary art, the **Musée de Saint-Paul.** ☎ *04-9332-8695. Open June–Sept., daily 10–7; rest of year, daily 10–noon and 2–6. Free.*

The narrow pedestrians-only Rue Grande, lined with antique shops, art galleries, boutiques and restaurants, is the main street of the village. Follow it to the utterly delightful urn-shaped **fountain** (3) that splashes away merrily in a tiny square.

Turn left and climb the steps to the 13th-century **Church** (4), heavily rebuilt during the 17th century. Its attractive interior contains some remarkable works of art, including a painting of St. Catherine attributed to Tintoretto at the far end of the north aisle. Step into the Treasury for a look at a few unusually fine items dating from the 12th to the 15th centuries. Nearby is the **Museum of Local History**, a waxworks created by craftsmen from the famous Grévin Wax Museum in Paris. ☎ *04-9332-4113. Open daily, 10–5:30 or 7. Closed mid-Nov. to mid-Dec. Admission 20FF.*

Amble over to the east ramparts. It is possible, if you're feeling sure-footed, to walk along the top of these for some good views. Continue on to the **South Gate Bastion** (5), from which you may—in clear weather—have a sweeping ***panorama** from the Alps to the Mediterranean.

Now meander back to the North Gate, exploring the hidden stepped alleys along the way. Return to the bus stop and follow the secondary road to the left. This leads, in half a mile (800 meters), to St. Paul's major attraction. Those with cars should follow the road signs instead.

***FONDATION MAEGHT** (6, off the map), ☎ *04-9332-8163. Open July–Sept., daily 10–7; rest of year, daily 10–12:30 and 2:30–6. Adults 45FF, students 35FF.*

A visit to the Maeght Foundation is an experience no lover of modern art should miss. Established in 1964 by a Paris gallery owner and publisher to promote an understanding of contemporary art, it is housed in a stunning cluster of buildings set atop a hill surrounded by pine forests. More than just a museum, the foundation embraces a wide range of artistic endeavors, with theaters, libraries, studios and other facilities on the premises. Its permanent collections cover works by many of the leading artists of this century. More important than this, however, are the renowned temporary exhibitions, usually devoted to the work of one particular artist.

Return to the bus stop, from which you can continue on to Vence or head back to Nice.

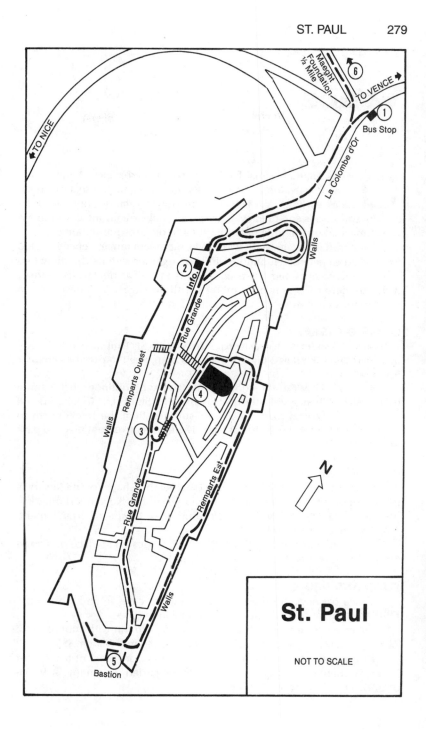

St. Paul

NOT TO SCALE

Vence

Once a Ligurian tribal capital of some importance, Vence, then known by its Roman name of *Vintium*, became the seat of a bishop as early as AD 374—a distinction it retained until 1790. Its ancient town walls and medieval quarter are still virtually intact, complete with a maze of quaint little passageways and picturesque squares.

Sheltered from the north winds by a mountain range, Vence is noted for its mild climate and luminous air. This, together with its charming Old Town, has long attracted artists and writers as well as numerous tourists. A daytrip here can easily be combined with one to St. Paul, described in the previous chapter.

GETTING THERE:

Buses connect Vence with Nice by way of St. Paul at nearly hourly intervals. The trip takes a bit less than one hour. See the previous chapter for details.

By car, follow the directions to St. Paul and continue on for three more miles to Vence. A faster route, bypassing St. Paul, is to take the A-8 Autoroute or coastal roads to Cagnes-sur-Mer, then the D-236 north to Vence. It is 14 miles northwest of Nice. The most convenient place to park is at Place du Grand Jardin.

PRACTICALITIES:

Vence may be visited at any time. The nearby Chapel of the Rosary is usually open on Tuesdays and Thursdays (except in November) only, but possibly more frequently during the summer or by special arrangement. Ask the tourist office about this.

The local **tourist office**, ☎ 04-9358-0638, is located at Place du Grand Jardin, near the bus stop.

FOOD AND DRINK:

Vence has several restaurants and outdoor cafés in and around the Old Town. Some of the better selections include:

Auberge des Seigneurs (Place du Frêne) An old inn with superb food. ☎ 04-9358-0424. X: Mon., Tues. lunch, mid-Nov. to mid-March. $$$

La Farigoule (15 Ave. Henri-Isnard, 2 blocks northwest of the tourist office) Authentic regional cuisine in a lovely garden restaurant. ☎ 93-58-01-27. X: Fri. off-season, Sat. lunch. $$

Chez Jordi (8 Rue Hôtel de Ville, a block south of the cathedral) A small but popular restaurant, so reserve. ☎ 04-9358-8345. X: Sun., Mon., mid-July to mid-Aug., late Dec. to mid-Jan. $$

SUGGESTED TOUR:

Numbers in parentheses correspond to numbers on the map.

Leave the **bus stop** (1) and stroll over to the **tourist office** (2), where you can ask about seeing the famous Chapel of the Rosary (7), designed and decorated by the artist Henri Matisse.

Place du Peyra (3), on the site of the ancient Roman forum, is reached via a medieval gateway standing next to a 15th-century tower. This delightful little square in the Old Town is enlivened by a gurgling urn-shaped fountain and several outdoor cafés.

Turn right and follow the map to the 11th-century former **Cathedral** (4), which still retains parts of its 5th-century predecessor, erected on the site of a Roman temple. The present structure was greatly altered during the 17th century. To the left of the main door there is an ancient inscription in honor of the 3rd-century Roman emperor Gordianus. Step inside to see the wonderfully satiric carvings on the 15th-century choir stalls. These are in a gallery that is sometimes open—just ask if it isn't.

Now follow the map around to **Place Godeau** (5), at the center of which stands a Roman column dedicated to the god Mars. Continue on and pass through the Porte d'Orient gate, then turn left and follow the line of the walls, re-entering the medieval quarter by way of Rue Pisani.

Meander along through the ancient narrow streets and exit the Old Town at the 13th-century Levis Portal. **Place du Frêne** (6), also known as Place Thiers, is noted for its enormously thick, centuries-old ash tree. Legend has it that this was planted in 1538 to commemorate a visit by François I. From the north end of the square you can get a good view of the nearby mountains and, if you can pick it out, the Chapel of the Rosary. The 15th-century **Château des Villeneuve**, near the Peyra Gate, is now restored and used for art exhibitions. ☎ *04-9358-7875. Open July–Oct., daily 10–6; rest of year, Tues.–Sun., 10–12:30 and 2–6. Admission 25FF.*

You may want to walk—or drive—to the nearby ***Chapel of the Rosary** (7, off the map), a bit less than one mile away. Designed and decorated by the noted artist Henri Matisse around 1950, this simple chapel is considered to be a great masterpiece of modern art and architecture. Check with the tourist office before making the trek as its opening times are very limited and subject to change. To get there just follow Avenue Henri-Isnard and Avenue des Poilus, then turn right on Avenue Henri-Matisse across a bridge and uphill to the *Chapelle du Rosaire.* ☎ *04-9358-0326. Usually open Tues. and Thurs., 10–11:30 and 2:30–5:30. Other times may be possible, especially in summer.*

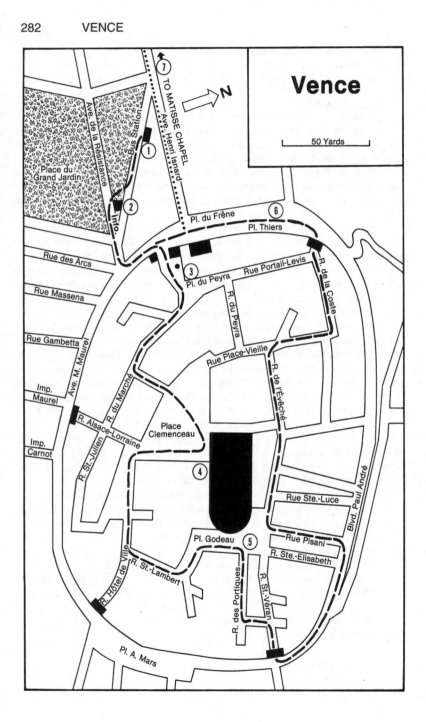

Vence

50 Yards

TO MATISSE CHAPEL

Ave. Henri Isnard

N

Bus Station

Info.

Place du Grand Jardin

Ave. de la Résistance

Pl. du Frêne

Pl. Thiers

Rue des Arcs

Pl. du Peyra

Rue Portail-Levis

R. de la Coste

Rue Massena

R. du Peyra

Rue Gambetta

Rue Place-Vieille

Ave. M. Maurel

R. du Marché

Imp. Maurel

R. Alsace-Lorraine

Place Clemenceau

R. de l'Évêché

R. St.-Julien

Imp. Carnot

Rue Ste.-Luce

Blvd. Paul André

Pl. Godeau

Rue Pisani

R. Hôtel de Ville

R. St.-Lambert

R. Ste.-Elisabeth

R. des Portiques

R. St.-Véran

Pl. A. Mars

Var Valley

L ittle known to foreign visitors, the narrow-gauge rail line through the Var Valley offers a magnificent visual treat coupled with an exciting ride. The private railway, properly known as the *Chemins de Fer de la Provence,* operates along a spectacular mountain route in the lower Alps between Nice and Digne. This same trip can also be made by car.

GETTING THERE:

Trains of the private railway depart from the Provence Station on Rue Alfred-Binet in Nice, just a few blocks north of the main station, ☎ 04-9382-1017. It is necessary to get to the station before 8:30 a.m. if you plan to make a whole day of it. Eurailpasses are accepted, and holders of the France Railpass or InterRail Pass are granted a 50% fare reduction. Be sure to pick up a current schedule to determine which stops can be made — and for how long. Schedules are also available at the main Nice station.

By car, you can cover most of the same route by following the N-202 north from the Nice Airport. There are difficult mountain roads between Scaffarels and St.-André-les-Alpes , but these can be bypassed by sticking to the N-202.

PRACTICALITIES:

Trains operate all year round, although on a reduced schedule in winter. The castle at Entrevaux is usually open from mid-June to mid-September, but closed on Mondays.

The tourist office in **Entrevaux,** ☎ 04-9305-4673 (in winter call the Town Hall at 04-9305-4004), is inside the town gate. The phone number in Nice for the Provence Railway is 04-9382-1017.

FOOD AND DRINK:

There are simple restaurants and cafés at each of the stops. Some of the better choices are:

De l'Avenue (in the village of Annot) A small country inn with meals. ☎ 04-9283-2207. X: Nov. through Mar. $ and $$

L'Amandier (N-202 at the station in Puget-Théniers) A great value, and convenient. ☎ 04-9305-0513. X: Sun. eve., Mon., Nov. $

SUGGESTED TOUR:

Numbers in parentheses correspond to numbers on the map.

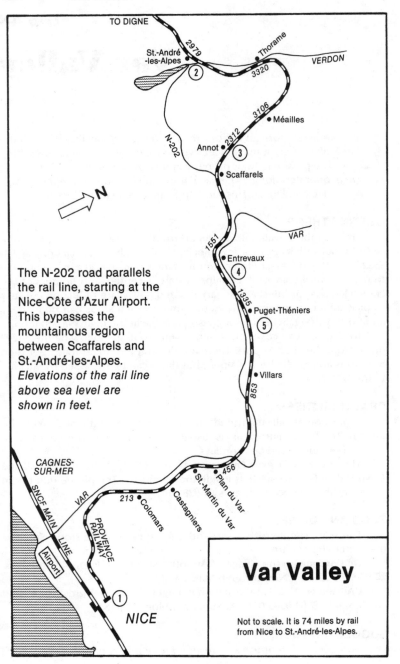

TO DIGNE

St.-André
-les-Alpes

2979

Thorame

VERDON

②

3320

3106

● Méailles

N-202

2312

Annot ●

③

Scaffarels ●

VAR

1551

● Entrevaux

④

1335

● Puget-Théniers

⑤

● Villars

853

N

The N-202 road parallels
the rail line, starting at the
Nice-Côte d'Azur Airport.
This bypasses the
mountainous region
between Scaffarels and
St.-André-les-Alpes.
*Elevations of the rail line
above sea level are
shown in feet.*

CAGNES-
SUR-MER

SNCF MAIN LINE

VAR

213 ● Colomars

456 ● Plan du Var

St.-Martin du Var ●

Castagniers ●

PROVENCE RAILWAY

Airport

①

NICE

Var Valley

Not to scale. It is 74 miles by rail
from Nice to St.-André-les-Alpes.

Board the train in **Nice** (1) and ride it all the way to **St.-André-les-Alpes** (2), a trip of about 2.5 hours, or 74 miles. Along the way you will climb through narrow gorges to an elevation of 3,353 feet, then begin a short descent to the pleasant little mountain resort. This is a fine place for a delightful country lunch, or you may decide to take the next train back to Annot or Entrevaux and eat there, depending on the schedule.

The wonderfully picturesque old town of **Annot** (3), founded in the 12th century, is another excellent place to have lunch. If you do stop there, be sure to check the schedule so you don't miss out on seeing Entrevaux.

The most visually exciting town along this route is **Entrevaux** (4), an ancient walled fortress approached via a drawbridge over the Var stream. Once a frontier between France and the Kingdom of Savoy, its present ramparts were built in 1695 by Vauban, Louis XIV's great military engineer. Wander through the unspoiled passageways to the 12th- and 17th-century former **Cathedral**, known for its richly-decorated interior. Perched high above the village is the mighty **Citadelle**—a castle that may be visited in summer by asking at the tourist office *(Bureau d'Accueil)*. There is also an interesting small **museum** of motor scooters in the village. ☎ *04-9305-4078. Open Apr.–Sept.*

If time permits, you may want to make a stop at **Puget-Théniers** (5) before returning to Nice. This lovely old town, dominated by the ruins of an ancient castle, has a fine 13th-century church and an attractive square. It is also a well-known center for steam-train activities.

APPENDIX

MENU TRANSLATOR

Abricot apricot
Agneau lamb
Aiglefin haddock
Ail garlic
Aïoli garlic mayonnaise
Alsacienne in the style of Alsace, often with sauerkraut, sausages and ham
Amande almond
Ananas pineapple
Anchois anchovies
Andouillette chitterling sausage
Aneth dill
Anguille eel
Anis aniseed
Arachides peanuts
Artichaut artichoke
Asperges asparagus
Assiette assortie mixture of cold hors d'oeuvre
Aubergine eggplant
Avocat avocado
Baguette long loaf of bread
Banane banana
Bar sea bass
Barbue brill
Basilic basil
Baudroie anglerfish

Béarnaise sauce with egg yolks, tarragon, shallots, butter, and white wine
Béchamel white sauce
Beignet fritter
Bercy sauce with white wine, shallots and herbs
Betterave beet
Beurre butter
Bifteck, biftek beefsteak
Bisque shellfish soup, chowder
Blanquette stew with egg and cream sauce
Boeuf beef
Bouef à la mode beef braised in red wine with vegetables
Boeuf Bourguignon beef stew in red wine with vegetables
Bombe fancy ice cream dish
Bordelaise in the style of Bordeaux with red wine, shallots, beef marrow, and mushrooms
Boudin blood sausage
Boudin blanc white sausage of veal, pork or chicken
Bouillabaisse fish and seafood stew

Bouquet shrimp
Bourguignonne in the style of
    Burgundy with red wine,
    onions, and bacon
Bourride fish and shellfish soup
    with aïoli
Brioche soft yeasty roll
Brochette skewered meat or fish
Caille quail
Canard duck
Caneton duckling
Carbonnade flamande beef
    braised
    in beer
Carotte carrot
Carpe carp
Carré d'agneau rack of lamb
Cassis blackcurrant
Cassoulet casserole of white
    beans with pork, goose, duck,
    and sausage
Céleri celery
Cèpes wild flat mushrooms
Cerises cherries
Cervelles brains
Champignons mushrooms
Chantilly sweet whipped cream
Chapon capon
Charcuterie cold cuts, pâtés,
    cured meats, and terrines
Chasseur hunter style
Châteaubriand thick fillet of beef
Chèvre goat or goat cheese
Chicorée curly endive
Chou cabbage
Choucroute sauerkraut
Choucroute garnie sauerkraut
    with pork, sausage, or other
    meats
Choufleur cauliflower
Ciboulettes chives
Citron lemon
Citron vent lime
Civet de lièvre jugged hare
Clémentine tangerine
Cochon pig

Concombre cucumber
Confit preserved
Confit de canard duck preserved
    in its own fat
Confiture preserves, jam
Consommé clear broth
Contre-filet sirloin steak
Coq cock, hen, or chicken
Coq au vin stewed chicken in red
    wine with mushrooms, onions,
    and bacon
Coquillage shellfish
Coquille St.-Jacques sea scallop
Cornichon small pickle
Côte chop or rib
Côtelette cutlet
Coupe de fruits fruit cup
Courgette zucchini
Crabe crab
Crème cream
Crème caramel custard
Crêpes thin pancakes
Cresson watercress
Crevette shrimp
Croissant flaky crescent-shaped
    roll
Croque-monsieur grilled ham and
    cheese sandwich
Cru raw
Crudités raw vegetable salad
Crustacés shellfish
Cuit cooked
Daube meat stew in wine stock
Daurade sea bream
Dijonnaise in the style of Dijon,
    with mustard
Dinde, dindon, dindonneau turkey
Échalote shallot
Écrevisses crayfish
Émincé thin slice
Endive endive
Entrecôte rib steak
Épices spices
Épinards spinach
Escalope thin slice
Escargots snails

Estragon tarragon
Faisan pheasant
Farci stuffed
Farine flour
Faux-filet sirloin steak
Fenouil fennel
Flageolets small green kidney beans
Flan custard tart
Foie liver
Foie gras goose liver
Fondue melted cheese dish
Forestière with mushrooms
Four oven
Frais, fraîche fresh, chilled
Fraises strawberries
Framboises raspberries
Frappé surrounded by crushed ice
Fricassée stewed or sauteed, braised in wine with cream
Frit fried
Frites French fries
Friture small fried fish
Fromage cheese
Fruits de mer seafood
Fumé smoked
Galantine cold meat, fish, or vegetables in jelly
Galette pancake with stuffing
Gambas large prawns
Garbure thick soup
Garni garnished
Gâteau cake
Gelée aspic
Gibelotte rabbit stewed in wine
Gibier game
Gigot d'agneau leg of lamb
Glace ice cream
Glacée iced or glazed
Graisse fat
Gratin crisp topping of cheese and bread crumbs
Grenouilles frogs (legs)
Grillade grilled meat
Grillée grilled

Groseille red currant
Haché, hachis minced, hashed
Hareng herring
Haricots beans
Haricots verts green beans
Homard lobster
Huile oil
Huîtres oysters
Jambon ham
Jardinière garnished with fresh vegetables
Julienne thin sliced vegetables
Jus juice
Lait milk
Laitue lettuce
Lamproie lamprey eel
Langouste spiny lobster
Langue tongue
Lapereau young rabbit
Lapin rabbit
Lard bacon
Légumes vegetables
Lentilles lentils
Loup sea bass
Macédoine diced mixed fruit or vegetables
Margret de canard duck steak or breast
Maïs sweet corn
Mandarine tangerine
Maquereau mackerel
Marrons chestnuts
Matelote freshwater fish stew
Menthe mint
Miel honey
Mirabelle yellow plum
Mornay cheese sauce
Morue salt cod
Moules mussels
Moutarde mustard
Mouton mutton
Myrtille blueberry
Navet turnip

Noisette hazelnut, or round piece
  of boneless meat
Noix nuts, walnuts
Nouilles noodles
Oeufs eggs
Oie goose
Oignons onions
Oseille sorrel
Oursins sea urchins
Paillard slice of veal or chicken
  breast
Pain bread
Palombe pigeon
Palourdes clams
Pamplemousse grapefruit
Panaché mixture of foods
Papillote cooked in parchment or
  foil
Parfum flavor
Paramentier dish with potatoes
Pastèque watermelon
Pâté cold minced meat or fish
  spread
Pâtes pasta
Pâtisserie pastry
Pêche peach
Perche perch
Perdrix partridge
Persil parsley
Petits-pois little green peas
Pied de porc pig's foot
Pigeonneau squab
Pignons pine nuts
Piments pimentos
Pintade guinea fowl
Pipérade omelette with peppers,
  onions, tomatoes, and ham
Piquante spicy
Pistache pistachio
Pistou purée of basil, garlic, and
  olive oil
Plateau de fromages cheese board
Poché poached
Poire pear
Poireau leek
Pois peas

Poisson fish
Poivre pepper
Poivron sweet bell pepper
Pomme apple
Pommes de terre potatoes
Pommes frites French fries
Porc pork
Porcelet young suckling pig
Potage soup
Pot-au-feu boiled beef and
  vegetable stew
Potée boiled pork and vegetables
Poularde capon
Poulet chicken
Poulpe octopus
Praire clam
Profiterole cream puff filled with
  chocolate
Provençale in the style of
  Provence, with garlic, tomatoes,
  and olive oil
Prune plum
Pruneau prune
Quenelles dumplings of fish or
  poultry
Quiche open pie with egg and
  cream plus filling
Raclette melted cheese dish
Radis radish
Ragoût stew
Raie skate
Raisins grapes
Ratatouille vegetable casserole
Rémoulade sauce of mayonnaise,
  capers, mustard, anchovies, and
  herbs
Rillettes potted meat
Ris de veau veal sweet breads
Riz rice
Rognons kidneys
Rosbif roast beef
Rôti roast
Rouget red mullet
Roulade meat or fish, rolled and
  stuffed
Safran saffron

Salade composée mixed salad
Salade Niçoise salad with tuna, olives, tomatoes, potatoes, and beans
Salade verte green salad
Salé salted
Saucisses fresh sausages
Saucisson dried sausage
Sauge sage
Saumon salmon
Sauté browned in fat
Sauvage wild
Scarole escarole
Sel salt
Sorbet sherbet
Soupe soup
Steak au poivre steak with crushed peppercorns
Steak haché chopped steak
Steak tartare minced raw beef
Sucre sugar
Suprême de volaille filet of chicken breast in cream sauce
Tarte pie

Terrine cold baked minced meat or fish
Tête de veau calf's head
Thon tuna
Thym thyme
Tomate tomato
Tournedos center cut beef fillet
Tranche slice
Truffes truffles
Truite trout
Vapeur steamed
Veau veal
Venaison venison
Viande meat
Vichyssoise cold potato and leek soup
Vinaigre vinegar
Vinaigrette oil and vinegar dressing
Volaille poultry
Vol-au-vent puff pastry case with stuffing
Yaourt yogurt

A GLOSSARY OF DINING TERMS

Meal repas
Breakfast petit déjeuner
Lunch déjeuner
Dinner diner

Headwaiter maître d'hôtel
Waiter monsieur
Waitress mademoiselle, madame
The menu, please la carte, s'il vous plaît
Set meal menu menu prix-fixe
Ordering items individually à la carte
Today's special plat du jour
Sampling of dishes or wines dégustation

The wine list la carte des vins
Another serving of ..., please encore un ..., s'il vous plaît
The check, please l'addition, s'il vous plaît
Drink included in price boisson comprise
Cover charge couvert
Tip included service compris, s.c., prix net
Tip not included service non com pris, s.n.c.
Gratuity pourboire

Plate assiette
Knife couteau

Fork fourchette
Spoon cuillère
Glass verre
Cup tasse
Napkin serviette

Drink boisson
Pre-dinner drink apéritif
After-dinner drink digestif
White wine vin blanc
Red wine vin rouge
Rosé wine vin rosé
Half-bottle demi-bouteille
Beer bière
Draft beer bière à la pression
Mineral water eau minérale
Carbonated gazeuse
Still non-gazeuse
Tap water eau fraîche, une carafe
  d'eau

Hot chaud
Cold froid
Very rare bleu
Rare saignant

Medium à point
Well done bien cuit
Sweet doux
Dry sec
Bread pain
Butter beurre
Salt sel
Pepper poivre
Mustard moutarde
Oil huile
Vinegar vinaigre

Coffee café
Small black coffee café express
Coffee with cream café crème
Breakfast coffee with milk café au
  lait
Tea thé
Lemon citron
Chocolate chocolat
Milk lait
Sugar sucre
Orange or tomato juice jus
  d'orange / de tomate

A RAIL TRAVELER'S GLOSSARY

Abonnement season ticket or pass
Aller to go one way
Aller et Retour round trip
A Partir from (date) on
Arrêt stop, halt
Arrivée arrival
Autobus, Autocar bus
Autorail railcar
Avec Supplément with surcharge
Banlieue suburban
  (commuter trains)
Billet ticket
Billet Simple ordinary one-way
  ticket
Bureau de Change currency

exchange
Changement change (of trains)
Chariot luggage cart
Composition des Trains train
  make-up
Composteur ticket validating
  machine
Compostez votre Billet validate
  your ticket
Consigne checkroom, left luggage
Consigne Automatique luggage
  locker
Contrôleur ticket collector
Correspondence connection
Couchette inexpensive sleeping

car with bunks
Couloir aisle (seat)
Dames women
Défense de Fumer no smoking
Demi-Tarif half fare
Départ departure
Deuxième Classe second class
Douane customs
Emporter to take out, as in items from snack bar
Enregistrement to send baggage ahead
Entrée entrance
Entrée Interdite do not enter
Étranger foreign
Facultatif optional, on request (train or bus stop)
Fenêtre window (seat)
Fêtes holidays
Fiches-Horaires free pocket-sized timetables
Fumeurs smoking
Gare station
Gare Routière bus station
Grandes Lignes main lines
Grève strike of workers
Gril-Express cafeteria car
Guichet ticket window
Hommes men
Horaire timetable
Jusqu'au until (date)
Libre free, available
Libre Service self service
Ligne line
Location de Voitures car rental
Métro subway
Messieurs men
Monter to board (the train)
Objets Trouvés lost-and-found
Occupé occupied

Place seat
Plein Tarif full fare
Poste-PTT post office, telephone service
Première Classe first class
Prochain next (departure)
Quai platform
Quotidien daily
RATP Paris Transit Authority
Remboursement refund
Renseignements information
RER Paris commuter rail lines
Réseau network, system
Réservation reservation
Retardé delay
Salle d' Attente waiting room
Sauf except
Sortie exit
Sortie de Secours emergency exit
SNCF French National Railroads
Tarif fare
Tous les Jours every day
Vers to
Voie track
Voiture car (of train or otherwise)
Voiture Directe through train to indicated destination
Voyage trip, travel
Voyager to travel
Voyageur traveler, passenger
Wagon railroad car
Wagon-Lit sleeping car
Wagon-Restaurant dining car

A DRIVER'S GLOSSARY

Accotement non Stabilisé soft shoulder

Allumez vos Phares turn on head lights

Arrêt Interdit no stopping

Attention caution

Au Pas slow

Autoroute high-speed limited-access highway, usually toll, indicated by letter "A" preceding route number

Autres Directions through traffic

Bifurcation junction

Carrefour crossroads

Carte Grise car registration papers

Carte Routière road map

Céder le Passage yield

Centre Ville to the center of town

Chaussée Déformée bad road surface

Chantier road construction

Chute de Pierres falling rocks

Circuit Touristique scenic route

Circulation Interdite no thoroughfare

Descente Dangereuse steep hill

Déviation detour (diversion)

Douane customs

Eau water

École school

Entrée Interdite no entrance

Essence gasoline (petrol)

Fin d'Interdiction end of restriction

Fin de Limitation de Vitesse end of speed restriction

Gravillons gravel road surface

Halte stop

Hauteur Limitée low clearance

Huile oil

Impasse dead-end road (cul-de-sac)

Interdiction de Doubler no passing

Interdiction de Stationner no parking

Itinéraire Bis alternative route

Limitation de Vitesse speed restriction

Location de Voitures car rental (hire)

Nids de Poule pot holes

Passage à Niveau grade crossing

Passage Interdit entry forbidden, no thoroughfare

Passage Protégé right-of-way at intersection ahead

Péage toll (road)

Pente Dangereuse steep incline

Permis de Conduire driver's license

Piétons pedestrians

Piste Reservée aux Transports Publics lane reserved for public transport

Pneus tires

Poids Lourds truck (lorry) route

Priorité à Droite vehicles coming from the right have the right-of-way

Priorité à Gauche vehicles coming from the left have the right-of-way

Ralentir reduce speed

Rappel previous sign still applies

Réservée aux Piétons pedestrians only

Réservée aux Transports Publics (lane) reserved for public transport

Rond Point traffic circle (roundabout)

Route Barrée road closed

Route Étroite narrow road
Route Glissante slippery road
Sauf (Seulement) Riverains (private road) for residents only
Sens Interdit wrong direction
Sens Unique one-way street
Serrez à Droite keep to the right
Serrez à Gauche keep to the left
Sortie exit
Sortie de Camions truck crossing
Stationnement Autorisé parking allowed
Stationnement Interdit no parking
Tenet vos Distances keep your distance
Toutes Directions all directions
Travaux road work
Verglas slippery road
Virages curves ahead
Voie de Dégagement private entrance
Voie Unique single-lane traffic
Voiture car, vehicle
Voiture à Louer rental car
Zone Bleue time-indicator disc required for parking
Zone Rouge tow-away zone

APPROXIMATE CONVERSIONS

1 Mile = 1.6 km
1 km = 0.6 miles
1 U.S. Gallon = 3.78 litres
1 Litre = 0.26 U.S. Gallons

DAYS OF THE WEEK

Lundi Monday
Mardi Tuesday
Mercredi Wednesday
Jeudi Thursday
Vendredi Friday
Samedi Saturday
Dimanche Sunday
Aujourd'hui today
Demain tomorrow

SEASONS

Saison season
Printemps Spring
Été Summer
Automne Autumn
Hiver Winter

Index

Special interest attractions are also listed under their category headings.

Daytrips

• OTHER EUROPEAN TITLES •

Daytrips LONDON

By Earl Steinbicker. Explores the metropolis on 10 one-day walking tours, then describes 45 daytrips to destinations throughout southern England, with excursions to the Midlands, West Country, and Wales — all by either rail or car. Expanded 6th edition, 352 pages, 62 maps. ISBN: 0-8038-9394-9.

Daytrips GERMANY

By Earl Steinbicker. 60 of Germany's most enticing destinations can be savored on daytrips from Munich, Frankfurt, Hamburg, and Berlin. Walking tours of the big cities are included. Expanded 5th edition, 352 pages, 67 maps. ISBN: 0-8038-9428-7.

Daytrips SWITZERLAND

By Norman P.T. Renouf. 45 one-day adventures in and from convenient bases including Zurich and Geneva, with forays into nearby Germany, Austria, and Italy. 320 pages, 38 maps. ISBN: 0-8038-9417-7.

Daytrips SPAIN & PORTUGAL

By Norman P.T. Renouf. Fifty one-day adventures by rail, bus, or car — including many walking tours, as well as side trips to Gibraltar and Morocco. All the major tourist sights are covered, plus several excursions to little-known, off-the-beaten-track destinations. 368 pages, 18 full-color photos, 28 B&W photos, 51 maps. ISBN: 0-8038-9389-2.

Daytrips IRELAND

By Patricia Tunison Preston. Covers the entire Emerald Isle with 55 one-day self-guided tours both within and from the major tourist areas, plus sections on shopping. Expanded 2nd edition, 400 pages, 57 maps. ISBN: 0-8038-2003-8.

Daytrips ITALY

By Earl Steinbicker. Features 40 one-day adventures in and around Rome, Florence, Milan, Venice, and Naples. 3rd edition, 304 pages, 45 maps, 69 B&W photos. ISBN: 0-8038-9372-8.

Daytrips HOLLAND, BELGIUM & LUXEMBOURG

By Earl Steinbicker. Many unusual places are covered on these 40 daytrips, along with all the favorites plus the 3 major cities. 2nd edition, 288 pages, 45 maps, 69 B&W photos. ISBN: 0-8038-9368-X.

Daytrips ISRAEL

By Earl Steinbicker. 25 one-day adventures by bus or car to the Holy Land's most interesting sites. Includes Jerusalem walking tours. 2nd edition, 206 pages, 40 maps, 40 B&W photos. ISBN: 0-8038-9374-4.

Daytrips

• AMERICAN TITLES •

Daytrips WASHINGTON, D.C.

By Earl Steinbicker. Fifty one-day adventures in the Nation's Capital, and to nearby Virginia, Maryland, Delaware, and Pennsylvania. Both walking and driving tours are featured. 368 pages, 60 maps. Revised 2nd edition. ISBN: 0-8038-9429-5.

Daytrips PENNSYLVANIA DUTCH COUNTRY & PHILADELPHIA

By Earl Steinbicker. Completely covers the City of Brotherly Love, then goes on to probe southeastern Pennsylvania, southern New Jersey, and Delaware before moving west to Lancaster, the "Dutch" country, and Gettysburg. There are 50 daytrips in all. 288 pages, 54 maps. ISBN: 0-8038-9394-9.

ABOUT THE AUTHOR:

EARL STEINBICKER is a born tourist who believes that travel should be a joy, not an endurance test. For over 35 years he has been refining his carefree style of daytripping while working in New York, London, Paris, and other cities; first as head of a firm specializing in promotional photography and later as a professional writer. Whether by public transportation or private car, he has thoroughly probed the most delightful aspects of countries around the world — while always returning to the comforts of city life at night. A strong desire to share these experiences has led him to develop the "Daytrips" series of guides, which he continues to expand and revise. Recently, he has been assisting other authors in developing additional "Daytrips" books, further expanding the series. He presently lives in the Philadelphia suburbs.